Comparative Consumer Sales Law

For many years, legislators around the world have responded to the particular needs of consumers by introducing dedicated rules for consumer sales contracts. In the European Union, a significant push came through the adoption of the Consumer Sales Directive (99/44/EC). Elsewhere in the world, legislation focusing on consumer sales contracts has been introduced, for example in New Zealand and Australia. This book offers a snapshot of the current state of consumer sales law in a range of jurisdictions around the globe. It provides an overview of the law in selected jurisdictions and compares the application of these rules in the context of two case scenarios.

Geraint Howells is Chair Professor of Commercial Law and Dean of the Law School at City University Hong Kong. His expertise covers consumer law and product liability, consumer safety and tobacco regulation, and he has written, co-authored and edited many books and journal articles.

Christian Twigg-Flesner is Professor of International Commercial Law at the University of Warwick, UK. He has expertise in consumer law, the Europeanisation of contract law, the digital revolution and contract law, and the harmonisation of commercial and contract law. He has published widely on EU consumer and contract law.

Hans-W. Micklitz is Professor of Economic Law, European University Institute, Italy. He has published widely in European private law, European and international consumer law and legal theory.

Chen Lei is Associate Professor and Associate Dean at the School of Law, City University of Hong Kong. He has published extensively in the fields of property law, contract law and Chinese legal history. He is an associate member of the International Academy of Comparative Law and a Fellow of the European Law Institute. Chen Lei is also a council member of the Chinese Civil Law Association and an executive council member of the Chinese Consumer Protection Law Association.

The editors express their appreciation to City University of Hong Kong for the funding support in making this book a reality. Special thanks to Karen Choi Po Yan for her research assistance and contribution.

Markets and the Law

Series Editor:
Geraint Howells, City University of Hong Kong

Series Advisory Board:
Stefan Grundmann – Humboldt University of Berlin, Germany, and European University Institute, Italy
Hans Micklitz – Bamberg University, Germany
James P. Nehf – Indiana University, USA
Iain Ramsay – Kent Law School, UK
Charles Rickett – Auckland University of Technology, New Zealand
Reiner Schulze – Münster University, Germany
Jules Stuyck – Katholieke Universiteit Leuven, Belgium
Stephen Weatherill – University of Oxford, UK
Thomas Wilhelmsson – University of Helsinki, Finland

Markets and the Law is concerned with the way the law interacts with the market through regulation, self-regulation and the impact of private law regimes. It looks at the impact of regional and international organisations (e.g. European Community and World Trade Organization), and many of the works adopt a comparative approach and/or appeal to an international audience. Examples of subjects covered include trade laws, intellectual property, sales law, insurance, consumer law, banking, financial markets, labour law, environmental law and social regulation affecting the market, as well as competition law. The series includes texts covering a broad area, monographs on focused issues, and collections of essays dealing with particular themes.

Other titles in the series:

Consumer Debt and Social Exclusion in Europe
Hans-W. Micklitz and Irina Domurath
ISBN 978-1-4724-4903-0

Codifying Contract Law
International and Consumer Law Perspectives
Edited by Mary Keyes and Therese Wilson
ISBN 978-1-4724-1561-5

The European Unfair Commercial Practices Directive
Impact, Enforcement Strategies and National Legal Systems
Edited by Willem van Boom, Amandine Garde and Orkun Akseli
ISBN 978-1-4724-2340-5

www.routledge.com/Markets-and-the-Law/book-series/ASHSER1252

Comparative Consumer Sales Law

Edited by Geraint Howells,
Christian Twigg-Flesner,
Hans-W. Micklitz and Chen Lei

LONDON AND NEW YORK

First published 2018
by Routledge
2 Park Square, Milton Park, Abingdon, Oxon OX14 4RN

and by Routledge
711 Third Avenue, New York, NY 10017

Routledge is an imprint of the Taylor & Francis Group, an informa business

© 2018 selection and editorial matter, Geraint Howells, Christian Twigg-Flesner, Hans-W. Micklitz and Chen Lei; individual chapters, the contributors

The right of Geraint Howells, Christian Twigg-Flesner, Hans-W. Micklitz and Chen Lei to be identified as the authors of the editorial material, and of the authors for their individual chapters, has been asserted in accordance with sections 77 and 78 of the Copyright, Designs and Patents Act 1988.

All rights reserved. No part of this book may be reprinted or reproduced or utilised in any form or by any electronic, mechanical, or other means, now known or hereafter invented, including photocopying and recording, or in any information storage or retrieval system, without permission in writing from the publishers.

Trademark notice: Product or corporate names may be trademarks or registered trademarks, and are used only for identification and explanation without intent to infringe.

British Library Cataloguing-in-Publication Data
A catalogue record for this book is available from the British Library

Library of Congress Cataloging-in-Publication Data
Names: Howells, Geraint G., author. | Twigg-Flesner, Christian, 1975– author. | Micklitz, Hans-W., author.
Title: Comparative consumer sales law / Geraint Howells, Christian Twigg-Flesner, Hans-W. Micklitz.
Description: Abingdon, Oxon [UK] ; New York : Routledge, 2017. | Series: Markets and the law | Includes bibliographical references and index.
Identifiers: LCCN 2017031427 | ISBN 9780754621317 (hardback)
Subjects: LCSH: Consumer protection—Law and legislation. | Sales. | European Parliament. Directive 1999/44/EC of the European Parliament and of the Council of 25 May 1999 on certain aspects of the sale of consumer goods and associated guarantees.
Classification: LCC K3842 .H69 2017 | DDC 343.07/1—dc23
LC record available at https://lccn.loc.gov/2017031427

ISBN: 978-0-7546-2131-7 (hbk)
ISBN: 978-1-315-57305-2 (ebk)

Typeset in Galliard
by Apex CoVantage, LLC

Contents

List of tables   vii
Notes on contributors   viii

Comparative consumer sales law – introduction   1
GERAINT HOWELLS AND CHRISTIAN TWIGG-FLESNER

1 **Consumer sales law in Australia**   15
GAIL PEARSON

2 **Consumer sales law in the European Union**   31
MATEJA DUROVIC

3 **Consumer sales law in Germany**   48
ANDRÉ JANSSEN

4 **Consumer sales law in Hong Kong**   69
CHEN LEI AND GERAINT HOWELLS

5 **Consumer sales law in People's Republic of China**   82
SHIYUAN HAN

6 **Consumer sales law in New Zealand**   95
CHRIS NICOLL

7 **Singapore consumer law**   113
GARY LOW

8 **Consumer sales law in the United Kingdom**   128
CHRISTIAN TWIGG-FLESNER

9 Consumer sales law in the United States   146
   LARRY A. DIMATTEO

10 Consumer sales law in Vietnam   165
   NGUYEN VAN CUONG

   Index   183

Tables

8.1	Remedies in respect of goods	135
9.1	Complaint categories 1 January 1–December 31, 2009 Federal Trade Commission (Released February 2010)	148
9.2	Complaint categories 1 January 1–December 31, 2015 Federal Trade Commission (Released February 2016)	149
9.3	Fraud complaints by company's method of contacting consumers (Calendar Years 2013–2015)	150

Contributors

Larry A. DiMatteo is the Huber Hurst Professor of Contract Law & Legal Studies, Warrington College of Business and Affiliate Professor of Law, Levin College of Law at the University of Florida.

Mateja Durovic is an Assistant Professor of the School of Law at the City University of Hong Kong.

Shiyuan Han is the Professor of Civil Law of the School of Law at Tsinghua University (Beijing) and the Director of European and Comparative Law Centre.

Geraint Howells is Chair Professor of Commercial Law and Dean of the Law School at City University Hong Kong.

André Janssen is an Associate Professor (visiting) of the School of Law at the City University of Hong Kong.

Chen Lei is the Associate Dean and Associate Professor of the School of Law at the City University of Hong Kong.

Gary Low is an Assistant Professor of Law at the Singapore Management University. He sits on the Central Committee of the Consumers Association of Singapore.

Hans-W. Micklitz is Professor of Economic Law, European University Institute, Italy. He published widely in European private law, European and international consumer law and legal theory.

Chris Nicoll is an Associate Professor at The University of Auckland in New Zealand. His expertise is commercial, insurance and maritime law.

Gail Pearson is Professor of Business Law at the University of Sydney.

Christian Twigg-Flesner is Professor of International Commercial Law at the University of Warwick.

Nguyen Van Cuong is the General Director of Institute of Legal Science, Ministry of Justice of Vietnam.

Comparative consumer sales law – introduction

Geraint Howells and Christian Twigg-Flesner

I. Introduction

In this book, we are seeking to gain an understanding of the state of consumer sales law in a selection of jurisdictions from around the world. Legal scholars based in Europe have, for many years, conducted their discourse on this topic within the content of the European Union's Consumer Sales Directive[1] and the – ultimately aborted – attempt to develop a Common European Sales Law.[2] We cover some of these developments in this book, as well as the state of play in two EU Member States: Germany and the United Kingdom. However, our real interest is in how EU consumer sales law compares with the legal rules on consumer sales in other key jurisdictions with active consumer markets, particularly in Asia, the USA and Australasia. We have therefore assembled contributions which examine the law on consumer sales contracts in Australia, China, Hong Kong, New Zealand, Singapore, the United States and Vietnam.

Our intention was to find out about both the legal rules, i.e. the 'law in the books', and the way these rules might apply to particular factual circumstances. For the latter, we opted for a case-scenario approach: we designed two factual (and fictional) scenarios about a consumer who has acquired something and encounters various post-purchase problems. The first scenario is a familiar scenario based around a motor vehicle with various issues, whereas the second reflects a more recent phenomenon: digital content. We asked each contributor to provide a summary of the main legal rules on consumer sales in their jurisdiction, and then provide a discussion of how current law would apply to the two factual scenarios. Our purpose was to discover whether possible differences in the design of the legal rules on consumer sales would invariably mean that this would also produce different outcomes in concrete cases, or whether there would be a high degree of congruence irrespective of the legal rules at issue. We summarise our main findings in this introductory chapter, but readers are encouraged to delve into the individual chapters for fuller analysis.

---

1 Directive 1999/44/EC.
2 See further, G. Howells, C. Twigg-Flesner and T. Wilhelmsson, *Rethinking EU Consumer Law* (London: Routledge, 2017), ch.5.

II. Consumer markets

There is no doubt that consumer sales form an important plank of the national economy. In the United States, the consumer goods market includes more than 3.6 million retail establishments having total sales of almost $2.5 trillion.[3] In the EU, consumer spending represents 57% of gross domestic product (GDP).[4] In many countries, consumer spending has risen off the back of the growth in GDP, employment and household income.[5] This growth is most marked in China where retail sales of consumer goods rose from 24.28 trillion yuan in 2013 to 27.19 trillion yuan in 2014.[6]

Shopping patterns are changing with, for instance, more consumer money being spent on services like restaurants and travel and less on goods. Shopping has also been affected by the growth of the internet. Everywhere, the rise in the use of the internet is being noted, and it is giving rise to new contractual issues related to the digital content, new online intermediaries and the shared economy. However, in some countries, this is not yet fully felt as the offline world is fighting back; in Singapore, for instance, the malls are positioning themselves as places of entertainment.[7] Indeed, whilst gains can be made for consumers by shopping across borders, a great deal of online shopping is still done in the domestic context. Predictions are though that online shopping will continue to grow given the spread of the internet, the widespread ownership of mobile devices, and the increased numbers of apps and intermediary platforms.

However, the increase in consumption has gone hand in hand with high and increasing numbers of consumer complaints. In the United States, they rose from 1,330,471 in 2009 to 3,083,379 in 2015. That is an increase of 232%.[8] In China, there were 258,555 complaints to the China Consumer Association in the first half of 2016. This rise in the number of complaints may be a positive feature if it represents consumers being aware of their rights and being able to use them.

The nature of the complaints varies somewhat between countries. In China, for instance the emphasis of complaint seems to be on quality and after-sales service, whereas in the United States, debt collection and internet-related factors like scams, identity theft and so on figure prominently.[9] Of course cars are an

---

3 See Select USA, US Department of Commerce, *Consumer Goods Spotlight* (Select USA), http://selectusa.commerce.gov/industry-snapshots/consumer-goods-industry-united-states.html, accessed 3 June 2017.
4 European Commission, *Consumer Conditions Scoreboard 2015* (European Commission, 2017), http://ec.europa.eu/consumers/consumer_evidence/consumer_scoreboards/11_edition/docs/ccs2015scoreboard_en.pdf, accessed 3 June 2017.
5 E.g. Nicoll (New Zealand), p. 95.
6 National Bureau of Statistics of China, *National Data*, http://data.stats.gov.cn/search.htm?s=社会消费品零售总额, accessed 30 May 2017.
7 K. Paterson, *Mall Culture Puts Singapore Ahead of the Global Ecommerce Game* (Singapore: Digital Market Asia, 14 November 2014).
8 See DiMatteo (United States), p. 149.
9 See DiMatteo (United States), pp. 148–9.

important source of complaints in many jurisdictions.[10] In several jurisdictions, telecommunications are seen as an increased area of consumer complaints.

It is clear that the consumer market is buoyant and dynamic. It is always going to give rise to some complaints. These may be predicted to continue to include some old chestnuts relating to cars and electrical appliances, but they will increasing be also about the new products generated by technology and the growth of the service sector and the novel problems created by new selling mediums. Addressing these problems needs not only legal rules that protect consumers, but also mechanisms to provide practical access to justice.

III. Access to justice of consumers

In all systems, there is a balance between public and private enforcement. In many systems, the emphasis is on individual redress in the first instance, but in some such as China, the role of the state in protecting consumer rights is to the fore. However, enforcement of individual right is the Achilles heel of consumer protection everywhere.[11] In the United States, the class action is seen as a means to assist consumer claims.[12] In many other countries studied, such a procedure is at best being discussed as something that should be encouraged, but is not yet available, at least in anything like the US model.[13]

Although some systems have special procedures for small claims that may make access to justice easier,[14] the lack of legal representation for consumers is a serious problem everywhere. In several countries, the consumer organisations are seen as having a role to assist litigation by providing advice and support to consumers with complaints.[15] They often perform a mediation function. This is part of a wider development of ADR. More often, it is seen as a practical means of providing redress where formal resolution would be problematic.

Public enforcement can be undertaken by a range of regulatory agencies at different levels in the governance structures of states. Public law can lead to a range of sanctions that might include criminal regulation. However, as the Australian report describes, the more typical modern approach is to adopt a responsive regulation mode that prefers to start with education and moves up through a hierarchy of lesser measures, such as seeking undertakings, with criminal sanction if available being a last resort. Publicity aimed at exposing traders to reputational risk is being experimented with in some systems.[16] There is also the risk that traders avoid sanction by closing down and opening under a new name.

10 For example, in Singapore, Australia and the European Union.
11 See Nicoll (New Zealand), p. 97.
12 See DiMatteo (United States), p. 150.
13 For example, the European Union does not have similar procedures.
14 See Nicoll p. 98 (New Zealand), Pearson (Australia) p. 18, DiMatteo (United States) p. 159.
15 See Han (China) p. 85, Low (Singapore), p. 116.
16 For example, see Pearson (Australia) p. 17 and Minister for Innovation and better Regulation, Second Reading Speech, Fair Trading Amendment (Information About Complaints) Bill 2015, 16 September 2015.

In some systems, criminal liability automatically gives rise to civil liability.[17] Public enforcement can therefore be a means of achieving redress for consumers. In the United Kingdom, a new set of enhanced consumer measures is available to regulators, including the ability to provide redress.[18] In Germany, in some instances, illegal profits can be skimmed off, but as the money reverts to the state, there is little incentive on consumer organisations to bring such actions.[19]

Many of the legal rules on consumer sales fit within similar patterns in the countries studied. This is not the case with redress mechanisms. There are similar problems, but different solutions are found – simplifying procedures, invoking ADR, class actions or relying on consumer organisations or public enforcement to achieve justice. Wide variations in the effectiveness of the systems also depends upon how much resources is directed to the agencies or how accessible small claims or ADR procedures are. Assessment of the protection afforded to consumers depends not so much on the law on paper, but the practice of law in the redress mechanisms available.

IV. Legal rules on consumer sales

One objective of this study was to find out more about the rules applicable to consumer sales contracts in the various jurisdictions. In particular, we wanted to discover whether there were dedicated legal rules for consumer sales contracts, or whether such contracts were subject to the rules applicable to non-consumer sales contracts.

Generally speaking, whilst none of the jurisdictions considered in this book have developed a completely separate consumer contract law, almost all of the jurisdictions have legal rules which regulate particular aspects of consumer sales contracts. The one exception is the United States, where there is no consistent approach to consumer-specific rules, although there are instances where state law, combined with federal level regulation, provides some rules which focus on consumer contracts (although the American Law Institute is working on a Restatement of the law on Consumer Contracts). In the European jurisdictions, there are consumer-specific rules which are heavily influenced by the EU's Consumer Sales Directive (1999/44/EC).[20] Both the German Civil Code and the UK's Consumer Rights Act 2015 (CRA 2015) contain rules which give effect to the EU's Consumer Sales Directive. In Germany, the implementation of that Directive became the impetus for a major reform of the Civil Code, and so the rules from the Directive are integrated into the rest of the Code's provisions.[21]

The United Kingdom, in particular, has significantly extended the reach of these provisions beyond consumer sales, to include also related other consumer supply

---

17 E.g., see Han (China), p. 84 and Nicoll (New Zealand), p. 99.
18 See Twigg-Flesner (UK), p. 5 and Enterprise Act 2002.
19 Janssen (Germany), p. 50.
20 Durovic (European Union), p. 36.
21 Janssen (Germany), p. 50.

transactions such as hire-purchase and hire (leasing). The primary driver behind the CRA 2015 was a reform of the rules applicable to consumer sales to simplify and modernise a previously complex legal regime. This may be compared to the (much earlier) Consumer Guarantees Act 1993 (CGA 1993) from New Zealand, which since 1993 deals with consumer sales contracts in a similar way to the CRA 2015 by having dedicated provisions on both the quality of goods and fitness for purpose, as well as a more extensive set of remedies than would be provided by the general (common) law of contract. Similar developments can be noted in some of the Asian jurisdictions, such as Singapore – indeed, the 2008 amendments to the Consumer Protection (Fair Trading) Act (CPFTA) intentionally resemble the EU's consumer sales rules.[22] The Chinese Law on the Protection of Consumer Rights and Interests (LPCRI) also contains rules specifically on consumer sales contracts and, interestingly, makes provision for punitive damages.

Another common feature of the legal rules on consumer sales is that these have emerged from the legal rules applicable to sales contracts generally. Thus, the common law countries featured in this book originally all had legislation on the sale of goods based on the British Sale of Goods Act 1893 with more recent legislation adopted to provide rules on particular aspects of consumer sales contracts, especially on the quality of goods and associated remedies. We can see such developments in both Australia and New Zealand, as well as in Singapore. In the latter jurisdiction, the legislator took the decision to align Singaporean law with the minimum consumer protection standards mandated in EU law, and so some rules are directly inspired by the EU's Consumer Sales Directive.

In a similar vein, the starting point for the EU's Consumer Sales Directive was the model provided by the (non-consumer) UN Convention on the International Sale of Goods 1980 (CISG) which has been ratified by the vast majority of the EU's member states. This also applies in the United States. In contrast, attempts there to introduce dedicated consumer rules have been unsuccessful, and so state legislation based on the (non-consumer) Uniform Commercial Code (UCC) applies to consumer sales contracts instead.

The two key aspects in respect of which common consumer sales rules have been introduced are (i) quality standards and (ii) remedies.

Quality standards

In the common law countries, there is an objective quality requirement which goods must comply with. Originally, this was merchantable quality, and whilst that test remains in Hong Kong – in Australia and New Zealand, this is now the 'acceptable quality' test, and in the United Kingdom and Singapore, it is 'satisfactory quality'. The factors deployed in determining whether goods reach this standard are generally similar and include fitness for common purposes,

---

22 Low (Singapore), p. 121.

durability, freedom from minor defects, safety and appearance/finish. The EU's minimum requirements in Art. 2 of the Consumer Sales Directive are similar but less extensive, covering matters such as fitness for common purposes and quality expectations regarding the goods in question and expectations shaped by public statements/advertising.

One interesting distinction is the nature of these quality, or conformity, requirements. In EU Law, the contractual agreement between the parties is prioritised, and the criteria for conformity with the contract are presumptive, but subject to the terms of the contract itself. In contrast, in the common law jurisdictions, including the United Kingdom, the quality requirement is objective and part of each contract irrespective of the agreement made between the parties though statements made by the parties may affect the assessment.

Remedies

As far as remedies are concerned, those jurisdictions which have consumer-specific rules tend to include rules which allow a consumer to require that goods are repaired or replaced. It is interesting that Australia and New Zealand provided for this even though the common law approach has traditionally been reluctant to embrace performance-based remedies, preferring instead to prioritise damages and termination. The UK's shift towards such remedies was driven by the need to give effect to the EU's Consumer Sales Directive, which also gives primacy to the performance-oriented remedies of repair and replacement.

There is usually less specificity when it comes to compensation for any additional losses, for example, food which has become unsafe to eat after a freezer has failed, or personal data lost because of a faulty computer. Generally, these matters are left to the general contract law rules on damages. German law, unlike the other jurisdictions featured in this study, makes an entitlement to claim damages subject to a fault-based test, whereas the other jurisdictions apply a strict liability approach. It is noteworthy that China has introduced a provision in Art.55 LPCRL for punitive damages in circumstances where fraud is involved in the supply of goods. In the other jurisdictions, there is no specific provision for punitive damages. However, despite this focus on performance-oriented remedies, there are instances when it is possible for a consumer to reject the goods and rescind the contract. Under the UK's CRA 2015, a consumer has 30 days from delivery to do so if there is a non-conformity.[23] In New Zealand, this is possible within a reasonable time where the failure to comply with the quality requirement is substantial,[24] or where the breach is not capable of being remedied.

---

23 Twigg-Flesner (UK), p. 141.
24 Nicoll (New Zealand), p. 104.

Parties liable

Finally, it is interesting to note that some jurisdictions have departed from the narrow contractual approach which permits a consumer to seek a remedy only from the business with which a contract was actually concluded (usually a retailer). Thus, in Australia and New Zealand, a consumer can bring a claim for a breach of the implied quality terms (or statutory quality guarantees) against the retailer or the manufacturer.

V. Factual scenarios

Whilst it is interesting to compare the legal rules applicable to consumer sales in a number of jurisdictions, it is only really through an examination of how these rules work in practice that it becomes possible to identify those areas where laws are on the same track, and where they follow different paths. To get a better understanding of how the legal rules in the various jurisdictions discussed in this book operate in the context of specific situations, we developed two case scenarios. The first is essentially a classic consumer sales problem involving a car with a range of problems: the first is a functional issue (a problem with the car's brakes and engine); the second is a failure of the car to live up to expectations built up through advertising, and the third is a failure to meet externally regulated emissions standards.[25]

The second scenario focuses on a more modern issue – the rise of so-called smart devices such as tablet computers which rely on apps, as well as the possibility to connect multiple devices (the 'internet of things' phenomenon). Although these are already a common feature of the consumer markets in many countries, there is still a debate about the extent to which this development has created novel legal issues which are as yet not sufficiently regulated. For example, the significance of apps downloaded directly onto devices via the internet has prompted discussion as to whether specific rules for 'digital content' are required, and if so, what the substance of such rules might look like.

In this section, we highlight the main findings, rather than offering a full comparison of how the different countries approach these issues. The reason for this is that there were no significant differences in the approaches adopted in the various jurisdictions. The more detailed discussions of these scenarios in the individual chapter flesh out the overview in this section, so readers will gain a fuller picture from reading all of the contributions. To some extent, this is not surprising, particularly in respect of contracts involving the sale of physical goods. However, even in the case of digital content, most of the jurisdictions will find a way of providing a remedy for the consumer – whether via dedicated rules, analogous application of sales rules, or ultimately via principles of general contract law.

---

25 Although this is not intended as a legal analysis of the car emissions scandal which broke in mid-2015, we thought that it would be worthwhile to get a general understanding of how the various jurisdictions might deal with this issue.

Scenario 1

> Alison has bought a new car from car retailer Billy. The car is made by manufacturer Reliable. The model is a R1 car, which was launched a few months previously. To promote the new model, Reliable launched a major advertising campaign under the slogan 'Top Reliability, Low Fuel Consumption, Best for the Environment'. One TV advert showed a family setting off on a holiday and travelling the entire length of the United Kingdom without stopping to refuel.
>
> When Alison bought her car, she explained that the primary purpose for buying the car would be to use it for the daily commute from home to work, a distance of 30 miles. Alison asked Billy whether the low fuel consumption would also show over short distances and was reassured that it would.
>
> After 3 weeks, Alison noticed that the brakes were slower to respond than when she first got the car. Also, the engine had started to make a howling noise whenever gears are changed at a low speed. Moreover, Alison realised that the car was using significantly more fuel than her previous car. Then, a news story broke which suggested that cars manufactured by Reliable failed to meet emissions standards by a significant margin.
>
> In your legal system, would A have recourse against Billy or Reliable and for what remedies as regards
>
> (i) The problems with the brakes and engine noise (would the position be different if the car was second-hand and 3 years old)?
> (ii) The higher-than-expected fuel consumption?
> (iii) Failure to meet emission standards?

(i) Problems with brakes and engine noise (and possible differences if car had not been new, but 3-year-old second-hand car)

This first issue concerns a mechanical issue with the goods: the brakes of the car are less responsive after 3 weeks of driving, and engine is making a noise whenever gears are changed. Although these issues were not noticed at the time of purchase, they arose soon after and could therefore be latent defects which manifested within a short period of time. Indeed, several jurisdictions have a rule (originally enacted in the EU's Consumer Sales Directive) which creates a presumption that any defect/non-conformity which arises within 6 months from the delivery are presumed to have existed at that point in time. This is the case in the EU jurisdictions,[26] as well as in Singapore (to match the EU's level of protection).[27]

Applying the relevant rules, all of these jurisdictions would conclude that this particular situation would amount to a breach of the relevant consumer sales law

---

26 I.e., Germany and the United Kingdom, as well as the rest of the EU.
27 Low (Singapore), p. 121.

rules, not least because of the fact that problems arose within a short period from the date of the sale. Although the precise test for determining this varies between the various jurisdictions, the ultimate conclusion would be that a consumer in this position is entitled to a remedy. All of the jurisdictions provide for repair or replacement (if possible). As an alternative, some jurisdictions also provide for the possibility of terminating the contract. In China, this is possible if two attempts at repair are unsuccessful. In Australia, termination would only be possible if the problem was deemed to be a major failure. In the United Kingdom, the consumer would still be able to reject the car and terminate the contract as fewer than 30 days had passed since the date of sale. In the various discussions, it is interesting to note that there was some variation as to the most appropriate remedy; Djurovic, for example, suggested that repair or replacement would not be appropriate because of the seriousness of the defects which would make either inefficient,[28] whereas others thought that repair would be worth exploring first.

One interesting matter to note is that several jurisdictions have adopted legislation specifically for cars. Thus, in the United States, most states have adopted legislation dealing with defects in a new car, which require a manufacturer or an authorised service agent to repair or ultimately buy back the vehicle if defects materialise within 24 months.[29] China has adopted the so-called 3R Provisions, which provide standards and associated remedies specifically in relation to cars used by consumers.[30] These provisions are quite detailed in terms of the seller's obligations to provide an appropriate remedy and further support.

In most jurisdictions, the consumer would only have a claim against the immediate seller of the goods. However, some jurisdictions permit an action against the manufacturer of the goods as an alternative. So in New Zealand, the consumer could claim against the manufacturer, provided that there are no acts or omissions on the part of someone else that have caused the breach.[31]

Finally, it is worth noting that in many instances, a consumer would be more likely to rely on the car manufacturer's warranty which will have been provided with the vehicle as a matter of standard business practice.[32]

If the car was a 3-year-old second-hand car, then most jurisdictions would modify the application of the relevant quality standard, which might result in a finding that there is no breach. This would seem to depend on an assessment of what sort of defects a consumer should reasonably expect when buying a second-hand car of this age.[33] However, the same legal rules would be applied overall, albeit with some modifications. In contrast, China has specific rules for second-hand vehicles below a certain age and mileage, which impose a mandatory guarantee of at least 3 months/5,000 kilometres.[34] These are therefore quite specific rules applicable to cars.

---

28 Durovic (European Union), p. 42.
29 DiMatteo (United States), p. 159. These are the so-called lemon laws.
30 Han (China), p. 87.
31 Nicoll (New Zealand), p. 96.
32 Cf. the brief discussion by Low (Singapore), p. 125.
33 Cf. e.g., Nicoll (New Zealand), p. 106.
34 Han (China), p. 90.

(ii) Higher-than-expected fuel consumption

The car had been marketed by the manufacturer as benefitting from low fuel consumption, and the consumer (Alison) also asked the retailer whether this would still be the case when the car was driven over short distances. It then transpires that the car uses more fuel than expected. We are not told if this is due to a defect with the particular car, or whether this model generally uses more fuel than the advertising campaign would suggest.

In many jurisdictions, the first route to seeking redress would be to rely on the requirement that goods must be fit for a particular purpose made known by a consumer. On the facts, the consumer had indicated that the car was required for a particular type of driving and that it should still maintain the indicated fuel consumption. Some jurisdictions would also take into account the general statement about fuel efficiency made in the advertising statements in determining whether the goods meet the consumer's reasonable expectations as to quality. In EU jurisdictions, this is a rule based on a specific provision in the Consumer Sales Directive.[35]

Several chapters note that the most appropriate remedy in this instance would depend on whether the lack of fuel efficiency affected only the particular car bought by the consumer in the scenario, or whether it affected the model of car more generally.[36] In the case of an isolated instance, repair or (more likely) replacement would be appropriate, whereas in the case of a wider problem, rescission of the contract would be favoured.

Some of the chapters note that there might also be separate recourse for misleading or incorrect statements made in advertising. In EU law, there are additional requirements to provide information about fuel efficiency, and failure to provide accurate information could be treated as an unfair commercial practice (although this would not necessarily provide a consumer with an individual remedy unless the EU Member State in question has provided for a private right of redress[37]). In Australia, express claims about the goods made in advertising could amount to a breach of a statutory guarantee that goods will comply with an express warranty made by a manufacturer.[38]

(iii) Failure to meet emissions standards

The third issue is that the car fails to meet emissions standards. These are externally determined criteria. From the consumer's perspective, the fact that the car was marketed as being 'best for the environment' may be a consideration.

In most jurisdictions, this issue could be dealt with as an aspect of quality in that failure to comply with relevant regulatory standards such as emissions rules would be a relevant factor in applying that standard. However, this might depend

---

35 Art.2(2)(d).
36 E.g. Janssen (Germany), p. 65.
37 In the United Kingdom, for example, the Consumer Protection from Unfair Trading Regulations 2008 were amended in respect of contracts concluded after October 2014 to provide consumers with a right to 'unwind' the contract or to claim a 'discount' in respect of contracts which were concluded as a result of a misleading practice.
38 S.59 ACL, see Pearson (Australia), p. 24.

on whether this is a separate issue or a consequence of the higher-than-expected fuel consumption of the car, because higher fuel consumption will invariably result in higher emissions.[39] If it is not possible to repair the car to correct this problem, either rejection of the car and rescission of the contract, or reduction of the price would be possible.

Also, there are specific rules regarding emission standards in place in most countries. Often, these have their own enforcement mechanisms, sometimes providing for the imposition of a fine on a car manufacturer who does not comply[40] and sometimes resulting in compensation for private buyers. In addition, failure to comply with emissions standards could mean that a car might not pass the mandatory inspection, which would amount to a non-conformity of the goods with the contract.[41]

Scenario 2

> David recently bought a new tablet computer made by Elizabeth. The tablet comes with a range of preloaded applications (software). One of these allows David to control various appliances around his home, such as his TV, digital recorder and central heating system. David is a keen runner, and so he decided to buy and download a new sports application onto his tablet which connects to his smartwatch and keeps track of where he has been running, his heart rate and blood pressure. The application cost $15. David went away on a running holiday for a week and made extensive use of the new application. However, after a few days, he noticed the blood pressure function had stopped working. An update was sent to patch up the problem, but he now understands the problem has recurred, but 6 months later, the company stopped trying to resolve the problem. However, he has stopped using the application because on returning home, David noticed that none of the TV programmes he had set to record were on his digital recorder. He then discovered that the central heating thermostat had been set to 32 degrees Celsius throughout. Finally, the tablet stopped connecting to the internet altogether. David sought advice from Fidelma, a computer specialist, and was correctly told that the application had interfered with other applications on the tablet, and also caused a failure of the Wi-Fi connector.
>
> In your legal system, would David have recourse (and with what remedies) for
>
> (i) The failure of the app and/or the failure to patch the problem?
> (ii) The interference of the sports application with the other apps on the tablet?
> (iii) The damage done to the Wi-Fi connector by the sports application?

---

39 Janssen (Germany), p. 66.
40 See e.g., Pearson (Australia), p. 24.
41 See e.g., Han (China), p. 91.

The second scenario focuses on a situation of more recent origin: the widespread use of smart devices and the popularity of applications. It was our intention to gauge how the various jurisdictions would approach this relatively new type of transaction, and also whether these jurisdictions have already made specific provision for contracts involving the supply of digital content. The number of jurisdictions with dedicated rules is small (the UK's CRA 2015 is a notable exception), and most of those who have made provision have generally extended the rules applicable to consumer goods to digital content by adopting wider definition of 'goods' (e.g. in Singapore, Australia and New Zealand).

(i) Failure of app and/or failure to patch the problem

This is essentially about flaws with the application itself and a failure by the company which produced the app to rectify this. It is not dissimilar to a situation involving physical goods (such as a cooker) which break down and where attempts to repair the problem have failed. The interesting issue is the extent to which the current legal framework can deal with problems with digital content.

In several jurisdictions (Singapore, Australia, New Zealand), the definition of goods has been extended to include computer software, digital content or intangibles, and consequently, the same rules as would apply to goods would be applied to the app. EU Law is (currently) not able to do so as the Consumer Sales Directive is limited to tangible items – although separate legislation on this has been proposed. The UK's CRA 2015, on the other hand, contains a chapter specifically for digital content. Whilst this generally maintains a parallel with the rules applicable to goods, there are some modifications to reflect the specificities of digital content.

In other jurisdictions, there are no specific rules in place, and so it is necessary to consider this issue under the general rules of contract or tort law. This could mean that rules applicable to the sale of goods might be applied by analogy, as is the case in China.[42] A different approach is currently suggested for Germany, where digital content downloaded directly via the internet would be treated as a contract for the acquisition of rights, which would then have the effect of bringing the rules on sales contracts back into play.[43]

(ii) Interference of sports application with other apps

This aspect deals with the impact downloaded applications/digital content can have on other applications already installed on a consumer's device. Here, the evidence shows that the sports app caused other apps to malfunction, suggesting that the sports app interfered with these other apps.

In most jurisdictions, there is no specific legal rule on this issue. Instead, this would be treated as a type of consequential loss, with any recovery subject to the

---

42 Han (China), p. 92.
43 Janssen (Germany), p. 67.

rules that would ordinarily be applied to damages.[44] However, there are specific rules in both Australia and the United Kingdom. In Australia, software may not damage other software or hardware. Also, it seems that, because software (and therefore digital content) is classified as 'goods' in Australia, the rules applicable to damage or personal injury caused by defective goods could apply here (although this would have to be a safety defect, rather than poor quality generally).[45] In the United Kingdom, s.46 of the CRA 2015 provides for an entitlement to compensation for damage caused by digital content to other digital content where such damage would not have occurred if the trader had exercised reasonable care and skill. Unlike consequential losses recoverable at common law for a breach of contract (strict liability), the threshold for liability is akin to a negligence standard in that not every damage caused is covered by s.46. Alternatively, a consumer can ask for repair where this is possible.

(iii) Damage to Wi-Fi connector by the app

The third issue is one which is unusual but does occasional arise: a flaw with the digital content on the consumer's device has an effect on the hardware itself and creates a failure of physical components.

As with the damage to digital content, the approach of most jurisdictions currently is to rely on general principles of contract law on damages for consequential losses. The special rules in Australia and in the United Kingdom mentioned above would be applicable to this situation, too.

VI. Conclusions

An interesting issue arises in terms of the discrepancies between the different jurisdictions with regard to the rules on consumer sales. One might have been tempted to assume that there is a lot of similarity among the common law legal systems, and perhaps also the EU countries, with distinct features in the Asian jurisdictions. However, as the various chapters in this book reveal, that difference cannot really be made out. This is most obviously so in the case of Singapore, which has deliberately aligned its consumer law with the provisions of EU law, but the substantive laws in all the jurisdictions we consider here are quite well aligned.

Overall, it seems that the level of substantive consumer protection, at least with regard to the aspects we examined in this book, is not as diverse as one might have expected. We can see considerable variation in the detail of the relevant legal rules, but once one turns to the outcomes which the application of such rules produces, we see far less divergence than might be assumed. Interestingly, the United States stands out for lacking a coherent approach to consumer protection

---

44 E.g., Low (Singapore), p. 127, Nicoll (New Zealand), p. 109, Janssen (Germany), p. 68.
45 See Pearson (Australia), p. 30.

at federal level, with individual states taking the lead in adopting state-level consumer protection rules. It will be interesting to see whether the American Law Institute's Restatement on Consumer Law might become a catalyst for change here. It was also interesting to note that there are parallels between jurisdictions in unexpected contexts: for example, both the United States and China have specific rules regarding the supply of new cars (the US 'lemon laws' at state level, and China's '3R' rules). A second example is the fact that many common law systems (Australia, New Zealand and the United Kingdom) have introduced remedies which focus on the trader's obligation to perform the contract (i.e. repair and replacement), whereas the traditional common law remedies in such instances would usually be limited to termination of the contract and/or a claim for damages.

As might have been expected, the true differences are lying in the design of the enforcement systems. Here much depends on the accessibility of courts and ADR bodies for the enforcement of individual claims. There seems to be a match between the type of substantive law and remedies (public/private) and the consumer market.

1 Consumer sales law in Australia

Gail Pearson

I. The Australian consumer market

The retail market for goods and services represents about 5% of gross domestic product (GDP) and employs about 10%.[1] Its relative importance is declining.[2] Food retailing is about 48% of the total, and household goods about 19%, followed by clothing and soft goods.[3] These figures exclude cars, car parts and fuel. Households spend less on consumer goods and more on services such as eating out.[4] After 2017, for the first time in 100 years, Australia will not have an automotive industry due to high cost manufacturing, and changing consumer preferences in a competitive market.[5] The market for smartphones, tablets and apps is buoyant with a high take-up rate.[6] The apps market is dominated by free and low cost apps, particularly social networking and weather apps, and the use of apps for smart appliances is growing.[7]

Retail is a multi-channel industry with bricks and mortar department stores, specialty stores, supermarkets and significant online distribution.[8] Retail establishments

---

1 Productivity Commission, *Productivity Update 2015*, www.pc.gov.au/research/ongoing/productivity-update/pc-productivity-update-2015/2014-australian-productivity Box 1.2. This does not include gas and electricity services or accommodation and food services; in 2011, the GDP figure was about 4% Productivity Commission, *Report No 56 Economic Structure and Performance of the Australian Retail Industry* (2011), p. 30.
2 Productivity Commission, *Research Report, Relative Costs of Doing Business in Australia* (September 2014), p. 41.
3 Ibid., pp. 38, 39.
4 Ibid., p. 48.
5 www.industry.gov.au/industry/IndustrySectors/automotive/Pages/default.aspx, accessed 18 January 2016.
6 Australian Government, Australian Communications and Media Authority, *Mobile Apps Emerging Issues in Media and Communications Occasional Paper 1* (March 2013), p. 7.
7 Ibid., pp. 8, 6.
8 In 2010, online sales were estimated at 6% or $12.6 billion of all retail sales within Australia and from overseas. Productivity Commission, 2011 p. XX11; Productivity Commission, 2014 pp. 37, 51. In 2015, around 90% of retailers operated a website. Australian Retailers Association and NetSuite Joint Study Reveals the Proliferation of Retail Channels is Making Customer Experience Management Difficult to Achieve, Frost & Sullivan, *The Customer Experience Challenge for Australian Retailers* (2015).

16 *Gail Pearson*

correlate with population distribution.[9] The impact of technology is significant,[10] and online shopping continues to grow. [11] Most is domestic.[12] Online shoppers also buy internationally at lower prices as part of the global retail trade.[13] Australia has more frequent online shoppers than some European countries, but fewer than the United Kingdom, United States, and Germany.[14]

Australia imports a high percentage of its retail items, including passenger cars.[15] One of the problems is car recalls due to faulty airbags for the driver and front passenger.[16] The market for apps is global. Australians download and buy apps from app stores or retail platforms provided by entities such as Apple and Google.[17] More people download onto mobile phones than tablets, and significantly more free apps than paid apps.[18] In-app promotion of further apps, particularly in games for children is a problem. Consumer sales problems as indicated by complaints data and advice contacts show problems with cars[19] by contrast with confidence in apps (although not in mobile and broadband plans and billing).[20]

9   The States of NSW and Victoria have 59.7% of retail establishments and 56.9% of the Australian population. Ibis World, *Consumer Goods Retail in Australia: Market Research Report* (July 2015), www.ibisworld.com.au/industry/default.aspx?indid=1720, accessed 18 January 2016.
10 Productivity Commission, 2014, p. 49f.
11 Roy Morgan Research, *The State of Australia's $37.8 b Online Shopping Landscape* (2 December 2015 Finding No 6591), www.roymorgan.com/findings/6591-online-shopping-in-australia-june-2015-201512012314, accessed 18 January 2016.
12 In a 2012 study, 73% of consumers said their online shopping was domestic NSW Government, Department of Fair Trading, *Consumer and SMB Attitudes to Online Shopping and Awareness of Security Measures* (Research Executive Summary, Stancombe Research and Planning, 2012).
13 Productivity Commission, 2011, p. XXIII.
14 Productivity Commission, 2014, p. 100.
15 Productivity Commission Inquiry, *Report No 70 Australia's Automotive Manufacturing Industry* (May 2014), p. 42. Australian Government, Australian Communications and Media Authority, *Mobile Apps Emerging Issues in Media and Communications Occasional Paper 1* (March 2013), p. 8.
16 In 2014, 168,000 cars were recalled. www.accc.gov.au/update/takata-airbag-recalls-affecting-australian-consumers, accessed 21 May 2015.
17 Australian Government Australian Communications and Media Authority, *Emerging Business Models in the Digital Economy – The Mobile Applications Market*(Occasional Paper May 2011), p. 12; Australian Government, Australian Communications and Media Authority, *Mobile Apps Emerging Issues in Media and Communications Occasional Paper 1* (March 2013), pp. 8, 9.
18 Australian Government, Australian Communications and Media Authority, *Mobile Apps Emerging Issues in Media and Communications Occasional Paper 1* (March 2013) p. 7.
19 Ibid.; Consumer Affairs Victoria 2014–2015, p. 13.
20 ACCC Annual Report 2014–2015, www.accc.gov.au/publications/accc-aer-annual-report/accc-aer-annual-report-2014-15/accc-and-aer-annual-report-2014–15/part-3-performance-program-11-accc/goal-2-protect-the-interests-and-safety-of-consumers-and-support-fair-trading-in-markets-affecting-consumers-and-small-business/21-deliver-priority-consumer-law-outcomes, accessed 1 February 2016.

II. Access to justice for consumers and enforcement of consumer law

Australia is a Federation, and the national consumer laws are administered in a multi-regulator framework.[21] Federal and state agencies, including the Australian Competition and Consumer Commission (ACCC), Consumer Affairs Victoria, and NSW Fair Trading, all take the initiative in different matters. Victoria is leading a national campaign to identify which businesses receive most complaints[22] and a recent New South Wales (NSW) law allows publication of such names.[23] The policy is public exposure as a form of reputational regulation similar to platform based ratings.[24] In online shopping, often the most effective form of consumer redress is a credit card chargeback. The project, led by Victoria, is to create nationally consistent information and guidance for the use of chargebacks.[25]

Australian regulators are influenced by 'responsive regulation' which escalates from education and persuasion for compliance, through to prosecution. They aim to reduce consumer harm by engaging with business and providing accessible educational material on consumer rights. Some state regulators are more likely to take regulatory action such as requiring a supplier to substantiate claims, or an Undertaking from a supplier [26] than direct enforcement. The ACCC takes strategic enforcement action, but there have been few consumer guarantees cases and instead litigation to prevent misrepresentations about the consumer guarantees.[27] This means the scope of the new consumer guarantee law is being worked out first in Tribunals rather than superior Courts.

Consumers can seek justice by dealing directly with the retailer; making a complaint to an External Dispute Resolution (EDR) scheme; complaining to a regulatory agency; approaching an Administrative Tribunal, a lower Magistrates Court or County Court, or, depending on the size and type of claim, a higher state Court or the Federal Court.

---

21 See *Director of Consumer Affairs Victoria v Dimmeys Stores* [2013] FCA 618 upholding this framework.
22 Consumer Affairs Victoria 2014–2015, p. 25.
23 Fair Trading Act 1987 NSW s 86AA.
24 Minister for Innovation and better Regulation, Second Reading Speech, Fair Trading Amendment (Information About Complaints) Bill 2015, 16 September 2015.
25 Ibid. On the Banking Code of Practice and bank compliance see Code Compliance Monitoring Committee, *Chargebacks Followup Inquiry Report* (October 2013), www.ccmc.org.au/cms/wp-content/uploads/2013/11/CCMC-Inquiry-Report-Chargebacks-Followup-October-2013.pdf, accessed 18 January 2016.
26 ACL s 218. See for example the Apple undertaking in connection with consumer guarantee rights. ACCC Register of Undertakings D13/178396 17 December 2013. An Undertaking may include a compliance programme, http://registers.accc.gov.au/content/index.phtml/itemId/1129114.
27 E.g. *Australian Competition and Consumer Commission v Avitalb Pty Ltd*.[2014] FCA 222; *Australian Competition and Consumer Commission* v *Hewlett Packard Australia Pty Ltd*. [2013] FCA 653.

Although EDR is well developed in certain sectors of the economy, there is no Retail Ombudsman. The Telecommunications Industry Ombudsman can take complaints about apps.[28] App stores themselves provide a consumer-regulatory system that filters quality with peer advice, recommendations and ratings.[29]

The agencies, through websites, telephone call centres and regional offices,[30] encourage consumers to deal directly with the supplier to resolve a problem and then, if necessary, step in.[31] NSW manages to resolve about 93% of complaints without resort to a Court or Tribunal.[32] Cross-border complaints are directed towards the International Consumer Protection and Enforcement Network.[33]

Many civil disputes involve consumer issues[34] and raise problems with inappropriate advisers and unmet legal needs.[35] Not all state jurisdictions have a civil and administrative Tribunal and in some states the appropriate forum is the Magistrates Court.[36] The NSW Civil and Administrative Tribunal (NCAT) has a Consumer and Commercial Division. It can hear consumer claims up to $40,000;[37] and is trialling online dispute resolution for consumer claims up to $5,000.[38] It is not bound by rules of evidence, nor is legal representation necessary.[39]

There are differences between the Tribunals regarding appeals to the Court.[40] Tribunal and Court fees are not a barrier for most, but the cost of representation for Court is a problem as there is little legal aid for consumer disputes.[41]

---

28 The ACCC lists relevant Ombudsman services at www.accc.gov.au/contact-us/other-helpful-agencies/industry-ombudsmen-dispute-resolution, accessed 18 January 2016; Australian Government, Australian Communications and Media Authority, *Mobile Apps Emerging Issues in Media and Communications Occasional Paper 1* (March 2013), p. 8.
29 Australian Government, Australian Communications and Media Authority, *Mobile Apps Emerging Issues in Media and Communications Occasional Paper 1* (March 2013), p. 9.
30 In Victoria, visits to the website have grown by 78% in the last 2 years, and this correlates with a decline in telephone calls. Consumer Affairs Victoria 2014–2015, pp. 11, 12.
31 The state agencies can negotiate an outcome for the consumer, www.accc.gov.au/contact-us/other-helpful-agencies/consumer-protection-agencies, accessed 18 January 2016.
32 NSW Fair Trading Year in Review 2013–2014, p. 11, www.fairtrading.nsw.gov.au/biz_res/ftweb/pdfs/About_us/Publications/Annual_reports/Year_in_Review_1314.pdf.
33 www.icpen.org/for-consumer-experts/what-we-do, accessed 18 January 2016.
34 Productivity Commission Report No 72, *Access to Justice Arrangements* (Overview 2014), p. 4, vol. 1, pp. 88, 89.
35 Ibid., vol. 1 pp. 98, 102.
36 www.accc.gov.au/contact-us/other-helpful-agencies/small-claims-tribunals#new-south-wales, accessed 19 January 2016.
37 *Fair Trading Act*, NSW 1987 Part 6A.
38 NSW Government, Department of Justice, *Annual Report 2014–2015*, p. 23, www.justice.nsw.gov.au/Documents/Annual%20Reports/DoJ_Annual_Report_2014-15.pdf.
39 *Civil and Administrative Tribunal Act 2013* (NSW) s 37, s 38, s45, Schedule 4 s 7, *Fair Trading Act* NSW 1987 s 13 (1) (b). It must observe rules of evidence in its enforcement jurisdiction and in imposing civil penalties: s 38(3). Leave for representation may be granted.
40 Productivity Commission, vol. 1, p. 380.
41 Productivity Commission Report No 72, *Access to Justice Arrangements* (2014), vol. 1, p. 533, pp. 550, 552; vol. 2 p. 641.

III. The legal framework for consumer sales

The *Competition and Consumer Act 2010* (Cth) (CCA) re-enacted the Trade Practices Act 1974 (Cth) and introduced changes in consumer protection rules. The Australian Consumer Law (ACL) is in Schedule 2 to the CCA. It applies to all sectors of the economy except financial services which are governed by other statutes.[42] There is provision for extra territorial jurisdiction.[43]

The structure of the ACL follows a conventional pattern of definitions followed by Parts for particular sets of protections. The following outlines this structure: Chapter 2, General Protections (misleading or deceptive conduct, unconscionable conduct and unfair contract terms provisions); Chapter 3, Specific Protections (including false representations, pyramid and other selling mechanisms, consumer guarantees and product safe provisions); Chapter 4, offenses; Chapter 5, Enforcement and Remedies.

Chapter 3.2 Division 1 contains the consumer guarantees. The consumer guarantees impose performance standards on a supply of goods to a consumer. In general, these require a supply 'in trade or commerce' to 'a consumer' that is not a sale by auction. There is a consumer if the value of the goods is $40,000 or less or if the goods are of a kind ordinarily used for personal, domestic or household purposes.[44] Neither instance applies if the goods were acquired for resupply or for using up or transforming them in trade or commerce.[45] The right of recovery is against the supplier. The guarantees cannot be excluded by contract.[46] It is not compulsory to display a sign alerting consumers to their rights regarding consumer guarantees, but this can, if necessary, be mandated.[47]

In contrast with implied terms in a contract, the consumer guarantees are not contractual terms, but statutory obligations. They are more akin to an obligation in tort than in contract. The obligations are familiar to sale of goods lawyers as they require conformity with good title,[48] undisturbed possession,[49] freedom from undisclosed security interests,[50] acceptable quality,[51] fitness for a disclosed purpose,[52] correspondence with description,[53] correspondence with the sample or demonstration model,[54] availability of spare parts and repairs for a reasonable

---

42 *Corporations Act 2001* (Cth); *National Consumer Credit Protection Act 2009* (Cth) and the *Australian Securities and Investments Commission Act 2001* (Cth) which echoes the ACL.
43 *Competition and Consumer Act 2010* (Cth) s 44AD.
44 ACL s 3 (1).
45 ACL s 3 (2).
46 ACL s 64.
47 ACL s 66.
48 ACL s 51.
49 ACL s 52.
50 ACL s 53.
51 ACL s 54.
52 ACL s 55.
53 ACL s 56.
54 ACL s 57.

period,[55] and compliance with express warranties given by manufacturer or supplier.[56] The consumer guarantees in the provision of services are due skill and care in rendering the service,[57] fitness for a communicated purpose,[58] and supply of the service within a reasonable time.[59]

To meet the standard of the consumer guarantee of acceptable quality, the goods must be fit for all purposes for which such goods are commonly supplied; acceptable in appearance and finish; free from defects; safe; and durable.[60] This is judged against what a reasonable consumer fully acquainted with the state of the goods and any hidden defects would find acceptable.[61] The nature of the goods, their price, any statements on labels or packaging, representations by the supplier or manufacturer and any other relevant circumstances must be taken into account.[62]

In addition to the mandatory consumer guarantees, some suppliers offer a warranty against defects to consumers. This is usually sold as an extended warranty that goods will be repaired, replaced or compensation provided if there is a problem.[63] Extended warranties must contain a statement that the consumer already has the benefit of the consumer guarantees, ensuring a clear distinction between the two.[64]

Chapter 3.3 concerns product safety. The first Division is about safety standards. Subsequent Divisions are largely about banning goods; compulsory and voluntary recall of goods; and safety warning notices. Division 5 has provisions that require suppliers to report goods or product related services associated with death or serious injury. Part 3.4 is about information standards for goods and services.

Part 3.5 sets out non-excludable manufacturer's liability for goods with safety defects that have been supplied in trade or commerce.[65] There is a safety defect if goods are not as safe as persons are entitled to expect taking into account warnings, as well as what might reasonably be expected to be done in relation to the goods.[66] There are four causes of action: the goods injure or kill a person;[67] cause loss to another person because an individual was injured or died;[68] damage or destroy other goods ordinarily used for a household purpose and used for such a purpose;[69] and destroy or damage land, buildings or fixtures ordinarily acquired for private use and so used or intended to be used as such.[70] The regulator may

---

55 ACL s 58.
56 ACL s 59, s 2 'express warranty'.
57 ACL s 60.
58 ACL s 61.
59 ACL s 62.
60 ACL s 54 (2) (a) (b) (c) (d) (e).
61 ACL s 54 (2).
62 ACL s 54(3).
63 ACL s 102.
64 Competition and Consumer Regulations 2010 (Cth) reg 90 (2).
65 ACL s 150.
66 ACL s 9.
67 ACL s 138.
68 ACL s 139.
69 ACL s 140.
70 ACL s 141.

take representative action.[71] Defences include absence of a safety defect at the time of supply by the actual manufacturer; compliance with a mandatory safety standard; inability to discover a safety defect because of the state of scientific or technical knowledge.[72] When offending goods are comprised in other goods, it is a defence if the safety defect is attributable only to the design of the other goods, the markings of the other goods or the manufacturer's instructions or warnings regarding the other goods.[73]

Chapter 4 has seven parts. A contravention of Chapter 2 or Chapter 3 provisions is not an offence.[74] The offenses largely replicate the civil contraventions in Chapter 3 and provide for defences. However, a contravention of the misleading or deceptive conduct, unconscionable conduct, unfair contract terms and consumer guarantee provisions do not lead to co requisite offenses. It is an offence if the supplier fails to comply with the prescribed form and content for a warranty against defects.[75] It is an offence to fail to comply with a substantiation notice issued by the regulator regarding a claim or representation made to promote the supply of goods.[76] Prosecutions must commence within 3 years, and if necessary, preference must be given to compensation rather than the fine.[77]

Chapter 5's heading is Enforcement and Remedies. There is a role for both regulator and consumer. The ACCC can enforce the civil provisions of the ACL by taking an undertaking;[78] requiring claims or representations about goods or services to be substantiated;[79] issuing a public warning notice about the conduct of a person;[80] asking the court to impose civil or pecuniary penalties (but not for failure to conform with the consumer guarantees);[81] seeking an injunction from the court;[82] seeking compensation from the court for loss suffered by a person because of the conduct of another person;[83] seeking redress for loss or damage suffered by non-party consumers;[84] seeking a non-punitive order from the court for a community service order, a compliance programme, or education and training programmes;[85] seeking an adverse publicity order from the court;[86] seeking an order from the court that a person be disqualified from managing a

---

71 ACL s 149.
72 ACL s 142.
73 ACL s 142 (d).
74 ACL s 217.
75 ACL s 192.
76 ACL s 206.
77 ACL s 212, s 213.
78 ACL s 218.
79 ACL s 219.
80 ACL s 223.
81 ACL s 224. Preference must be given to compensation rather than the pecuniary penalty: ACL s 227.
82 ACL s 232 (2).
83 ACL s 237.
84 ACL s 239.
85 ACL s 246.
86 ACL s 247.

corporation (but not for failure to conform with a consumer guarantee nor for manufacturer's liabilities for safety defects);[87] and seeking a declaration from the court that a contractual term is an unfair term.[88]

A person can recover damages for conduct that contravenes all provisions in ACL Chapters 2 and 3.[89] There is a separate part for consumer guarantees remedies.[90] Remedies are available against both the supplier and the manufacturer.[91] These differ if there was a major failure to achieve the performance standards.[92] Irrespective of it being a major failure, a consumer can recover damages for failure to comply with a guarantee if it was reasonably foreseeable that the failure would cause the loss or damage.[93] It is a major failure if a reasonable consumer fully acquainted with the nature and extent of the defects would not have acquired the goods; there is a significant departure from the description, sample or demonstration model; the goods are substantially unfit for the purpose for which such goods are commonly supplied or for the disclosed and communicated purpose, and they cannot be easily remedied to be made fit; or if the goods are of unacceptable quality because they are unsafe.[94]

If it is not a major failure and can be remedied the consumer may require the supplier to remedy the failure.[95] If the supplier does not do this, the consumer can have the defect remedied and recover costs from the supplier.[96] The consumer can reject the goods, subject to notification requirements, in three situations: (1) the supplier fails to remedy a non-major failure defect;[97] (2) the goods cannot be remedied;[98] and (3) the lack of performance is a major failure.[99] An alternative to rejecting the goods if they cannot be remedied or it is a major failure is compensation for the difference in price and value of the goods.[100]

IV. Factual scenarios

Scenario 1

The car has been supplied to A by the retailer, B who acquired it from the manufacturer, R. The manufacturer made statements in an advertising campaign. The

---

87 ACL s 248.
88 ACL s 250.
89 ACL s 236.
90 ACL Part 5–4.
91 ACL ss 259–266; ss 271–273.
92 Judicial comment refers to the 'complexity' of the provisions. *Director of Consumer Affairs Victoria v The Good Guys Discount Warehouses (Australia) Pty Ltd.* [2016] FCA 22 at [31].
93 ACL s 259 (4), s 259 (6).
94 ACL s 260.
95 ACL s 259 (2). There is an exception for the guarantees of spare parts and repairs, and the express warranty that becomes a statutory guarantee.
96 ACL s 259 (3).
97 ACL s 259 (2) (b) (ii).
98 ACL s 259 (3).
99 ACL s 259 (3) (a).
100 ACL s 259 (3) (b).

buyer communicated the purposes in buying the car. The retailer made representations about the performance of the car. A short time after the sale, there were problems with the individual car and a news story about cars manufactured by D. A has bought a new car that does not accord with statements as advertised by the manufacturer nor as represented by the retailer. A should approach her state-based Tribunal (in NSW this will be NCAT). As an applicant, she bears the standard of proof, on the balance of probabilities, to establish faults in the car.

This is a consumer sale. It is a sale by a retailer and not by auction. A has bought the car to commute to work and not for resupply. If the price of the car is under $40,000, it is certainly a consumer sale. If it is over $40,000, the car would be 'goods of a kind ordinarily bought for personal, domestic of household purposes'.[101] Under the ACL, action can be brought against the retailer and the manufacturer for failure to comply with the consumer guarantees.[102]

(i)(a) Brake and engine noise (new car)

A should claim that the car fails to meet the consumer guarantee of acceptable quality. At the time of writing, there is no superior court decision analysing acceptable quality.[103] A reasonable consumer fully acquainted with the slow brakes and howling engine noise in a new car 3 weeks after the sale is unlikely to regard the car as acceptable even though it is well known that the elasticity of brakes changes as a new car is driven and diesel-fuelled cars make a noise in low-gear changes. Howling might be a matter of degree. That this developed so quickly after the sale may lead to a finding of lack of acceptability, particularly as the statements made about the reliability of the car will be taken into account and the slow brakes may mean the car is becoming unsafe.

(i)(b) Brake and engine noise (second-hand car)

If the car were bought second-hand and was 3 years old, would it be of acceptable quality? A buyer of a second-had car cannot expect a new car. A reasonable consumer would expect to find some problems. In a Tribunal decision, a new car that developed a 'clunk' sound and shaking in the engine more than two and a half years after the sale was found to be of acceptable quality at the time of the sale.[104]

---

101 ACL s 3. See the discussion in *Bunnings Group Limited (formerly Bunnings Pty Ltd) v Laminex Group Limited* [2006] FCA 682 at [81] – [108].
102 Action against the manufacturer is for acceptable quality, description, repairs and spare parts, and express warranties. ACL s 271.
103 There are two court decisions *Burton v Chad One Pty Limited* [2013] NSWDC 301; *Cary Boyd v Agrison Pty Ltd (Civil)* [2014] VMC 23 and many Tribunal decisions particularly in NCAT and VCAT. Although referred to, whether or not the goods were of acceptable quality was not at issue in *Australian Competition and Consumer Commission v Valve Corporation (No 3)* [2016] FCA 196.
104 *Salim Investments Pty Ltd v MCM Autos Pty Ltd & Mazda Australia Pty Ltd.* [2015] NSW-CATCD 115.

(ii) Higher-than-expected fuel consumption

A should argue that B has not met consumer guarantee of fitness for a disclosed purpose. An explicitly communicated the purpose of using the car for a daily 30-mile commute and also by making enquiries about the low fuel consumption implicitly communicated the purpose of a car with a low fuel consumption.[105]

There may be an argument regarding failure of the guarantee of correspondence with description. The claims about reliability, fuel consumption and environmentally best, may go, not only to qualities, but to the kind of car.[106]

(iii) Failure to meet emissions standards

Depending on the veracity of the news story, the car may have failed to meet emission standards. This may also be a failure of acceptable quality as a reasonable consumer knowing that the car does not meet emission standards is unlikely to regard the car as acceptable. The existence of emission standards would be a relevant circumstance to be taken into account.[107] The accumulation of problems with the brakes, engine and fuel emissions strengthens the argument that the car is not of acceptable quality and A has a remedy against the retailer.

A may consider, but is unlikely to have a successful argument, that the car has a safety defect. Failure to meet emission standards may be unsafe for the environment, but to establish manufacturer's liability for the car having a safety defect, it would be necessary to establish that the car caused injury, death or damage to property.[108] There is no evidence that the emissions have caused any injury.

It is a contravention of the ACL to supply goods that do not comply with safety standards.[109] Emissions are governed by Australian Design Rules under the *Motor Vehicle Standards Act 1989*.[110] They are also mandatory safety standards for the ACL.[111] Both the manufacturer and retailer are potentially liable for a pecuniary penalty if treated as a civil matter[112] or an offence with a maximum penalty of $1.1 million.[113]

---

105 ACL s 55 (2) (a).
106 In *Ferraro v DBN Holdings Aust Pty Ltd v T/as Sports Auto Group* [2015] FCA 1127, a second-hand sports car did not correspond with description, and the court ordered that the buyer could retain the car, which was security for bank finance, until the refund was paid. The car was required to be kept locked, undriven and insured.
107 ACL s 54 (3).
108 ACL ss138, 139, 140, 141.
109 ACL s 106; *Electrolux Home Products Pty Ltd v Delap Impex KFT* [2015] FCA 62.
110 www.comlaw.gov.au/Details/F2011L02016/Supporting%20Material/Text.
111 Lack of safety for 'acceptable quality' does not require injury, http://minister.infrastructure.gov.au/pf/releases/2015/October/pf005_2015.aspx.
112 ACL s 106.
113 ACL s 194.

The assertions in the advertisement

The manufacturer made assertions about the quality, performance and characteristics of the goods[114] in an advertisement, namely that the car had low fuel consumption, was extremely reliable and best for the environment. Any assertion or representation made in connection with the promotion of the supply of the goods which has the natural tendency to induce a person to acquire the goods is an express warranty.[115] A was clearly influenced by these assertions as she asked subsequent questions.

A should argue that by making these express assertions, R has not met the consumer guarantee that the manufacturer will comply with any express warranty made by the manufacturer.[116]

A should also claim against the manufacturer for misleading or deceptive advertising.[117] R 'engaged in conduct' which was 'in trade or commerce'. The claims were directed towards the car-buying public and will be tested against the perceptions of that group except those who unreasonably fail to take care of themselves. The conduct is assessed as a whole in the light of relevant circumstances; does not have to be intentionally misleading; and it is unnecessary to prove that any particular person was misled.[118] The environmental and fuel claims are likely to be successful.[119] The reliability claim may be more problematic as, despite the slower braking and noise, the car may be reliable and may turn on 'top'. If the advertising statements are treated as representations as to the future that is that the car will be reliable, will have good fuel consumption and will be best for the environment, the ads will be misleading or deceptive unless there were reasonable grounds for making the representations.[120]

Remedies

A may wish to reject the car and obtain a refund. It is less likely, but she may wish to claim the difference between the price and value of the car.[121] A should argue there is a major failure due to unacceptable quality, including failure to meet

---

114 ACL s 2 'express warranty'.
115 ACL s 2.
116 ACL s 59.
117 ACL s 18.
118 *Campbell v BackOffice Investments Pty Ltd.* [2009] HCA 25; *Butcher v Lachlan Elder Realty Pty Ltd.* [2004] HCA 60. See *Australian Competition and Consumer Commission v Trading Post Australia Pty Ltd.* [2011] FCA 1086 [31] – [40] and *Australian Competition and Consumer Commission v Valve Corporation (No 3)* [2016] FCA 196 [212] – [228].
119 By consent, the Federal Court declared that advertisements by car manufacturer GM Holden contravened the prohibition on misleading or deceptive conduct when it made 'Grrrrrreen' marketing claims for Saab. ACCC, *Saab 'Grrrrrreen' Claims Declared Misleading by Federal Court* Media Release, MR 267/08 18 September 2008.
120 ACL s 4.
121 ACL s 259 (3) (a), s 263, s 259 (4).

the emission standards,[122] substantial lack of fitness for purpose that cannot be remedied, departure from description, and due to an accumulation of problems with the car.[123] In order to reject, she must notify the supplier and take the car to the retailer.[124]

The retailer may wish to repair the car. He will need to argue either that the guarantees have been met or that any failures do not constitute a major failure. He will argue that the car is safe, that the slow brakes, engine noise at a low speed gear change and higher-than-expected fuel consumption can all be remedied, and that if there is any departure from description or lack of fitness, this is not significant or substantial.

Failure to meet the express warranty/guarantee is not a major failure, and in addition to seeking a refund, A may also claim damages against the manufacturer for this failure.[125] This is in addition to damages or alternate remedies such as an injunction for misleading or deceptive conduct.

Scenario 2

David bought a tablet with preloaded apps (including for smart appliances) and downloaded another app for $15 (for sports). Within 1 week of supply, the sports app interfered first with the preloaded smart appliance apps and second with the Wi-Fi connector so that the tablet could not connect to the internet. The new sports app stopped working within 2 weeks, was patched with an update, and after 6 months, there were no further updates from the supplier. David stopped using it, and the app seller stopped trying to fix it. There is no information about the sports app contract or licence agreement. (We assume the app has been installed correctly.) The sports app does not work properly, and it has caused the preloaded apps and the Wi-Fi connector not to work. It does not appear to have damaged the tablet itself or the smartwatch.

---

122 The statutory nexus between lack of acceptability and a major failure rests on safety. It has been suggested that all failures to reach the standard of 'acceptable quality' will be a major failure as a reasonable consumer knowing of defects which make goods unacceptable would not buy them. See *Prestige Auto Traders Australia Pty Ltd v Bonnefin* [2017] NSWSC 149 at [135] – [142].
123 In *Saltalamaccia v Tayser Automotive Group Pty Ltd Trading as Nunawading Great Wall* (Civil Claims) [2014] VCAT 1463 at [59] a series of faults may result in a finding of lack of acceptable quality.
124 ACL s 262, s 263 provided returning the car is possible. s 259 (3) (a), s 263, s 259 (4). In *Ferraro v DBN Holdings Aust Pty Ltd v T/as Sports Auto Group* [2015] FCA 1127, a second-hand sports car did not correspond with description and the court ordered that the buyer could retain the car, which was security for bank finance, until the refund was paid. The car was required to be kept locked, undriven and insured.
125 ACL s 271(5).

Under the ACL, goods include computer software.[126] Apps are software and therefore goods.[127] Software is severable from the service it supplies.[128] The tablet, the preloaded apps and the new downloaded sports app are all goods for the purposes of the ACL. The update is code, thus software and therefore goods.

Initial commercial software plus updates and modifications under the agreement have been treated as the goods, not the supply of further goods.[129] This would indicate that an update under an initial agreement for an app should be an incident of that app. This distinction is important for if an update were the supply of another good, it may be possible to argue that it was for the purpose of being used up or transformed and therefore not an acquisition by a consumer. However, the using up or transforming exception to a consumer acquisition must be in trade or commerce, which is not the case here.[130]

(i) Failure of the app and failure to patch the problem

The consumer guarantees under the ACL apply to the sports app as this is a consumer sale. The ACL guarantees of fitness for the disclosed purpose, acceptable quality and facilities to repair goods are relevant.

David disclosed the purpose of the sports app to connect to a smartwatch to keep track of heart rate and blood pressure, presumably by implication.[131] In contrast with the Sale of Goods Act implied term,[132] the ACL does not have a proviso regarding a sale under a trade name, so it is not an issue if David selected the app under its trade name. The app worked at the time of supply but stopped working after a week or so. Fitness for purpose is judged at the time of supply.[133] How long does an app have to work? There is no failure of fitness for purpose

---

126 ACL s 2 'goods' (e); See *Australian Competition and Consumer Commission v Valve Corporation (No 3)* [2016 FCA 196 per Edelman J. [126] – [157] and especially [137].
127 On the meaning of app see *Apple Inc. v Registrar of Trade Marks* [2014] FCA 1304 at [180] – [188]. A supplier may be liable for software supplied with hardware, *Australian Competition and Consumer Commission v Avitalb Pty Ltd.* [2014] FCA 222.
128 *Bing! Software v Bing Technologies* [2009] FCAFC 131 at [15].
129 *JR Consulting & Drafting Pty Ltd & Anor v Cummings & Ors* [2014] NSWSC 1252 at [82]. In *JR Consulting* the software was on a disc and not downloaded. But it should make no difference if an update is provided to software that was initially provided by disc or download.
130 ACL s 3 (2) (b).
131 ACL s 55 (2). A disclosed purposes may be made known expressly or by implication. A buyer can make known a purpose via the description by which the goods are acquired *Grant v Australian Knitting Mills Ltd.* [1935] UKPCHCA 1; (1935) 54 CLR 49 at p. 60.
132 Sale of Goods Act 1923 (NSW) s 19 (1); *Tre Cavalli Pty Limited v The Berry Rural Co Operative Society Limited* [2013] NSWCA 235.
133 Relevant information known at the time of the trial can be taken into account to assess what is reasonable for a consumer to expect. *Prestige Auto Traders Australia Pty Ltd v Bonnefin* [2017] NSWSC 149 at [132].

merely because software requires updating.[134] If the update is an incident of the goods and not a separate supply, in the situation where an app works at first, there is a problem, an update fixes it, does this mean the app is fit for the purpose? If the update fails to fix the problem, does this mean the app is not fit for the purpose? The latter appears to be the case with David's sports app.

The sports app will not be of acceptable quality.[135] It is not fit for all the purposes for which such an app is commonly supplied. Even if a court were to find no failure to comply with fitness for the disclosed purpose, it may still find lack of acceptable quality due to lack of durability, safety and freedom from defects.[136] Fifteen dollars for an app is not a cheap app, so consideration of the price is unlikely to help the supplier or manufacturer.

An update to an app may be a facility to repair goods.[137] If so, the guarantee that the manufacturer take reasonable steps to ensure such a facility is reasonably available for a reasonable period after the supply or initial download is not met as it is standard for updates to be provided for considerably longer than 6 months. David was not given notice that facilities to repair would not be available.[138]

There have been unsuccessful attempts to argue failure to disclose risks or withdrawal of support for software is unconscionable conduct.[139] Peremptorily shutting down support for software was not unconscionable where the conduct was 'the outcome of a period of disputation between two commercially sophisticated parties'.[140] David is not a commercially sophisticated party and has an argument that the supplier acted unconscionably in the supply of goods[141] by failing to disclose intended conduct such as stopping resolution of the problem and risks to David,[142] and by not acting in good faith.[143] David's case is strengthened if the supplier's conduct is inconsistent with its conduct towards others who acquired the sports app.[144]

---

134 *TMA Australia Pty Ltd v Indect Electronics & Distribution GmbH* [2015] NSWCA 343 at [48] – [54]. The commercially supplied software required an authenticity check update every 3 months. The acquirer argued there was a breach of fitness for purpose because the software would not operate continuously for the life of the system without update. The Court rejected this argument. This was because the software contained that feature. This contrasts with the situation where the software could not install through no fault of the computer, and the Tribunal said this did not oust the obligation that the software be fit for the purpose. *Gibson v I Product International (General)* [2012] NSWCTTT 204.
135 ACL s 54.
136 ACL s 54 (2).
137 ACL s 58 (1). This is harder to argue if the app plus software together amounts to goods.
138 ACL s 58 (2).
139 ACL ss 20, 21. In *JR Consulting & Drafting Pty Ltd & Anor v Cummings & Ors* [2014] NSWSC 1252 mere moral fault was not unconscionable; *TMA Australia Pty Ltd v Indect Electronics & Distribution GmbH* [2015] NSWCA 343.
140 *TMA Australia Pty Ltd v Indect Electronics & Distribution GmbH* [2015] NSWCA 343 at [148].
141 ACL s 21.
142 ACL s 22 (i) (i), (ii).
143 ACL s 22 (l).
144 ACL s 22 (f).

If there is a failure to meet the performance standards of the consumer guarantees, David will argue that there has been a failure to remedy the failure,[145] as this can be classified as a major failure. The option to reject the app seems unviable. If David uninstalls the app, is this rejection of the goods? How does one reject a downloaded app and its update and return it to the supplier?[146] If David does successfully reject the app, he may elect a refund or a replacement.[147] Neither these options, nor recovery of the difference between price and value seem useful.

(ii) Interference with other apps

The sports app interfered so that the appliance apps did not work so this can be characterised as loss or damage to other goods.[148] Liability depends on the characterisation of the app maker as a manufacturer. Can the platform, the app supplier, or the app developer be a manufacturer? If making software and an app can fall under 'produce' or 'process', there will be a manufacturer.[149] The person who permitted a business name or brand to be applied to the new app, including the platform, can be the manufacturer.[150]

The sports app will have a safety defect as the community at large entitled to expect that a newly downloaded app will not interfere with existing apps so that they do not work to operate the household appliances.[151] There were no warnings that the sports app may interfere with other apps. Goods are not expected to be absolutely risk free and safety is a matter of degree. Absence of any warning has been taken into account in reaching conclusions on a safety defect.[152] If the sports app were held to be defective, the app 'manufacturer' may argue that the state of scientific knowledge at the time the app was supplied, that is downloaded, was not such to discover the defect, that is, that the sports app could interfere with preloaded apps. If it were not possible to discover that there was some code in the sports app that interfered with preloaded software then the manufacturer may have a defence.[153] As a further defence, the sports app manufacturer could

---

145 ACL s 259 (2) (b) (i).
146 ACL s 263 (2) requires a consumer who has rejected the goods to return them to the supplier. There are some exceptions. One is if they have already been retrieved by the supplier. Can a supplier retrieve an app?
147 ACL s 263 (4).
148 ACL s 140. If this is characterised as the sports app software interfering with the service, but not the software provided by the appliance apps, the manufacturer's liability regime does not apply.
149 ACL s 7 (1) (a).
150 ACL s 7(1).
151 ACL s 9.
152 *Peterson v Merck Sharpe & Dohme (Aust) Pty Ltd.* [2010] FCA 180 at [191–192], [198].
153 ACL s 142 (c); *Peterson v Merck Sharpe & Dohme (Aust) Pty Ltd.* [2010] FCA 180 at [208].

also explore whether the sports app is goods comprised in other goods, that is the tablet and if the defect could be attributable to the tablet.[154]

(iii) Damage done to the Wi-Fi connector

The argument for manufacturer's liability for damage to the Wi-Fi connector will be similar to that for interference with the preloaded apps. It is immaterial that one is hardware and the other software. The community is entitled to expect that software will not damage either hardware or other software.[155] A finding that the app is unsafe supports argument for a major failure to meet the consumer guarantee standard of acceptable quality.

V. Specific issues in Australia

The new consumer guarantees of the ACL exist alongside the implied terms of the state-based Sale of Goods Acts, some of which have specific provisions for consumer sales.[156] The ACL applies to faulty goods (including software) and conduct.[157] It will not apply to the telecommunications service aspect of an app.[158]

---

154 ACL s 142 (d).
155 ACL s 140.
156 E.g. Sale of Goods Act 1923 (NSW) s 62, s 64.
157 Other relevant codes and legislation are the e Payments Code for online payments; the Privacy Act 1988 for dealing with personal data; the Broadcasting Services Act 1992 for content; and the Telecommunications Act 1997 for particular segments such telecommunications service providers and content providers. See Australian Government, Australian Communications and Media Authority, *Mobile Apps Emerging Issues in Media and Communications Occasional Paper 1* (March 2013) pp. 14, 15.
158 ACL s 65(1) (b); s 65 (2).

2 Consumer sales law in the European Union

Mateja Durovic

I. The European Union consumer market

The European Union (EU) is the largest economy of the world, and consumer spending represents 57% of its gross domestic product (GDP).[1] The EU consists of 28 Member States with a total population of around 510 million people. It has been established and developed around the idea of the common market with a free flow of goods, services, people and capital among the Member States. Together with the strengthening of the internal market, the European Union as of year 1975 has also started setting up its common consumer law and policy.[2] On the one hand, the efforts and reasons behind the development of EU consumer law have been based on the necessity to have a uniformed legal framework for consumer protection in all EU Member States which would, through contribution to the legal certainty, encourage cross-border trade and strengthen further the internal market. On the other hand, the rise of EU Consumer Law has occurred in order to achieve a high level of consumer protection from which all citizens in the EU would profit. Eventually, the final outcome is that, today, the European Union has got the most advanced system of consumer protection in the world.[3]

Despite a well-developed legal framework for consumer protection, consumers' awareness in the EU of their consumer rights while acting at the market is still limited. This is why the European Commission has launched the Consumer Awareness Campaign.[4] When it comes to consumer satisfaction, the European Commission regularly publishes two Consumer Scoreboards: Consumer Conditions Scoreboard and Consumer Markets Scoreboard. These two documents contain the results of the assessment of consumer satisfaction with the market and

---

1 Consumer Conditions Scoreboard 2015, 5, http://ec.europa.eu/consumers/consumer_evidence/consumer_scoreboards/11_edition/docs/ccs2015scoreboard_en.pdf.
2 Preliminary Programme of the European Community for consumer protection and information policy OJ C 92, 25.4.1975, 2–16.
3 On EU Consumer Law, see H. Micklitz, N. Reich, P. Rott and K. Tonner, *EU Consumer Law* (2014), Intersentia, Cambridge; S. Weatherill, *EU Consumer Law and Policy*, 2nd ed. (2013), Edward Elgar Publishing, London.
4 Consumer Awareness Campaign, http://ec.europa.eu/justice/newsroom/consumer-marketing/events/140317_en.htm.

provide the output for the future consumer policy. According to the latest available Consumer Markets Scoreboard, consumer satisfaction seems to be higher in case of the market of goods than in case of the market of services.[5] Among particular types of consumer goods, the books, magazines and newspapers, non-alcoholic drinks and bread, cereals, rice and pasta market are the three types of the goods placed at the market in case of which the best performance and consumer satisfaction has been recorded. Contrary to this, meat and meat products, fuel for vehicles and second-hand car market are the three markets of goods with the lowest performance and level of consumer satisfaction.[6] Cars are, generally speaking, consumer goods where particular number of consumer complaints have been present. Particularly significant is the case of the cars manufactured by the company Volkswagen, which, due to the secretly installed illegal device air pollutant emission standards, turned out not to be in conformity with the specifications of the sales contract. This widely spread illegal practice of Volkswagen was discovered in 2015, and currently, this is one of the most important pending consumer issues in Europe as millions of consumers have bought this car model.

Present focus of EU Consumer Law and Policy is to provide an adequate regulatory response to the development of the market, modern technologies, digital economies and new shopping techniques. This goal may be clearly identified as a priority in the Digital Single Market strategy which the European Commission adopted in May 2015.[7] The supply of digital content and the online shopping are becoming increasingly popular consumer activities in the EU, but there is not yet a piece of uniform European consumer legislation that deals with this particular issue. Consequently, in December 2015, the European Commission published its two legislative proposals: Proposal for a Directive on certain aspects concerning contracts for the supply of digital content[8] and Proposal for Directive on certain aspects concerning contracts for the online and other distance sales of goods.[9] Both of these Proposals are currently being assessed and discussed by the relevant stakeholders.

II. Access to justice for consumers in the European Union

Consumer access to justice as one of the human rights in the EU

In the EU, the right of any person to have an adequate and efficient protection of his or her consumer rights has been equalised with a human right which thus

---

5 10th Consumer Markets Scoreboard 2014, 5, http://ec.europa.eu/consumers/consumer_evidence/consumer_scoreboards/10_edition/docs/consumer_market_brochure_141027_en.pdf.
6 Ibid., p. 11.
7 A Digital Single Market Strategy for Europe – COM(2015) 192 final.
8 COM(2015) 634 final.
9 COM(2015) 635 final.

deserves particularly high level of protection.[10] Consumer's right to access to justice in cases when his or her consumer rights have been infringed is guaranteed both through the provisions of the Charter of Fundamental Rights of the European Union, as the most important codex of human rights of the European Union,[11] and by the rules of the European Convention of Human Rights, as one of the most significant global instruments for protection of human rights, to which all of the 28 EU Member States are contracting parties.[12]

In practice, consumer access to justice takes place in the EU Member States before the national authorities. EU Law only imposes a mandatory obligation on each of the EU Member States to secure consumers' access to justice when their consumer rights have been infringed.[13] The enforcement powers of the European Union are limited and concentrated primarily on the coordination of cooperation between the European Commission and the national authorities responsible for the enforcement of consumer protection laws in all areas of consumer law of the EU Member States.

The legal framework for the cooperation has been set up through the provisions of Regulation 2006/2004 on consumer protection cooperation.[14] The principal goal of the Regulation is to ensure that EU consumer law is applied equally and that consumers have an effective access to justice throughout the European Union. Moreover, the European Court of Justice (ECJ) plays an increasingly important role in clarifying what are the obligations of the Member States is securing the effective access to justice of consumers.[15] Eventually, BEUC, the European Consumer Organisation, which connects the national consumer organisations is also an important institution which helps coordination of the pan-European enforcement of consumer law.[16]

Individual redress

Common European rules on individual consumer redress are rather limited. EU Member States are left with what is called 'procedural authomy' to define themselves legal frameworks which will secure consumer access to justice. The

---

10 I. Benöhr, *EU Consumer Law and Human Rights* (Cambridge: Cambridge University Press, 2013).
11 Articles 38 and 47 Charter of Fundamental Rights of the European Union.
12 Articles 6 and 13 ECHR.
13 Joined Cases C-317/08 to C-320/08 *Rosalba Alassini e.a. v. Telecom It Spa e.a.* [2010] ECR I-02213, para 61.
14 Regulation (EC) No 2006/2004 of the European Parliament and of the Council of 27 October 2004 on cooperation between national authorities responsible for the enforcement of consumer protection laws (the Regulation on consumer protection cooperation) [2004] OJ L 364/1.
15 S. Wrbka, *European Consumer Access to Justice Revisited* (Cambridge: Cambridge University Press, 2014).
16 M. Durovic, "The Apple Case: The Commencement of Pan-European Battle Against Unfair Commercial Practices" (2013) 9 *European Review of Contract Law* 253.

procedural autonomy is, however, not absolute, but limited by two principles: the principle of equivalence and the principle effectiveness. The principle of equivalence requires that the rules of EU Member States used for enforcement of EU consumer law should not be less favourable than those governing similar situations subject to domestic law. The principle of efficiency means that the national rules of EU Member States should not make it impossible in practice or excessively difficult to exercise the rights conferred by EU Consumer law. Through the interpretation of the principles of equivalence and effectiveness, the ECJ has substantially shaped and limited procedural autonomy of the EU Member States.[17] The most influential is the development of *ex officio* doctrine, that is identification by the ECJ of different sets of obligations that the national courts are supposed to assess by their own motions while applying EU Consumer law as developed in a particular Member State.[18]

One of few common European rules that touches upon the individual enforcement is Regulation 861/2007 on small claim procedure.[19] This Regulation is aimed to address particularities of consumer claims which are typically of low value, where consumer misses an incentive to start court proceedings. This is why this Regulation has established special procedure rules for consumer disputes which are based on simplicity, speed and proportionality. However, the effects of this Regulation in practice are rather limited as insufficient number of national authorities apply it, followed by the lack of familiarity of its provisions by the lawyers and general public. This Regulation is currently under a revision process.

Following the tendency of the development of diverse forms of out-of-court settlements of consumer disputes, the European Union has itself established a common European legal framework on consumer arbitration. That was done through the adoption of Directive 2013/11/EU on alternative resolution of consumer disputes which entered into force in 2013. EU Member States are obliged to secure the existence of an operational scheme of consumer arbitration. Importantly, this Directive is focused on securing adequate legal framework for consumer arbitration in case of cross-border disputes among different Member States. However, it has laid down some general principles that consumer arbitration in the EU needs to fulfil. For instance, that is the case with the requirements related to the expertise, independency, impartiality, transparency, effectiveness, fairness, liberty and legality that any entity in charge of running consumer arbitration and the arbitration procedure itself, always need to fulfil.

---

17 Case C-415/11 *Mohamed Aziz v Caixa d'Estalvis de Catalunya, Tarragona i Manresa (Catalunyacaixa)* [2013], para 50; Case C-565/11 *Mariana Irimie v Administraţia Finanţelor Publice Sibiu and Administraţia Fondului pentru Mediu* [2013], para 23; Case C-32/12 *Soledad Duarte Hueros v Autociba SA and Automóviles Citroën España SA* [2013], para 31; Case C-413/12 *Asociación de Consumidores Independientes de Castilla y León v Anuntis Segundamano España SL* [2013], para 30.
18 V. Trstenjak, "Procedural Aspects of European Consumer Protection Law and the Case Law of the CJEU" (2013) 21 *European Review of Private Law* 451.
19 Regulation 861/2007 on small claim procedure, *OJ L 199, 31.7.2007*, pp. 1–22.

In addition to the general consumer arbitration legislation, a set of specific European rules deals with the online consumer arbitration. That is Regulation 524/2013 on online resolution of consumer disputes which started applying in 2016.[20] The online consumer arbitration is used in case of consumer disputes which have arisen from online transactions, in particular the online transactions performed by market players from different EU Member States. This is in line with EU tendency to focus its legislative efforts on cross-border consumer transactions. It is, somehow, expected that consumers who perform their economic activities online have also possibilities to an online resolution of disputes that arise from these online activities. Online resolution of consumer disputes is thus seen as an excellent and most efficient manner to resolve consumer disputes which have arisen from the online commercial transactions.

Collective redress

In line with a tendency of collective redress becoming an increasingly popular instrument to secure consumers' access to justice worldwide, the European Union has provided some rules on collective redress. These rules are more extensive than in case of individual redress, but incomplete, leaving to a large extent to the EU Member States freedom to choose their national models for collective redress.

The most important piece of the European legislation is Directive 2009/22/EC on injunctions which secures that in each Member State there exists a possibility of an effective injunction procedure and issuing of measures of cessation or prohibition whenever collective interests of consumers have been harmed.[21] Despite the fact that Directive 2009/22/EC is focused on cross-border consumer disputes, its provisions are also relevant for the national laws of EU Member States as this Directive needs to be seen as a benchmark according to which national rules on collective redress have to be evaluated.[22]

Subsequently to Directive 2009/22/EC on injunctions, the European Union has published Recommendation 2013/396/EU on collective redress.[23] This Recommendation suggests that each EU Member State should adopt a legal framework for collective redress of consumers. The choice regarding the model of the collective redress is, however, left to the Member States which may freely decide on that.[24]

20 Regulation 524/2013 on online resolution of consumer disputes, *OJ L 165, 18.6.2013*, pp. 1–12.
21 Directive 2009/22/EC of the European Parliament and of the Council of 23 April 2009 on injunctions for the protection of consumers' interests (Codified version) [2009] OJ L110/30 1.5.2009, pp. 269–275.
22 H.W. Micklitz, "A Common Approach on the Collective Enforcement of Unfair Commercial Practices and Unfair Contract Terms" in W. Van Boom, A. Garde and O. Akseli (eds.), *The European Unfair Commercial Practices Directive – Impact, Enforcement Strategies and National Legal Systems* (UK: Ashgate, 2014).
23 Recommendation 2013/396/EU on collective redress, OJ L 201, 26.7.2013, pp. 60–65.
24 For a more detailed explanation, see: C. Hodges, "Collective Redress: A Breakthrough or a Damp Sqibb?" (2014) 34 *Journal of Consumer Policy* 67.

III. EU legal framework for consumer sales

In the European Union, the most significant source of the common European rules on consumer sales is Directive 1999/44/EC on consumer sales and associated guarantees (Sales Directive). This Directive was adopted in 1999, and all of the twenty-eight EU Member States have transposed the provisions of this Directive into their national legal systems. The provisions of the Sales Directive apply to contracts for the sale of consumer goods concluded between a seller, as any natural or legal person who, under a contract, sells consumer goods in the course of his trade, business or profession, and a consumer, a natural person who is acting for purposes which are not related to his trade, business or profession.[25]

Consumer goods are defined as any tangible movable item, with the exception of goods sold by way of execution or otherwise by authority of law, water and gas where they are not put up for sale in a limited volume or set quantity and electricity.[26] In all cases when a particular sales contract falls within the scope of the Sales Directive, EU Law requires *ex officio* application of the Directive's provisions in order to secure an effective protection to the consumers as it was pointed out by the ECJ in its case law.[27]

The Sales Directive is a directive which requires only minimum harmonisation.[28] Its minimum harmonisation nature means that EU Member States are free to provide a higher level of protection than the one envisaged by the directive, which is especially relevant when it comes to the conformity period and hierarchical order of the remedies to be used in case of the lack of conformity.[29] Besides the Sales Directive, an additional set of rules relevant for consumer sales is contained in Directive 2005/29/EC on unfair commercial practices, Directive 93/13/EEC on unfair contract terms and Directive 2011/83/EU on consumer rights which all together complete European legal framework for consumer sales.

In case of sales of consumer goods, one of the most important issues is the question of guarantee, that is, the existence of seller's liability for occurrence of any defects of the sold goods. Under EU Law, a distinction is to be made between the legal (or statutory) guarantee and the commercial guarantee. The legal guarantee is a mandatory guarantee which is granted to the consumer by the Sales Directive for the period of, at least (as EU Member States may envisage a longer period in line with the minimum harmonisation approach), two years during which seller is liable for the lack of conformity with the contract of the sold goods.

The commercial guarantee is an additional guarantee provided by the seller himself or herself, either free of charge or for remuneration, which provides a

---

25 Article 1(2)(a) and (c) Sales Directive.
26 Article 1(2)(b) Sales Directive.
27 Case C-497/13 *Froukje Faber v Autobedrijf Hazet Ochten BV* (2015).
28 Article 8(2) Sales Directive.
29 H. Schulte-Nolke, C. Twigg-Flesner and M. Ebers (eds.), *EC Consumer Law Compendium* (Munich: Sellier, 2007).

higher level of protection to consumer than the legal guarantee.[30] Some of the examples of commercial guarantee include cases of the longer period of duration of the conformity requirement than the mandatory 2 years or the existence of a possibility given to consumer to freely terminate the contract without the need to firstly exhaust other remedies for the lack of conformity. In practice, commercial practice plays an important role as it does not only provide an additional protection to consumer, but it also stimulates fair competition of the traders at the market.[31]

The seller is prohibited from presenting the legal guarantee as a specific feature of the consumer goods. Moreover, the seller is obliged to inform consumer about the existence and meaning of the legal guarantee and, in cases when the commercial guarantee is offered, the manners in which it provides a higher level of protection than the legal guarantee.[32] Otherwise, the seller will be liable for engagement in misleading practices under Directive 2005/29/EC on unfair commercial practices (UCPD).[33] One of most important and successful consumer law cases in the European Union dealt exactly with such kind of misleading practices, the Apple case.[34]

The legal guarantee is binding, and its application can never be excluded by the contractual parties.[35] A clause in consumer contract which is aimed to in any manner limit or completely exclude the legal guarantee is contrary not only to the Sales Directive, but such a term would be also considered as unfair, and thus, it will be contrary to the provisions of Directive 93/13/EEC on unfair contract terms and would also represent an illegal practice under the provisions of the UCPD.[36]

According to the Sales Directive, the seller is liable for any lack of conformity which becomes apparent within the period of 2 years as of the day of the delivery of the goods.[37] The lack of conformity needs to have existed at the moment when the purchased goods were delivered to the consumer.[38] During the first 6 months from the delivery of the goods, it is presumed that the lack of conformity existed at the moment of delivery.[39] In order to win in his or her claim, the consumer is

---

30 Article 2(1)(14) CRD.
31 M.C. Bianca and S. Grundmann, *EU Sales Directive* (Antwerp et al.: Intersentia, 2002), p. 221.
32 Article 5(1)(e) CRD.
33 Article 5(5) and point 10 of Annex I UCPD.
34 M. Durovic, "The Apple Case: The Commencement of Pan-European Battle Against Unfair Commercial Practices" (2013) 9 *European Review of Contract Law* 253.
35 Article 7 Sales Directive.
36 Case C-453/10 *Jana Pereničová and Vladislav Pereníč v SOS financ spol. s r. o.* [2012].
37 Article 5(1) Sales Directive.
38 Case C-32/12 *Soledad Duarte Hueros v Autociba SA and Automóviles Citroën España SA* [2013] ECR I-0000, para 27; Case C-404/06 *Quelle AG v Bundesverband der Verbraucherzentralen und Verbraucherverbände* [2008] ECR I-02685, para 26; Joined Cases C-65/09 and C-87/09 *Gebr. Weber GmbH v Jürgen Wittmer and Ingrid Putz v Medianess Electronics GmbH* [2011] ECR I-05257, para 43.
39 Article 5(3) Sales Directive.

only required to prove the existence of the lack of conformity and that it became physically apparent, within 6 months of delivery of the goods.[40] After the expiry of the period of 6 months, the burden of proof shifts, and in order to succeed in his or her claim, consumer needs also to prove that the cause of the lack of conformity or its origin are attributable to the seller.

Under EU Law, the lack of conformity will exist when the acquired goods, first, do not comply with a description provided by the seller or as it was shown in a sample or model; second, when they do not fit the specific purposes for which consumers purchased them and which the seller accepted; third, when the goods are not fit for the purpose such products are normally used for; fourth, when the quality and performance of the goods are not in accordance with seller's, producer's or producer's representative public statements about the goods, in particular taking into consideration advertising and labelling.[41]

However, in certain cases, consumer's claim will not be successful. In the case where the consumer was aware, or could not reasonably be unaware of, the lack of conformity, or if the lack of conformity has its origin in materials supplied by the consumer.[42] In addition to this, consumer will neither succeed in cases when the seller has succeeded to prove that he was not, and could not reasonably have been, aware of a particular public statement about consumer goods or that by the time of conclusion of the contract the statement had been corrected, or that the decision to buy the consumer goods could not have been influenced by the statement.[43]

In case of occurrence of the lack of conformity, EU Law envisages two tiers of remedies.[44] First, the consumer has the right to ask for the replacement of defective goods or its repair. Second, in cases when consumer's claim for replacement or appropriate is not appropriate or replacement or repair have not been completed within reasonable period of time or they cause significant inconvenience to the consumer, the consumer can opt for contract termination or diminution of the paid price. The choice between the remedies within a specific tier is always on consumer.

In case of the first tier, repair or replacement of defective goods always needs to be done within reasonable period of time, free of charge and without significant inconvenience to the consumer. Seller is prohibited of imposing of any kind of cost on consumer who requires replacement or repair of the goods.[45] The seller is obliged to bear all cost of removing defective goods and instalments of the new ones with which the defective ones are to be replaced. The seller will be exempted from this obligation only in cases when the replacement represents

---

40 Case C-497/13 Froukje Faber V Autobedrijf Hazet Ochten BV of 4 June 2015, para 70–71.
41 Article 2(2) Sales Directive.
42 Article 2(3) Sales Directive.
43 Article 2(4) Sales Directive.
44 Article 3 Sales Directive.
45 Case C-404/06 *Quelle AG v Bundesverband der Verbraucherzentralen und Verbraucherverbände* [2008] ECR I-02685.

a disproportionate cost for the seller.[46] Such an approach has been adopted to secure a fully effective protection of consumer in case of defective goods. Any behaviour of seller contrary to these rules will represent an unfair commercial practice, in particular an aggressive commercial practice as defined by the UCPD, because in such a manner, seller imposes an onerous obstacle to consumer to enforce his or her contractual rights.[47]

In case when none of the options of the first tier are possible, for example due to the fact that the goods cannot be repaired and the seller does not have any goods to replace the defective one, consumer may opt between diminishing of the price and contract rescission. As the Sales Directive is dedicated to protect contractual relationships between seller and consumer, the contract rescission has been given only as a subsidiary option, as part of the second tier of remedies.[48] Consumer's right to terminate the contract is further limited by prohibition of contract rescission in cases when the lack of conformity is minor.[49]

In case of consumer's choice to terminate the contract, the seller is not allowed to demand any kind of compensation from consumer for the usage of goods which turned out not to be in conformity with the contract.[50] Seller's liability for defective goods cannot be exempted on the ground that the lack of conformity is the outcome of the act or omission of the producer, intermediary or previous seller in the contractual chain. In such cases, the seller is still liable to the consumer, but the Sales Directive entitles the seller to ask for compensation from the producer, intermediary or the previous seller. The conditions and manners for enforcing these rights of the seller are left to be defined by the national laws of the Member States.[51]

IV. Factual scenarios

Scenario 1

Under EU Law, Alison is to be considered as a consumer, Billy is a seller and Reliable is a producer. In case of all three situations of Scenario 1, Alison may base her claim and ask for the appropriate remedies which are given to her on the ground of the provisions of the Sales Directive and the UCPD. Under the Sales Directive, Alison does not have remedies against Reliable. However, Reliable may be found liable for its engagement in the unfair commercial practices under the UCPD.

---

46 Joined Cases C-65/09 and C-87/09 *Gebr. Weber GmbH v Jürgen Wittmer and Ingrid Putz v Medianess Electronics GmbH* [2011] ECR I-05257.
47 Article 9(1)(d) Directive 2005/29/EC on unfair commercial practices.
48 H.W. Micklitz, J. Stuyck and E. Terryn (eds.), *Cases, Materials and Text on Consumer Law* (UK: Hart Publishing, 2010), p. 361.
49 Article 3(6) Sales Directive.
50 Case C-489/07 *Pia Messner v Firma Stefan Krüger* [2009] ECR I-7315.
51 Article 4 Sales Directive.

(i)(a) Brake and engine noise (new car)

Under the Sales Directive, the principal obligation of Billy is to deliver the car to Alison which is in conformity with the specification of the contract they have concluded.[52] Otherwise, if the delivered car turns out to be defective, Billy will be liable for the lack of conformity, and Alison may use some of the remedies. The Sales Directive identifies four cases when it will be considered that delivered goods are not in conformity with the contract. In case of her problems with the car brakes, it seems that Alison may successfully argue that the acquired car shows the presence of the lack of conformity on the ground of, at least, three bases.

First, the fact that the car's brakes have deteriorated within such a short period of time, shows that they are not completely fit for the particular use for which Alison bought the car, which is her daily commute. Billy was clearly aware of this specific purpose before conclusion of the contract. Second, the improperly working brakes show also that the car is not fit for the purpose for which cars are normally used, which is a safe driving. Third, when it comes to quality and performance of the acquired car that Alison could expect, it seems that an obvious lack of conformity is present too. This is especially true if the publicly made advertising 'Top Reliability, Low Fuel Consumption, Best for the Environment' is taken into consideration. Problematic breaks would certainly comply with the 'top reliability' statement. The present engine noise, under the condition that it is just a noise which does not affect in any manner the safety and operability of the car, is a less serious defect than the brakes issue. However, the engine noise would still represent a justified ground for Alison to prove the presence of the lack of conformity, but the available remedies may be different from the case of unreliable brakes.

A necessary pre-condition for Alison to win her case is to prove that the defect has occurred within the period of 2 years. This condition is in this specific case easily fulfilled as the car defects have occurred 3 weeks after the delivery of the car which established a presumption that the lack of conformity existed at the time of delivery of the car. Moreover, as the defect has occurred within the first 6 months as of the car delivery, as his defence Billy would need to prove that the cause or origin of the lack of conformity of the car is an act or omission which took place after the delivery of the goods.[53] An example of valid proof would be to demonstrate that Alison used improperly, contrary to the given instructions, the car after she had bought it. However, in this case, it seems that chances of Billy succeed to do something like this are minimal.

The exception to this general rule on burden of proof under the Sales Directive are the cases when this presumption is incompatible with the nature of the goods or the nature of the lack of conformity, which is an exclusion which cannot be applied in case of Alison's car purchase.[54] Accordingly, to succeed in her

---

52 Article 2(1) Sales Directive.
53 Case C-497/13 Froukje Faber V Autobedrijf Hazet Ochten BV at [73].
54 Article 5(3) Sales Directive.

case, Alison just needs to show that the breaks problem and engine noise became physically apparent before the expiry of the 6 months period of the delivery of the car. That is obvious in this case, so Alison would not have any problems in proving her claim. Contrary to this Alison does not need to prove that the cause or origins of the lack of conformity are attributable to Billy.[55]

Under EU Law, as a remedy for the defective car, Alison may ask first for the car repair or replacement. Replacement in this case will effectively remedy the lack of conformity only under the condition that all these characteristics occur exclusively in case of Alison's car and not in case of all cars of the same model. Similarly, the repair as an option will have a purpose if it is possible to fix the brakes and to fix the engine noise, so that Alison can use the car for her daily commute.

In case of both of these remedies, it is essential that the car gets replaced or repaired within a reasonable period of time or without significant inconvenience for Alison. Significant inconvenience would be the case, for instance, if Billy requires Alison to drive her car a few hundred miles away from her home to a particular car service where it is going to be repaired. Otherwise, if the repair or replacement are not executed within a reasonable period of time or without significant inconvenience, Alison may use her second-tier remedy and rescind the contract.

However, in this case, the efficiency of repair and replacement to remedy the existing car defects seem to be quite unlikely. This is why Alison will have to rely on one of the remedies of the second tier which are the price diminution or contract recession. In certain cases, recession would be hardly possible as it would be, for example, in case of minor defect. Accordingly, the fact that engine had started to make a howling noise whenever gears are changed at a low speed is most probably to be considered as a minor defect, under the condition that the safety and operability of the car are not affected.[56] This is why Alison might only ask for price diminution. For the brakes problem, this can hardly be considered as a minor defect. This is why Alison might ask also for the rescission unlike in case of the engine noise. However, even if Alison requires only contract recession and it turns out that rescission is not possible as the defect is considered as minor, the national court of EU Member States before which the proceeding takes place is obliged to, *ex officio* (by its own motion) grant the price reduction to Alison.[57]

Contract rescission also remains a possibility if neither repair nor replacement can be performed within reasonable period of time or without significant inconvenience for Alison. In case of car replacement or rescission of the contract, Billy cannot ask any money for the fact that Alison used the car. This is because the Sales Directive requires that consumer have effective protection in the context of remedies, and the existence of any requirement for compensation for the car usage

---

55 Case C-497/13 Froukje Faber V Autobedrijf Hazet Ochten BV at [70] and [71].
56 Article 3(6) Sales Directive.
57 Case C-32/12 Soledad Duarte Hueros Autociba SA Automóviles Citroën España SA at [39] – [41].

would diminish the effectiveness of the remedies.[58] If Billy causes any obstacles to Alison regarding the performance of her remedies for the lack of conformity, this will also represent a form of unfair commercial practice under the UCPD.[59] In such a manner, EU Law secures the effectiveness of consumer protection.

(i)(b) Brake and engine noise (second-hand car)

In case of the car being second-hand and 3 years old, a possibly different legal position of Alison than in case of new car would depend on the applicable law of specific EU Member State. For second-hand goods, the Sales Directive itself does not provide any different conformity requirements than for the conditions for the new consumer goods. The Sales Directive only provides that EU Member States may exclude from the scope of application the second-hand goods sold at public auction where consumers have the opportunity of attending the sale in person.[60]

However, this exception does not seem to be applicable to this case as Alison bought the car directly from Billy, and not at an auction. In addition to this, according to the Sales Directive, EU Member States are entitled to envisage a shorter minimum period of time of legal guarantee for the purchase of the second-hand goods. However, the envisaged period can never be for less than 1 year.[61] Again, as the lack of conformity has occurred only 3 weeks after the delivery of the car, the fact whether specific EU Member State has adopted this exception is not of any practical relevance for this case. This means that for this particular case, the car age would not matter unless a connection with the conformity can be established.

(ii) Higher-than-expected fuel consumption

In case of higher-than-expected fuel consumption of the acquired car, the situation is similar to the case of the brakes problem and the engine noise as the presence of lack of conformity is obvious here. The car Alison bought does not comply with the description given by the seller and does not possess the qualities of the goods which the seller held out to the consumer as a model as the car consumes more fuel. Second, Alison made clearly her intention to buy a car with low fuel consumption that she would use for his daily commuting. Billy was fully aware of that and reassured Alison that the car will be fine. The fact that the car is using significantly more fuel is certainly something that is very important to Alison so this is certainly a huge defect. Unless this is a problem which is present only in case of the specific car that Alison bought, the replacement with another car of the same model does not seem to be option. Price diminution or contract rescission seem to be the only options.

---

58 Ibid. at [30].
59 Article 9(1)(d) UCPD.
60 Article 1(3) Sales Directive.
61 Article 7(1) Sales Directive.

For the EU rules on the fuel consumption, an important source of law is Directive 1999/94/EC of consumer information on fuel economy and CO_2 emissions (*Car labelling Directive*) requires that all new cars are provided with the information on fuel consumption. Importantly, the Car labelling Directive does not apply in case of second-hand cars, but only on new cars. In this scenario, there are two possible alternatives. First is the case if Billy failed to provide that information to consumer. In that case, Billy would be liable under the rules of the UCPD both for misleading actions, as he falsely reassured Alison about low fuel consumption and, for misleading omission, as he failed to provide relevant information to Alison which is required by the Car labelling Directive.

Second, if the car Alison bought had been labelled with the information in the manner required by the Car labelling Directive about fuel consumption, Billy cannot be liable for misleading omissions under the UCPD, but only for misleading actions as he provided a false information to consumer about the fuel consumption. For the application of the provisions of the UCPD, it is necessary to demonstrate that Alison as a deceived consumer acted as an average consumer, that is the European required standard of required consumer of a reasonably well-informed and reasonably observant and circumspect consumer.[62] The fairness of a commercial practice is always to be assessed in comparison to the average consumer whom a commercial practice reaches or to whom it is addressed, which represents the principal benchmark.[63] The required standard of behaviour of average consumer Alison does not seem to be a problem in this case as it may be observed that Billy reassured Alison.

Alison, under the provisions of the UCPD, does not have any private law remedies. However, EU Member States have developed different private law remedies that Alison may use in addition to the remedies available under the Sales Directive.[64] Some of the countries have envisaged that consumers who have concluded the contract as a result of an unfair commercial practices may ask for the contract termination. This kind of remedy may be more beneficial, if applicable, to Alison in comparison with the remedies under the Sales Directive as it enables Alison to immediately terminate the contract without the need to ask first for the replacement or repair, being allowed to rescind the contract only after she has asked for repair and replacement, two remedies which are highly unlikely capable of remedying the existing lack of conformity.

(iii) Failure to meet emissions standards

Again, as in case of the brakes deterioration, engine noise and high fuel consumption, Alison primarily relies on the remedies given by the Sales Directive. Similarly, as in case of the high fuel consumption, it seems that neither replacement

---

62 Recital 18 UCPD.
63 Articles 5–8 UCPD.
64 M. Durovic, *European Law on Unfair Competition and Contract Law* (UK: Hart Publishing, 2016).

nor repair are capable of effectively remedying the lack of conformity. This is why Alison may only rely on contract rescission as an effective remedy. A less likely option may also be the price diminishment.

In addition to this, EU Law rules on car emission standards require the car manufacturers to always equip the cars they produce in such a manner to respect the emission requirement in normal use.[65] Moreover, EU Law explicitly prohibits the use of defeat devices, defined as

> any element of design which senses temperature, vehicle speed, engine speed (RPM), transmission gear, manifold vacuum or any other parameter for the purpose of activating, modulating, delaying or deactivating the operation of any part of the emission control system, that reduces the effectiveness of the emission control system under conditions which may reasonably be expected to be encountered in normal vehicle operation and use.

Member States are obliged to enforce this prohibition.[66]

Same as in case of fuel consumption, the Car labelling Directive requires that the CO2 emission values must be displayed on a label attached to the windscreen of all new passenger cars at the point of sale, on posters and other promotional material, and in specific printed guides, which have to be published to provide consumers with relevant information on all car brands and models. Failure to disclose any of this information will again represent misleading omission as a form of unfair commercial practice under the UCPD and thus will be prohibited. Accordingly, Alison may use some of the private law remedies, if any, granted to her by the national laws of EU Member States as she has concluded her consumer contract under the impact of unfair commercial practice.

Scenario 2

This scenario is focused on the legal consequences of the supplied digital content to David, as a consumer, that turned out to be defective. Besides being defective, the supplied digital content also caused the additional damage to David's other products.

For the protection of consumers in case of supplied digital content, EU Law currently does not have a specific piece of legislation. Some sector-specific rules for the digital content are contained in a more general consumer legislation, but these rules are rather limited. This is why EU consumer policy is now focused on the development of particular consumer law regimes for the digital content and online sale of goods, as envisaged in the Digital Single Market Strategy adopted

---

65 Article 5(1) Regulation on type approval of motor vehicles with respect to emissions from light vehicles (Regulation (EC) No 715/2007).
66 Article 5(2) Regulation on type approval of motor vehicles with respect to emissions from light vehicles (Regulation (EC) No 715/2007).

by the European Commission in May 2015.[67] One of the principal goals set up by the Strategy is to adopt a set of harmonised EU rules for protection of consumers in case of the supply of digital content. Consequently, a Proposal of the Directive on contracts for the supply of digital content was published in December 2015.[68] It is still not known when the Proposal will be adopted.

(i) Failure of the app and failure to patch the problem

As a result of the lack of a specific European piece legislation for the provision of digital content, David needs to rely on remedies given to him by the existing directives. However, David cannot apply the most powerful remedies for the defective established by the Sales Directive. The defective application was not provided on a tangible medium, but David directly downloaded it on his tablet. The issue is that the application cannot be subsumed under the definition of consumer goods provided by the Sales Directive and accordingly falls outside of its scope of application.[69] The Sales Directive only covers the application provided on a tangible medium. Accordingly, David cannot use the remedies for the lack of conformity granted by the Sales Directive unless the EU Member State whose law applies to this case has broaden its scope application while transposing the Directive's provisions into their national legal systems.

In the lack of possibility to base his claim on the Sales Directive, David may use remedies granted to him by Directive 2011/83/EU on consumer rights (CRD) and by the UCPD. The CRD applies to any contract concluded between a trader and a consumer.[70] The download of application made by David is a form of online contract under the CRD. The CRD has established a specific system of protection of consumer in online consumer contracts as types of contracts where consumer's weakness in the contractual relationship with the trader is particularly noticeable. For online consumer contracts, the CRD grants to consumers two principal rights: the right to be informed and the right to withdraw from a contract. Both of these rights are relevant for David and his case. Some rules on contracts concluded online are also contained in Directive 2000/31/EC on e-commerce.[71] However, in this particular case the provisions of this Directive do not give to David any higher level of protection or better remedies than the CRD. This is why the provisions of this Directive will not be examined.

Under the CRD, the contract on download of digital content are neither to be classified as a sales contract nor as a service contract. The CRD defines the digital content as the data which are produced and supplied in digital form, such

---

67 COM (2015) 192 final http://ec.europa.eu/priorities/digital-single-market/, http://ec.europa.eu/priorities/digital-single-market/.
68 COM (2015) 634 final, http://ec.europa.eu/justice/contract/files/directive_-digital_content.pdf.
69 Article 1(2)(b) Sales Directive.
70 Article 3 CRD.
71 OJ L 178, 17.7.2000, p. 1.

as computer programmes, applications, games, music, videos or texts, irrespective of whether they are accessed through downloading or streaming, from a tangible medium or through any other means.[72]

Before conclusion of his contract and download of the application, David was supposed to be informed by the supplier about the functionality, including applicable technical protection measures, of digital content he was downloading.[73] In addition to this, the CRD enlists a number of mandatory pre-contractual information requirements that the supplier of digital content was obliged to disclose to David.[74] The CRD itself does not provide sanctions for the failure to provide information, but this has been left to be regulated by the EU Member States under the condition that the applicable sanctions are effective, proportionate and dissuasive.[75] Accordingly, David will have to rely on the remedies provided by EU Member States, for instance those on consent defects.

Failure to provide information to David will also represent a misleading omission under the UCPD, as a form of unfair commercial practice for which the supplier of digital content will also be liable.[76] Being an online contract, the CRD requires that David had to receive a written confirmation of his transaction. The confirmation must be presented on a paper or on another durable medium such as an e-mail, fax or similar.

Besides the right to be informed, David may profit from another right given to him by the provisions of the CRD: the right of withdrawal. For David, the right of withdrawal may represent an easily accessible and efficient remedy for downloaded defective application.[77] The right to withdraw enables David to freely, without any negative consequences or costs, terminate the contract within the prescribed period of time.

If the digital content has been downloaded, the CRD provides that the trader must obtain the express consent from the consumer to waive the right of withdrawal. David will not have his right to withdraw if he has explicitly acknowledged that he loses his right of withdrawal.[78]

In case of digital content which is not supplied on a tangible medium, the 14-day withdrawal period starts as of the day of the conclusion of the contract.[79] If David decides to enforce his right of withdrawal, the supplier of digital content needs to refund consumer within 14 days of the withdrawal. If the supplier failed to provide David about the information about the existence of his right of withdrawal, which is not known from the facts of this particular case, David's right to withdraw will be prolonged for 1 additional year.[80]

---

72 Recital 19 CRD.
73 Article 6(1)(r) CRD.
74 Article 6(1) CRD.
75 Article 24 CRD.
76 Article 7 UCPD.
77 M.B. Loos, "Rights of Withdrawal" in G. Howells and R. Schulze (eds.), *Modernising and Harmonising Consumer Contract Law* (Munich: Sellier, 2009), pp. 245–249.
78 Article 16(1)(m) CRD.
79 Article 9(2)(c) CRD.
80 Article 10(1) CRD.

(ii) Interference with other apps

The CRD has imposed on the trader, as one of the mandatory pre-contractual information requirements, the duty to provide information regarding the interoperability of the digital content on how the digital content may be reasonably expected to operate with relevant hardware and software.[81] This information needs to be provided to consumer in a clear and comprehensible manner. The trader is supposed to provide not all information regarding the interoperability, but only the information he is aware of or can reasonably be expected to have been aware of.

In this case, the information that the particular application may affect other hardware or software is certainly something that the supplier of the digital content was supposed to be aware of and inform David accordingly. The burden to prove that the information has been provided is on the trader.[82] In case if the trader failed to provide that information, David may rely on different remedies which are granted to him by the national laws of EU Member States for failure to disclose information, for example those on consent defects as this has remained the competence of EU Member States. In addition to this, the failure to provide information by trader represents a misleading omission under the UCPD.[83] David may also have some private law remedies for misleading omission granted by the national laws.[84] Again, the easiest way for David to terminate the contract would be to use his right of withdrawal under the condition that it may be performed.

(iii) Damage done to the Wi-Fi connector

For the damage done to the Wi-Fi connector by the downloaded sports application, EU Law itself does not grant to David any kind of particular remedy. This has been left to be regulated by the national laws of the EU Member States. Depending on what has been chosen as the national approach, the damage done to the Wi-Fi needs to be remedied and calculated either on a contract-based measure or a tort-law-based measure in line with the applicable national law.

V. Specific issues in the European Union

Everything relevant for consumer sales under EU Law has already been mentioned and covered by this book chapter.

---

81 Article 6(1)(s) CRD.
82 Article 6(9) CRD.
83 Article 7 UCPD.
84 M. Durovic, "The Impact of Directive 2005/29/EC on Unfair Commercial Practices on Contract Law" (2015) 23(5) *European Review of Private Law* 862–878.

3 Consumer sales law in Germany

André Janssen

I. The German consumer market[1]

Germany is Europe's largest economy, and it has a strong consumer market which includes the sale of goods, services as well as digital products (e.g. music, games, anti-virus software and cloud storage) and which has increased rapidly in the recent years. Unfortunately, unlike several other countries (see for example the United Kingdom with the Department for Business, Innovation and Skills) comprehensive surveys providing overall data on how consumers participate in the market and what problems they encounter are absent in Germany. However, what can be said is that the e-commerce market for consumer goods has quickly grown over the last decade and is expected to continue to grow in the future. The downside of this development however, is that many physical shops, especially the small- and medium-sized ones in smaller cities suffer due to a lack of clients and are forced to close down as a consequence. This shift from offline to online shopping led to an increased awareness of the danger that online shopping may lead to 'dead' or at least empty city centres.

In addition to what has just been said, the sale of digital contents can be identified as another fast-growing market (which due to its nature does not affect offline sales and does not contribute to dying city centres). In particular, this sector – the sale of digital contents – seems to give rise to a high number of legal conflicts. Thirty-nine per cent of German consumers who came across the four popular types of digital contents (music, games, anti-virus software and cloud storage) in the past 12 months had encountered at least one problem relating to either the quality, access or terms and conditions of the contents they had paid for.[2] Moreover, 27% of them had at least one problem with the content they did not pay for with money.[3] These numbers seem to be considerably higher than the other sectors of the (German) consumer sales market, especially the online and offline purchase of consumer goods.

---

1 Status as per 1 December 2016.
2 See http://ec.europa.eu/justice/contract/files/digital_contracts/digital-contracts_factsheet-de_en.pdf.
3 See http://ec.europa.eu/justice/contract/files/digital_contracts/digital-contracts_factsheet-de_en.pdf.

II. Access to justice for consumers and enforcement of consumer law

1. Individual enforcement by the consumers

A German consumer who encounters a problem with the purchased good or service will normally contact the trader, who is his or her contracting partner, directly – and in the vast majority of these cases, he or she proposes an acceptable solution. If this informal procedure fails to resolve the consumer's complaint, an alternative dispute resolution mechanism can be a reasonable option. With the 2016 so-called *Verbraucherstreitbeilegungsgesetz*, the German legislator has implemented the Directive 2013/11/EU on Alternative Resolution of Consumer Disputes.[4] The independent competent private mediation bodies (Verbraucherschlichtungsstellen) are strongly regulated – similar to ordinary courts. They must have their own code of procedure and are subject to strict information duties.[5] Settling/resolving disputes through alternative dispute resolution is optional for both parties and free of charge for the consumer.[6] Furthermore, a lot of companies are subject to (voluntary) trade dispute resolution schemes, for example the insurance ombudsman for the insurance sector. Beside the just mentioned general consumer arbitration legislation, the Regulation 524/2013 on Online Resolution of Consumer Disputes[7] regulates online consumer arbitration. It started to apply in all EU Member States in 2016. The Regulation applies – in a nutshell – in cases of consumer disputes which have arisen from online transactions. It particularly focuses on those online transactions which are performed by market players from different EU Member States.

Of course, the consumers can also enforce their rights through litigation in civil courts. Most of the consumer complaint cases will be dealt with in the local courts (the so-called *Amtsgerichte*) as they normally deal with claims with values up to 5.000 €.[8] If the value of the claim is above that sum, the case will be assigned to the local courts (so-called *Landgerichte*). In contrast to the first scenario, the consumer needs to be represented by a lawyer at the local court level. Section 15a of the Introductory Act to the Civil Act (the so-called *Einführungsgesetz zum Bürgerlichen Gesetzbuch*) foresees a particularity for claims with a value up to 750 €: it makes it mandatory for the Länder on those small claims to commence an arbitration in front of a recognised arbitration committee (so-called *Gütestelle*) before starting litigation. The practical relevance is however very low as most of the Länder do not introduce such a requirement. For cross-border small claims procedure, see sections 1097 et seq. of the Civil Procedure Act, which needs to

---

4 Directive 2013/11/EU of the European Parliament and of the Council of 21 May 2013 on alternative dispute resolution for consumer disputes and amending Regulation (EC) No 2006/2004 and Directive 2009/22/EC (Directive on consumer ADR).
5 See sections 5, 7(3)(4), 10 Verbraucherstreitbeilegungsgesetz.
6 See sections 15, 23 Verbraucherstreitbeilegungsgesetz.
7 Regulation 524/2013 on Online Resolution of Consumer Disputes.
8 See section 23(2)(a) Gerichtsverfassungsgesetz.

be introduced due to the Regulation 861/2007 on Small Claim Procedure.[9] However, their practical relevance is until now limited.[10]

2. Collective enforcement of consumer law

The German legal system does not only rely on the individual enforcement of consumer legislation as just presented. The Injunctions Act (the so-called *Unterlassungsklagengesetz*) of 2002[11] grants particular eligible bodies the right to require refrainment and withdrawal from practices infringing consumer protection legislation.[12] According to section 3 of the Injunctions Act, these eligible bodies are the qualified entities (76 private consumer associations),[13] associations with legal personality for the promotion of commercial interests, and the Chambers of Trade and Industry or the Chambers of Crafts and Labour. If the trader does not refrain and withdraw from practices infringing consumer protection legislation, the eligible bodies can file a claim in the local court in whose district the defendant has his or her place of business.[14]

The rights of the eligible bodies are normally limited to refrainment and withdrawal as just mentioned. However, in unfair commercial practices contexts[15] (and partly also in competition law)[16] the legislatior also grants the eligible bodies the right to confiscate illegal profits. They can sue traders who intentionally use illegal commercial practices and thereby making a profit to the detriment of numerous purchasers, and have them surrender such profits to the federal budget. Nevertheless, as the (financial) incentive for those eligible bodies is low and that the intent of the trader needs to be proved, the practical relevance remains low.

III. The legal framework for consumer sales in Germany

1. General information

The most important piece of legislation in the area of private law in Germany is the German Civil Code (the so-called *Bürgerliches Gesetzbuch* – BGB, hereafter 'Civil Code'), which originates from 1900. The present German (consumer) sales law is mainly the result of the biggest reform in the German Civil Code history, the Reform of the Law of Obligations of 2002 (the so-called *Schuldrechtsreform*).[17]

---

9 Regulation 861/2007 on small claim procedure. The Regulation is under revision.
10 For the general reasons for the lack of empirical data see http://www.svr-verbraucherfragen.de/wp-content/uploads/Schmidt-Kessel_Gutachten.pdf
11 It implements the Directive 2009/22/EC of the European Parliament and of the Council of 23 April 2009 on injunctions for the protection of consumers' interests.
12 See sections 1 et seq. Injunctions Act.
13 See also section 4 Injunctions Act.
14 See section 6 Injunctions Act.
15 See section 10 Act Against Unfair Competition.
16 See section 34a Act Against Restraints of Competition.
17 See the Gesetz zur Modernisierung des Schuldrechts vom 26. November 2001 (BGBl. I 3138).

The initial legal incentive for this reform was the obligation of the German legislator to implement the Directive 1999/44/EC on certain aspects of the sale of consumer goods and associated guarantees (hereafter 'Consumer Sales Directive').[18] During that time, the legislator had to make an important decision between the 'small solution' (the so-called *kleine Lösung*) and the 'big solution' (the so-called *große Lösung*).[19] The first option would have been a minimalistic implementation of the Consumer Sales Directive, in the form of a Consumer Act. The second option would have been implementing a separate Consumer Sales Law part within the Civil Code without changing the overall structure and objectives of the Civil Code. Taking the implementation of the Consumer Sales Directive as an opportunity to modernise and reform the German law of obligations (including the general sales law) thoroughly, the German legislator chose the latter. Hence, the law of obligations and the sales law as we see it today is the result of this chosen 'big solution': the Consumer Sales Directive was implemented in the (general) sales law starting with sections 433 et seq. of the Civil Code. In principle, the content of the Directive was made applicable to all sorts of sales contracts (including business to business, business to consumer and consumer to consumer). Only the sections 474 et seq. of the Civil Code contain some provisions that are only applicable to business to consumer sales contracts (e.g. the reversed burden of proof in section 476 of the Civil Code). In general, the German Consumer Sales Law mainly deals with the general sales law with some particular Consumer Law elements provided by sections 474 et seq. of the Civil Code. The sales law provisions do not only apply to the sale of things but also to the purchase of rights according to section 453 of the Civil Code (the so-called *Rechtskauf*)[20] and to contracts dealing with the supply of movable things to be produced or manufactured under section 651 of the Civil Code (the so-called *Werklieferungsvertrag*).[21]

---

18 The full title is Directive 1999/44/EC of the European Parliament and of the Council of 25 May 1999 on certain aspects of the sale of consumer goods and associated guarantees.
19 See on that for example Däubler-Gmelin, Die Entscheidung für die so genannte Große Lösung bei der Schuldrechtsreform, Neue Juristische Wochenschrift (NJW) 2001, 2281 et seq.; Zimmermann, Schuldrechtsmodernisierung? Juristenzeitung (JZ) 2001, 171 et seq.
20 Section 453 Civil Code (purchase of rights) reads:

(1) The provisions on the purchase of things apply with the necessary modifications to the purchase of rights and other objects.
(2) The seller bears the costs of creation and transfer of the right.
(3) If a right comprising the right to possession of a thing is sold, the seller is obliged to deliver the thing to the buyer free of material and legal defects.

21 Section 651 Civil Code (Application of sale of goods law) reads:

The provisions of sale of goods law are applicable to a contract dealing with the supply of movable things to be produced or manufactured. Section 442(1) sentence 1 also applies to these contracts if the defect is caused by the material supplied by the customer. To the extent that the movable things to be produced or manufactured are not fungible things, sections 642, 643, 645, 649 and 650 apply, subject to the proviso that the applicable point of time under sections 446 and 447 takes the place of acceptance.

2. Non-conformity

Section 433 of the Civil Code outlines the typical contractual duties of parties to a purchase agreement: The buyer is (a) obliged to pay the seller the agreed purchase price and (b) to accept delivery of the thing[22] purchased (section 433(2) of the Civil Code). The seller of the thing is obliged (a) to deliver the thing to the buyer, (b) to procure ownership of the thing for the buyer, and he must (c) procure the thing for the buyer free from material and legal defects (section 433(1) of the Civil Code).[23]

Section 434 of the Civil Code[24] defines material defects in a subjective-objective manner (the so-called *subjektiv-objektiv Sachmangelbegriff*).[25] Comparing this provision with the relevant articles of the CISG (article 35 CISG) and the Consumer Sales Directive (article 2 Consumer Sales Directive), it becomes clear that the German legislator had strongly relied on them (especially the latter one). Section 434(1)1 of the Civil Code states that a thing is free from material defects if, upon the passing of the risk, the thing has the agreed quality. This is the subjective notion of material defect (the so-called *subjektiver Sachmangelbegriff*).[26]

---

22 Only corporeal objects are things as defined by law (see section 90 of the Civil Code).
23 Section 433 Civil Code (typical contractual duties in a purchase agreement) reads:

(1) By a purchase agreement, the seller of a thing is obliged to deliver the thing to the buyer and to procure ownership of the thing for the buyer. The seller must procure the thing for the buyer free from material and legal defects.
(2) The buyer is obliged to pay the seller the agreed purchase price and to accept delivery of the thing purchased.

24 Section 434 Civil Code (material defects) reads:

(1) The thing is free from material defects if, upon the passing of the risk, the thing has the agreed quality. To the extent that the quality has not been agreed, the thing is free of material defects 1. if it is suitable for the use intended under the contract, 2. if it is suitable for the customary use and its quality is usual in things of the same kind and the buyer may expect this quality in view of the type of the thing. Quality under sentence 2 no. 2 above includes characteristics which the buyer can expect from the public statements on specific characteristics of the thing that are made by the seller, the producer (section 4(1) and (2) of the Product Liability Act [Produkthaftungsgesetz]) or his assistant, including without limitation in advertising or in identification, unless the seller was not aware of the statement and also had no duty to be aware of it, or at the time when the contract was entered into it had been corrected in a manner of equal value, or it did not influence the decision to purchase the thing.
(2) It is also a material defect if the agreed assembly by the seller or persons whom he used to perform his obligation has been carried out improperly. In addition, there is a material defect in a thing intended for assembly if the assembly instructions are defective, unless the thing has been assembled without any error.
(3) Supply by the seller of a different thing or of a lesser amount of the thing is equivalent to a material defect.

25 Section 435 Civil Code deals with the legal defects instead. It reads: The thing is free of legal defects if third parties, in relation to the thing, can assert either no rights, or only the rights taken over in the purchase agreement, against the buyer. It is equivalent to a legal defect if a right that does not exist is registered in the Land Register.
26 In Common Law terminology 'express terms'.

To the extent that the quality has not been agreed, the thing is free according to section 434(1)2 of the Civil Code of material defects if it is either (objective notion of the material defect or the so-called *objektiver Sachmangelbegriff*):[27]

- suitable for the use intended under the contract (no. 1, intended use), or
- suitable for the customary use and its quality is usual in things of the same kind and the buyer may expect this quality in view of the type of the thing (no. 2, customary use).

Customary use under no. 2 includes characteristics which the buyer can expect from the public statements on specific characteristics of the thing that are made by the seller, the producer or his or her assistant, including without limitation in advertising or in identification, unless the seller was not aware of the statement and also had no duty to be aware of it, or at the time when the contract was entered into it had been corrected in a manner of equal value, or it did not influence the decision to purchase the thing (see section 434(1)3 of the Civil Code). It is also a material defect if the agreed assembly by the seller (or persons whom he used to perform his obligation) has been carried out improperly. In addition, there is a material defect in a thing intended for assembly if the assembly instructions are defective, unless the thing has been assembled without any error (see for both section 434(2) of the Civil Code). It is according to section 434(3) of the Civil Code also a material defect if the seller supplies a different thing or of a lesser amount of the thing. With this provision the German legislator tried to bring an end to some old legal discussions before the reform of the law of obligations.

3. Rights of the buyer and limitation period

If the seller delivers defective things to the buyer the latter has according to section 437 of the Civil Code[28] in principle the following rights:[29]

- (1) Right to cure,
- (2) Right to revoke the contract,
- (3) Right to reduce the price, or
- (4) Right to damages.[30]

---

27 In Common Law terminology 'implied terms'.
28 Section 437 Civil Code (rights of buyer in the case of defects) reads:
> If the thing is defective, the buyer may, provided the requirements of the following provisions are met and unless otherwise specified,
> (1) under section 439, demand cure,
> (2) revoke the agreement under sections 440, 323 and 326(5) or reduce the purchase price under section 441, and
> (3) under sections 440, 280, 281, 283 and 311a, demand damages, or under section 284, demand reimbursement of futile expenditure.

29 The words rights and remedies are used equivalently in this context.
30 The right to demand reimbursement of futile expenditure (see section 437 no. 3 Civil Code) has been omitted here due to its minor relevance in legal practice.

The buyer's primary remedy is the right to cure, the so-called *Nacherfüllung* (see sections 437 no. 1, 439 Civil Code). According to section 439(1) Civil Code, the buyer can choose between repairment (the so-called *Nachbesserung*, the non-conformity of the sold thing gets remedied) or replacement (the so-called *Nachlieferung*, the seller supplies another thing free of defects). In principle, the seller may refuse repairment or replacement (or even both) only when curing the defect would be unreasonable for him or her (see section 439(3) Civil Code).[31] When deciding whether a cure is unreasonable, account must be taken in particular of the value of the thing when free of defects, the importance of the defect and the question as to whether recourse could be had to the alternative kind of cure without substantial detriment to the buyer. The seller must pay the costs of curing the defect, especially transport costs, toll fees, material costs, and labour costs etc. (see section 439(2) Civil Code).

Beside the right to cure, the buyer also has the right to revoke the contract (see sections 437 no. 2, 440, 323, 326(5) Civil Code, the so-called *Rücktritt*) and the right to reduce the price (see section 437 no. 2, 441 Civil Code, so-called *Minderung*). The right to revoke the contract is excluded when the breach of duty is trivial (see section 323(5)2 Civil Code). In principle, both remedies come into play only if the buyer has set a reasonable deadline for the seller to cure the defect, and this deadline expires without the defect being cured (see sections 437 no. 2, 323(1) Civil Code, so-called *Nachfrist*). However, the German law recognises several exemptions to this important Nachfrist-procedure, in which the buyer no longer has to set a deadline for the seller to cure the defect. These exemptions are (sections 437 no. 2, 440, 323, 326(5) Civil Code):

- Seller seriously and definitively refuses to perform.[32]
- Existence of a so-called *Fixgeschäft*: Seller was supposed to perform on a certain day, and this performance was of interest to the buyer on this very day only.

---

31 Section 439 Civil code (cure) reads:

(1) As cure the buyer may, at his choice, demand that the defect is remedied or a thing free of defects is supplied.

(2) The seller must bear all expenses required for the purpose of cure, in particular transport, workmen's travel, work and materials costs.

(3) Without prejudice to section 275(2) and (3), the seller may refuse to provide the kind of cure chosen by the buyer, if this cure is possible only at disproportionate expense. In this connection, account must be taken in particular, without limitation, of the value of the thing when free of defects, the importance of the defect and the question as to whether recourse could be had to the alternative kind of cure without substantial detriment to the buyer. The claim of the buyer is restricted in this case to the alternative kind of cure; the right of the seller to refuse the alternative kind of cure too, subject to the requirements of sentence 1 above, is unaffected.

(4) If the seller supplies a thing free of defects for the purpose of cure, he may demand the return of the defective thing in accordance with sections 346 to 348.

32 Section 323 Civil Code (revocation for non-performance or for performance not in conformity with the contract) reads:

- After weighting the interests of both parties, the immediate revocation of the contract without the Nachfrist-procedure is justified.
- Costs for curing the defect are unreasonable for the seller and because of this, he or she refuses to do it.
- Unsuccessful cure (attempt to remedy a defect that fails twice is deemed to be such an unsuccessful cure, see section 440 Civil Code).[33]
- Curing the defect is impossible.

The German Sales Law is also aware of the right of the buyer to damages against the seller (see sections 440, 280, 281, 283 and 311a Civil Code). Unlike the basic Common Law concept, the right to damages is a fault-based liability in Germany. Section 276(1) of the Civil Code lays down that the obligor (in this

---

(1) If, in the case of a reciprocal contract, the obligor does not render an act of performance which is due, or does not render it in conformity with the contract, then the obligee may revoke the contract, if he has specified, without result, an additional period for performance or cure.
(2) The specification of a period of time can be dispensed with if

    1   the obligor seriously and definitively refuses performance,
    2   the obligor does not render performance by a date specified in the contract or within a period specified in the contract, in spite of the fact that, according to a notice given by the obligee to the obligor prior to conclusion of the contract or based on other circumstances attending at the time of its conclusion, the performance as per the date specified or within the period specified is of essential importance to the obligee, or
    3   in the case of work not having been carried out in accordance with the contract, special circumstances exist which, when the interests of both parties are weighed, justify immediate revocation.

(3) If the nature of the breach of duty is such that setting a period of time is out of the question, a warning notice is given instead.
(4) The obligee may revoke the contract before performance is due if it is obvious that the requirements for revocation will be met.
(5) If the obligor has performed in part, the obligee may revoke the whole contract only if he has no interest in part performance. If the obligor has not performed in conformity with the contract, the obligee may not revoke the contract if the breach of duty is trivial.
(6) Revocation is excluded if the obligee is solely or very predominantly responsible for the circumstance that would entitle him to revoke the contract or if the circumstance for which the obligor is not responsible occurs at a time when the obligee is in default of acceptance.

33 Section 440 Civil Code (special provisions on revocation and damages) reads:

    Except in the cases set out in section 281(2) and section 323(2), it is also not necessary to specify a period of time if the seller has refused to carry out both kinds of cure under section 439(3) or if the kind of cure that the buyer is entitled to receive has failed or cannot reasonably be expected of him. A repair is deemed to have failed after the second unsuccessful attempt, unless in particular the nature of the thing or of the defect or the other circumstances leads to a different conclusion.

case the seller) is *only* responsible for intention and negligence.[34] A person acts negligently if he or she fails to exercise the reasonable care (see section 276(2) Civil Code). However, the Schuldrechtsreform of 2002 introduced an important reversal of the burden of proof. According to section 280(1)2 Civil Code, the obligor's fault is presumed unless he or she can prove that he or she was *not* responsible for the breach of duty.

The German law of obligations distinguishes – in a nutshell – between two different kinds of right to damages. The right to damages may be asserted *in lieu of performance* (the so-called *Schadensersatz statt der Leistung*). In principle, this requires the buyer to first set a reasonable deadline for the seller to perform or to cure the defect and that subsequently, this deadline expires without a successful performance or cure. Hence, to exercise the right to revoke the contract and price reduction, the buyer needs to obey the Nachfrist-procedure. For example, in a case where the brakes of a car are defective, the buyer can only ask for Schadensersatz statt der Leistung (for the defective brakes) if the deadline to cure expires without success. The right to claim or damages may also be asserted *in addition to performance* (the so-called *Schadensersatz neben der Leistung*). In that case, the buyer does not have to set a deadline for the seller to perform or cure but, instead, directly asks for damages or more precisely for Schadensersatz neben der Leistung. The reason being the Nachfrist-procedure would be useless since the damage is not something that can be remedied through performance or cure by the seller. For example, when due to the defective brakes the driver of the car (who also bought the car) gets injured. Here, the damages in addition to performance would be for example the costs for the hospital.

The limitation period for all mentioned remedies in German Sales Law (or more general in cases where a moveable item was sold) is 2 years. It begins upon delivery of the thing (see section 438(1) no. 3, (2) Civil Code).[35]

---

34 Section 276 Civil Code (responsibility of the obligor) reads:

(1) The obligor is responsible for intention and negligence, if a higher or lower degree of liability is neither laid down nor to be inferred from the other subject matter of the obligation, including but not limited to the giving of a guarantee or the assumption of a procurement risk. The provisions of sections 827 and 828 apply with the necessary modifications.

(2) A person acts negligently if he fails to exercise reasonable care.

(3) The obligor may not be released in advance from liability for intention.

35 Section 438 Civil Code (limitation of claims for defects) reads:

(1) The claims cited in section 437 nos. 1 and 3 become statute-barred 1. in thirty years, if the defect consists a) a real right of a third party on the basis of which return of the purchased thing may be demanded, or b) some other right registered in the Land Register, 2. in five years a) in relation to a building, and b) in relation to a thing that has been used for a building in accordance with the normal way it is used and has resulted in the defectiveness of the building, and 3. otherwise in two years.

(2) In the case of a plot of land the limitation period commences upon the delivery of possession, in other cases upon delivery of the thing.

4. Particularities for consumer sales contracts

Sections 474 et seq. Civil Code (introduced in 2002 after the reform of the law of obligations) provide for some important deviations from the ordinary sales law rules in cases of consumer sales. These are contracts by which a consumer buys a movable thing from an entrepreneur or where the subject matter of the sales contract comprises, in addition to the sale of a movable thing, the provision of a service by the entrepreneur (see section 474(1) Civil Code).[36] The two most important deviations from the general sales law can be found in sections 475 and 476 of the Civil Code. The former section basically forbids the entrepreneur to circumvent or to deviate from the general sales law rules to the disadvantage of the consumer.[37] However, for second-hand moveable things the limitation period

---

(3) Notwithstanding subsection (1) nos. 2 and 3 and subsection (2), claims become statute-barred in the standard limitation period if the seller fraudulently concealed the defect. In the case of subsection (1) no. 2, however, claims are not statute-barred before the end of the period there specified.

(4) The right of revocation referred to in section 437 is subject to section 218. Notwithstanding the fact that a revocation is ineffective under section 218(1), the buyer may refuse to pay the purchase price to the extent he would be so entitled on the basis of revocation. If he makes use of this right, the seller may revoke the agreement.

(5) Section 218 and subsection (4) sentence 2 above apply with the necessary modifications to the right to reduce the price set out in section 437.

36 Section 474 Civil Code (concept of sale of consumer goods; applicable provisions) reads:

(1) Sales of consumer goods are contracts by which a consumer buys a movable thing from an entrepreneur. A contract will likewise constitute a sale of consumer goods where its subject matter comprises, in addition to the sale of a movable thing, the provision of a service by the entrepreneur.

(2) The following rules of this subtitle have concomitant application for the sale of consumer goods. This does not apply to second-hand things that are sold at a publicly accessible auction which the consumer may attend in person.

(3) Where no period of time has been determined for the respective performance to be rendered pursuant to section 433 and none can be inferred from the circumstances given, the obligee may only demand the rendering of such performance, in derogation from section 271(1), without undue delay. In this case, the entrepreneur must deliver the thing at the latest thirty days after the contract has been concluded. The parties to the contract may effect the respective performance immediately.

(4) Section 447(1) applies subject to the proviso that the risk of accidental destruction and accidental deterioration shall devolve to the buyer only if the buyer has instructed the forwarder, carrier or other person or body tasked with carrying out the shipment and the entrepreneur has not named this person or body to the buyer previously.

(5) Section 439(4) applies to the purchase contracts regulated by this subtitle subject to the proviso that benefits are not to be surrendered or substituted by their value. Sections 445 and 447(2) do not apply.

37 Section 475 Civil Code (deviating agreements) reads:

(1) If an agreement is entered into before a defect is notified to the entrepreneur and deviates, to the disadvantage of the consumer, from sections 433 to 435, 437, 439 to 443 and from the provisions of this subtitle, the entrepreneur may not invoke

can be reduced to one year. Section 476 Civil Code on the other hand stipulates an important shift of the burden of proof for consumer sales contracts.[38] If, within the first six months after the date risk is passed, a material defect manifests itself: It is presumed that the thing was already defective when risk had passed, unless this presumption is incompatible with the nature of the thing or of the defect.[39]

5. Standardised digital content

Unlike some other European countries, German Contract Law does not provide for any particular rules on the sale of digital contents yet. The German legislator seems to be awaiting for two directives to come: the Directive on certain aspects concerning contracts for the supply of digital content[40] and the Directive on certain aspects concerning contracts for the online and other distance sales of goods.[41] However, they are still only proposals. Hence, the present German situation for the sales of digital contents is as follows: If the buyer purchases a storage medium which contains standardised digital content, sections 433 et seq. Civil Code are applicable as this is a normal sale of a thing according to section 90 Civil Code.[42] However, for direct downloads or the use of standardised digital contents (e.g. apps) against money, the mentioned sections are not directly applicable as the sold items are by their nature immaterial. As mentioned, the German Sales Law does not provide for any particular provisions for these kinds of contracts. This gap is filled by identifying this kind of digital content contracts as a purchase of rights under section 453 Civil Code.[43] This makes sections 433 et seq. Civil Code applicable to this kind of contracts – they are treated, as far as possible, as 'regular' sales contracts.

---

    it. The provisions referred to in sentence 1 apply even if circumvented by other constructions.

(2) The limitation of the claims cited in section 437 may not be alleviated by an agreement reached before a defect is notified to an entrepreneur if the agreement means that there is a limitation period of less than two years from the statutory beginning of limitation or, in the case of second-hand things, of less than one year.

(3) Notwithstanding sections 307 to 309, subsections (1) and (2) above do not apply to the exclusion or restriction of the claim to damages.

38 Section 476 Civil Code (shifting the burden of proof) reads:

    If, within six months after the date of the passing of the risk, a material defect manifests itself, it is presumed that the thing was already defective when risk passed, unless this presumption is incompatible with the nature of the thing or of the defect.

39 See also European Court of Justice, Case C-497/13, *Froukje Faber* v. *Autobedrijf Hazet Ochten BV*.
40 COM(2015) 634 final.
41 COM(2015) 635 final.
42 Beck Online Großkommentar/Wilhelmi, section 453 BGB no. 171, 177. For non-standardized digital content, the sections 631 Civil Code et seq. for contracts to produce work are applicable.
43 Beck Online Großkommentar/Wilhelmi, section 453 BGB no. 171, 177; Staudinger/Beckmann (Sellier, 15th edition 2014), section 453 BGB no. 72.

IV. Factual scenarios

Scenario 1

a. Recourse against the manufacturer Reliable

Under the German legal system, Alison cannot successfully sue the manufacturer Reliable as they did not establish any contractual relationships. A direct action of the buyer against the producer of defective products in the absence of any contract does not exist. The doctrine of privity of contract is still what prevents such a direct action at the moment. The German legislator only recognises the contractual liability of the final seller of the defective goods. However, he or she established in conformity with the requirements of article 4 of the Consumer Sales Directive a mandatory right to redress on part of the seller if the goods were already defective upon delivery (see section 478 Civil Code).[44] Thus, at the end, the producer should be liable for those defective products – but it is a liability alongside the contractual chains and not a direct action of the buyer against the producer.[45]

In addition, there is neither a liability of the manufacturer under the German Product Liability Act (the so-called *Produkthaftungsgesetz*) nor under general

---

44 Section 478 Civil Code (recourse of the entrepreneur) reads:

  (1) If an entrepreneur has been obliged to take back a newly manufactured thing sold by him because it is defective, or if the consumer has reduced the purchase price, it is not necessary for the entrepreneur to fix the period of time which would otherwise be necessary in order to enforce the rights set out in section 437 with regard to the defect asserted by the consumer against the entrepreneur who sold the thing to him (supplier).
  (2) Where a newly manufactured thing is sold, the entrepreneur may demand of his supplier reimbursement of the expenses which the entrepreneur had to bear in relation to the consumer under section 439(2), if the defect asserted by the consumer already existed upon the passing of the risk to the entrepreneur.
  (3) In the case of subsections (1) and (2) above, section 476 applies, subject to the proviso that the period begins when the risk passes to the consumer.
  (4) The supplier may not rely on an agreement made before the defect was notified to the supplier which, to the disadvantage of the entrepreneur, deviates from sections 433 to 435, 437, 439 to 443 or from subsections (1) and (3) above or from section 479, if the obligee with the right of recourse is not given another form of compensation of equal value. Sentence 1, notwithstanding section 307, does not apply to an exclusion or restriction of the claim to damages. The provisions referred to in sentence 1 apply even if circumvented by other constructions.
  (5) Subsections (1) to (4) above apply with the necessary modifications to claims of the supplier and of the other buyers in the supply chain against their sellers if the obligors are entrepreneurs.
  (6) Section 377 of the Commercial Code [Handelsgesetzbuch] is unaffected.

45 See more detailed M. Ebers, A. Janssen and O. Meyer (eds.), *European Perspectives on Producers' Liability: Direct Producers' Liability for Non-conformity and the Sellers' Right of Redress* (Munich: Sellier, 2009).

tort law. Both section 1 of the Product Liability Act[46] and general tort law provision section 823 Civil Code[47] require that the defective product caused harm to *another's* legal right (e.g. body, health, other property). These provisions do not cover any losses the buyer suffered because of the defectiveness of the product as such. In theory, the only way in this scenario to get damages from the manufacturer is through section 826 Civil Code. It reads as follows: '*A person who, in a manner contrary to public policy, intentionally inflicts damage on another person is liable to the other person to make compensation for the damage*'. Thus, the requirements for such a liability are very strict and have not been met in the scenario as there is no evidence showing that the manufacturer *intentionally* (especially with regard to the false information given in the TV advert) caused Alison any kind of loss. In conclusion, Alison does not have any right against the manufacturer Reliable.

---

46 Section 1 Product Liability Act (liability) reads:

(1) In such case as a defective product causes a person's death, injury to his body or damage to his health, or damage to an item of property, the producer of the product has an obligation to compensate the injured person for the resulting damage. In case of damage to an item of property, this shall only apply if the damage was caused to an item of property other than the defective product and this other item of property is of a type ordinarily intended for private use or consumption und was used by the injured person mainly for his own private use or consumption.

(2) The producer's liability obligation is excluded if

1 he did not put the product into circulation,
2 under the circumstances it is probable that the defect which caused the damage did not exist at the time when the producer put the product into circulation,
3 the product was neither manufactured by him for sale or any other form of distribution for economic purpose nor manufactured or distributed by him in the course of his business,
4 the defect is due to compliance of the product with mandatory regulations at the time when the producer put the product into circulation or
5 the state of scientific and technical knowledge at the time when the producer put the product into circulation was not such as to enable the defect to be discovered.

(3) The obligation to pay damages of the producer of a component part is also excluded if the defect is attributable to the design of the product in which the component has been fitted or to the instructions given by the manufacturer of the product. The first sentence shall apply to the producer of a raw material mutatis mutandis.

(4) The injured person bears the burden of proving the defect, the damage and the causal relationship between defect and damage. If it is disputed whether the obligation to pay compensation is excluded pursuant to paragraph 2 or 3, the producer bears the burden of proof.

47 Section 823 Civil Code (liability in damages) reads:

(1) A person who, intentionally or negligently, unlawfully injures the life, body, health, freedom, property or another right of another person is liable to make compensation to the other party for the damage arising from this.

(2) The same duty is held by a person who commits a breach of a statute that is intended to protect another person. If, according to the contents of the statute, it may also be breached without fault, then liability to compensation only exists in the case of fault.

b. Recourse against the retailer Billy

Alison and Billy have concluded a valid sales contract under sections 145, 433 et seq. Civil Code. As Billy is an entrepreneur and Alison acts as a consumer, the additional special consumer sales law provisions of the sections 474 et seq. are applicable. There are three possible grounds for Alison to lodge a complaint: first, the problems with the brakes and engine noise (in the new and second-hand car scenario), the higher-than-expected fuel consumption and finally the failure to meet emission standards. Each compliant will be considered separately even if in practice all these complaints would be taken together to decide whether the car has a material defect and what kind of remedies would be available in case of non-conformity.

(I)(A) BRAKE AND ENGINE NOISE (NEW CAR)

The problems with the brakes and the engine noise are classical sales law matters. Both are material defects under German law. Alison could argue under section 434(1)2 no. 1 Civil Code that the car is not suitable for the *intended use under the contract*. She explained to Billy that she needed the car for the particular purpose of going to and from work every day (twice a day 30 miles). It was obvious to Billy that this particular purpose would be relevant to the general use of the sold car. As the sold car had problems with the brakes and showed unusual engine noises, Alison could argue that the sold car is not fit for the particular purpose under section 434(1)2 no. 1 Civil Code. In addition, she could also instead try to demonstrate that the car shows material defects under section sections 434(1)2 no. 2 Civil Code.[48] This provision outlines that a thing is free of material defects if it is suitable for *customary use*, and its *quality is usual* in things of the same kind, and the *buyer may expect* this quality in view of the type of the thing. Both problems (especially the problem with the brakes) make the car unsuitable for customary use. Brand new cars usually do not show these kinds of problems, and it is reasonable for buyers of new cars to expect cars free from such problems – they can expect a new car that is flawless (especially when the functioning of the brakes are relevant to safety).[49] As it is a consumer sales contract and the material defects manifested themselves within the first six months of the passing of risk (here three weeks after delivery), it is presumed that the car was already defective when risk was passed (see section 476 Civil Code).

The primary remedy of Alison would be the right to cure according to sections 437 no. 1, 439 Civil Code. In principle, she can either ask for repairment or replacement as both remedies are 'possible' (see sections 437 no. 1, 439(3)1

---

48 The relationship between section 434(1)2 no. 1 and no. 2 Civil Code is somewhat unclear but cannot be discussed here in more detail (see Beck'scher Online-Kommentar BGB/Faust, section 434 BGB no. 53 et seq.).
49 The manufacturer's advertising campaign referring to 'top reliability' could in theory be taken into account according to section 434(1)3 Civil Code as part of the overall assessment of whether the car has a material defect. However, this statement is too general to have any legal consequences under German law. It is a mere puff.

Civil Code). Both remedies are possible in the German law sense that the car can be repaired or replaced by another flawless new car (assuming that Alison's car is the only one that has the described problems and not all cars of that model). However, Billy may refuse to provide the kind of cure chosen by the Alison if this cure is only possible at disproportionate expenses (see sections 437 no. 1, 439(3)1–3 Civil Code). If one remedy is disproportionate, the claim of the buyer will be restricted to the alternative kind of cure. If both kinds of cure are disproportionate, the seller can even refuse both. To decide whether repairment and/or are disproportionate, it must be taken into account in particular:

- the value of the thing when free of defects,
- the importance of the defect, and
- the question as to whether recourse could be had to the alternative kind of cure without substantial detriment to the buyer.

Bearing in mind these mentioned aspects, taking into consideration that we do not have all relevant information and that it should be decided on a case by case basis, it seems to be more likely that a replacement may only possible at disproportionate costs. Considering the fast depreciation in value of a new car once it has been used, the repairment of Alison's car would probably be significantly cheaper than replacing it and could be done without any substantial detriment to Alison. In conclusion, Alison would probably be restricted to repairment.

If Alison sets a reasonable deadline for Billy to cure the defects and the deadline expires without the defects being cured, she can also revoke the contract (see section 437 no. 2, 440, 323, 326(5) Civil Code) or reduce the contract price under section 437 no. 2, 441 Civil Code. There are no facts at hand which indicate that an exemption from this Nachfrist-procedure is justified in the given case. As the material defects are not trivial under section 323(5) 2 Civil Code, the right to revoke the contract is not excluded.

Alison also has the right to damages in lieu of performance (Schadensersatz statt der Leistung) for the defective brakes and the engine noise. However, to exercise this right, an unsuccessful Nachfrist-procedure is needed as just discussed. In addition (and without the Nachfrist-procedure) to the rights mentioned, Alison might be able to claim damages in addition to performance (Schadensersatz neben der Leistung) if any additional losses as a consequence of the material defects have occurred (but not indicated here in this scenario). For both kinds of damages, one has to recall that Billy must have breached the contract intentionally or negligently (section 276(1) Civil Code) as the German law has a fault liability system (section 280(1) Civil Code). From the case at hand, it cannot be determined whether Billy acted with fault or not. However, Alison may rely on the reversed burden of proof for this aspect. According to section 280(1)2 Civil Code the obligor's fault (in this case Billy) is presumed unless he can prove that he was not responsible for the breach of duty. Thus, it would be Billy's task to proof that he was not responsible for the material defects. At least from the facts of the scenario 1, it cannot be concluded that this is the case. All remedies mentioned are not time-barred under section 438 Civil Code.

(I)(B) BRAKE AND ENGINE NOISE (SECOND-HAND CAR)

The relevant provisions for this alternative scenario (car is second-hand and three years old) are the same as just discussed. To decide whether there is a material defect section 434(1) Civil Code is decisive. If we start with section 434(1)2 no. 2 Civil Code, the question this time is also whether the car at hand is suitable for *customary use*, has the *quality which is usual* in things of the same kind and the *buyer may expect* this quality. There is no doubt that the standards to be met are different for new and second-hand items, especially cars.[50] Negative characteristics of a sold good might constitute as material defect for new but not for second-hand products. For second-hand cars, it is decisive whether or not the flaws shown exceed the normal wear and tear for cars of that type and age.[51] Normal wear and tear do not constitute as material defects.[52] As we do not have all relevant information (e.g. how slow are the breaks working, intensity of the noise of the engine), it is not easy to make a final decision. However, it seems more likely that both flaws (the problems with the brakes and the engine noise) do exceed the normal wear and tear of a 3-year-old second-hand car. A car of that kind may be louder than a brand new one, but Alison should not expect howling noises whenever gears are changed at a low speed. The same applies to the brakes as this is a safety sensitive aspect. Even a buyer of a second-hand car can expect the brakes to work flawlessly and that such wear parts would have been renewed in the past if necessary.[53] In conclusion, we do have probably two material defects according to section 434(1)2 no. 2 Civil Code even if the car is second-hand and 3 years old. Arguably, the sold second-hand car is also not suitable for Alison's intended use under the contract according to section 434(1)2 no. 1 Civil Code.

In general, Alison has the same remedies as in the original scenario, and the practically important section 476 Civil Code (reversed burden of proof) is also applicable to second-hand goods. However 'replacement' would normally not be available as it is a second-hand good (so-called *Stückschuld*) which makes this kind of cure 'impossible' in the understanding of the law (section 437 no. 1, 439(3)1 Civil Code). In that case, Alison is restricted to repairment of the car because of the impossibility of the replacement. A decision whether replacement is disproportionate is unnecessary in that case.

(II) HIGHER-THAN-EXPECTED FUEL CONSUMPTION

Turning to the next complaint, the higher-than-expected fuel consumption, there are two possible starting points for Alison to argue that it is a material defect: (a) the advertising campaign of Reliable under the slogan 'Top Reliability, Low Fuel Consumption, Best for the Environment' including the TV advert, and/or

---

50 Beck'scher Online-Kommentar BGB/Faust, section 434 BGB no. 64.
51 Beck'scher Online-Kommentar BGB/Faust, section 434 BGB no. 64.
52 Bundesgerichtshof, Neue Juristische Wochenschrift 2006, 434 no. 19.
53 Oberlandesgericht Koblenz, Neue Juristische Wochenschrift 2007, 1828.

(b) Alison made known a particular purpose to Billy, and he reassured that the low fuel consumption would also show over short distances.

Customary quality under section 434(1)2 no. 2 Civil Code also includes under section 434(1)3 Civil Code the characteristics which the buyer can expect from the public statements on specific characteristics of the thing that are made by the producer. Evaluating the whole advertising campaign (slogan 'Low Fuel Consumption' and TV advert) one would come to the conclusion that the statements made are not only a 'mere puff' but characterise the quality of the car as such. Assuming that Alison's car did not meet the quality standards mentioned in the advertising campaign, it is defective in the meaning of the law. Also the German Supreme Court (the so-called *Bundesgerichtshof*) decided on several occasions that a higher-than-expected fuel consumptions constitutes a material defect.[54] Billy could also not exempt himself from liability as the possible grounds for exemptions under section 434(1)3 Civil Code are not given here ((a) seller was not aware of the statement and also had no duty to be aware of it; (b) at the time the contract was concluded the statement had been corrected in an equal manner; (c) or the statement did not influence the purchaser's decision). Nevertheless, Billy did not give any additional guarantee under section 443 Civil Code.[55] Statements of the producer might be relevant in the context of section 434(1)3 Civil Code, but if the seller more or less only repeats the producer's statements (as did Billy here), the German Supreme Court stated that this is often not a guarantee under section 443 Civil Code.[56] Instead, or in addition to that, Alison could argue that she made a particular purpose known to Billy under section 434(1)2 no. 1 Civil Code during the sales conversation and that he reassured that the low fuel consumption would also show over short distances. The particular purpose here is not the daily commute from home to work as such, but that the car shows a low fuel consumption also over short distances – which is not the case.

---

[54] Bundesgerichtshof, Neue Juristische Wochenschrift 1996, 1337; Bundesgerichtshof, Neue Juristische Wochenschrift 1997, 2590.

[55] Section 443 Civil Code (guarantee) reads:

(1) Where the seller, the producer or some other third party enters into obligation, in addition to his statutory liability for defects, by way of making a declaration or in relevant advertising that was available prior to the purchase agreement being concluded or at the time of its conclusion, such obligation being in particular to reimburse the purchase price, to exchange the thing, to repair it or to provide services in this context should the thing not exhibit the quality or not fulfil other requirements than those concerning its freedom from defects, in each case as described in the declaration or in the relevant advertisement (guarantee), the buyer shall be entitled, in the case of a guarantee having been given, and notwithstanding his statutory claims, to the rights under the guarantee in relation to the person who has given the guarantee (guarantor).

(2) To the extent that the guarantor gives a guarantee as to the thing having a specified quality for a specified period (guarantee of durability), the presumption will be that a material defect which appears during the guarantee period triggers the rights under the guarantee.

[56] Bundesgerichtshof, Zeitschrift für Wirtschaftsrecht (ZIP) 1996, 599.

Coming to the remedies we can generally refer to the comments made above even though some particularities need to be stressed. As a first remedy, Alison has the right to cure, either repairment or replacement. If her car is the only one that has this material defect (the high fuel consumption), she can – subject to the proportionality criterion of the section 439(3) Civil Code – either ask for a repairment or replacement of the car as both remedies are 'possible'. Understanding the case like this, one could refer to the comments made under the brakes and engine noise problem-scenario for the other remedies (right to revoke the contract, price reduction, and right to damages).

The situation gets more complicated when the problems affecting her car is affecting every car of that model Alison bought. In that case, her car cannot be replaced by another flawless one as they all carry the same defect. Considering the given facts, this understanding of the scenario seems to be more likely. Here a replacement would be impossible under sections 434(3)1 Civil Code. Repairment of Alison's car however, does not seem to be impossible (reducing the fuel consumption) but is more likely that this kind of cure is only possible at disproportionate expenses under section 439(1) 1–3 Civil Code.[57] In that case, Billy cannot replace the car and may refuse to repair it, which would result in Alison not having a right to cure. However, in principle, she still has the right to revoke the contract, reduce the price or ask for damages in lieu of performance (Schadensersatz statt der Leistung). As the right to cure here is either impossible (replacement) or probably only possible at disproportionate costs (repairment) a Nachfrist-procedure would be useless. Section 440 Civil Code rules that in such a case, it is not necessary to specify a period of time to the seller to cure the non-conformity. Thus, Alison could directly choose between the three remaining remedies. To avoid a revocation of the contract, Billy could try to argue that the defect is only trivial under sections 437 no. 2, 323(5)2 Civil Code. However, the German Supreme court had already made clear that exceeding the fuel consumption indicated by the producer by 10% is already sufficient not to be considered as trivial.[58] Even though the exact facts of the case are silent to how much Alison's car is really consuming (in comparison to the producer's indications), it is likely that it has a significantly higher fuel consumption. It will be described below that fuel consumption and emission go hand in hand. As the cars failed to meet emissions standards by a *significant* margin, it can be assumed that they also consume significantly more fuel. In conclusion, in addition to price reduction and damages, Alison is also possibly entitled to revoke the contract. Billy could try to avoid damages if he can prove that he was not responsible for the breach of duty under section 280(1) 1, 2 Civil Code.

---

57 In case the costs for repairing the car are not disproportionate, Alison has to choose repairment as the right to cure first. Then no further differences to the what have been said before.
58 See Entscheidungen des Bundesgerichtshofs in Zivilsachen (BGHZ) 132, 55, 62; Münchener Kommentar zum BGB/Westermann (C.H. Beck, 6th edition 2012), section 437 BGB no. 12.

(III) FAILURE TO MEET EMISSIONS STANDARDS

The last complaint of Alison is that – assuming that the facts given in the news reports are correct – the sold car (and the whole model as such) fails to meet the emission standards by a significant margin. The core question here under German law is whether this is separate complaint at all (which can lead to the independent assumption of a material defect) or whether it is just a natural consequence of the higher-than-expected-fuel-consumption. If the latter assumption is correct, the failure to meet emission standards cannot lead to an independent material defect of its own besides the higher-than-expected fuel consumption. The Oberlandesgericht Hamm explained in its 2011 decision using the expertise of a technical expert that fuel consumption and emission '*go technically and mathematically hand in hand*'.[59] The more a car is consuming the higher the emissions are. Thus, it concluded that the failure to meet emission standards is not a separate material defect, but just a consequence of the excessively high fuel consumption.[60] Applying the Oberlandesgericht Hamm case here, the fact that the car's emissions is too high does not give Alison an additional reason to claim against Billy (alongside the reasons already mentioned before).

Scenario 2

David and the software supplier concluded a valid contract according to the sections 145 et seq. Civil Code. The latter had the obligation to provide the standardised sports software, while David had to pay the agreed sum of $15. The first issue that has to be dealt with is the nature of this contract as German law does not provide any particular provisions for these kinds of contracts. Sections 433 et seq. Civil Code are not directly applicable to direct downloads or use of standardised digital content (e.g. apps) against money as the sold items are by their nature immaterial. However, as already described before, this gap is filled by identifying these contracts as purchase of rights contracts under section 453 Civil Code.[61] This makes the general sales law provisions (sections 433 et seq. Civil Code) in principle applicable to this kind of contracts. Questionable is (as David is a consumer and the supplier an entrepreneur) whether the additional special consumer sales provisions of the sections 474 et seq. Civil Code are applicable here. According to the jurisprudence and the leading opinion in legal literature, these provisions are applicable even if the software itself is not to be considered as a moveable thing which is normally the prerequisite for their applicability.[62]

---

59   Oberlandesgericht Hamm, 09.06.2011–28 U 12/11, ADAJUR Dok.Nr. 94361.
60   Oberlandesgericht Hamm, 09.06.2011–28 U 12/11, ADAJUR Dok.Nr. 94361.
61   Beck Online Großkommentar/Wilhelmi, section 453 BGB no. 171, 177; Staudinger/Beckmann (Sellier, 15th edition 2014), section 453 BGB no. 72.
62   See Entscheidungen des Bundesgerichtshofs in Zivilsachen (BGHZ) 102, 135, 141; 109, 97, 100; Münchener Kommentar zum BGB/Lorenz (C.H. Beck, 7th edition 2016), section 474 BGB no. 10.

In conclusion, the same provisions in the first scenario also apply here. Factually, David's complaints deal with a possible defectiveness of an application which he bought and downloaded and its further negative consequences.

(i) Failure of the app and failure to patch the problem

David bought and downloaded the sport application onto his tablet which connects to his smartwatch from the supplier. The application was supposed to keep track of (a) where he was running, (b) his heart rate and (c) his blood pressure. However, after only a few days, David noticed that the blood pressure readings have failed. As it can be assumed that the function 'blood pressure reading' was already an explicit part of the contract conclusion period, the downloaded application does not have the agreed quality. According to the contractual agreement, the supplier had the obligation to deliver an application that includes a working blood pressure reading. As this is not the case, the download has a material defect under section 453(1), 434(1)1 Civil Code (subjective notion of the material defect). There is no need to refer to the objective notion of the material defect under the rest of section 434 Civil Code.

What kind of remedies David has depends on the understanding of the given facts. Due to the technical circumstances of the case, it can be assumed that all downloaded applications of that kind are defective and not only David's. So, the first remedy is the right to cure. David has either the right to repairment or replacement. However, as we assume that all downloaded applications are defective a replacement becomes impossible under sections 453(1), 437 no. 1, 439(1)(3)1 Civil Code. Repairment remains the only possible right to cure. The problem with repairment is that it would arguably only be at disproportionate expenses under section 439(3)1 Civil Code.[63] The price of the application is only $15, and the cost to repair it is probably much higher. In conclusion, the supplier can refuse both kind of cure (sections 453(1), 437 no. 1, 439(3)3 Civil Code). Consequently, David can choose among revocation, price reduction and damages in lieu of performance (Schadensersatz statt der Leistung) as there is no requirement to follow the Nachfrist-procedure in that case (see sections 453(1), 437 no. 1, 440 s. 1 German Civil Code). The right to revocation is also not excluded by section 453(1), 437 no. 2, 323(5)2 Civil Code as the breach at hand is not trivial in comparison with the overall functions of the application. For the right to damages, one has to again bear in mind that the supplier must have breached the contract intentionally or negligently (sections 280(1), 276(1) Civil Code). Here it cannot be determined from the case whether the supplier acted with fault or not. However, David may rely on the reversed burden of proof for this aspect under German law. According to section 280(1)2 Civil Code the obligor's fault is presumed unless he can prove that he was not responsible for the breach of duty. Thus, it would be the supplier's task to prove that he was not responsible for the breach of contract.

---

63 If repairment should not be considered as being disproportionate, David must ask for it first.

(ii) Interference with other apps

The defective application of the supplier has negatively affected other applications of the tablet, especially the remote operation of David's TV recorder and the central heating system (which led to the fact that the central heating thermostat had been set to 32 degrees Celsius all along). The appropriate remedy for David would be *damages in addition to performance*, which opposite to the damages in lieu of performance does not require a Nachfrist-procedure. For the issue regarding the supplier's fault, it can be referred to the explanations made above for the damages in lieu of performance. Let us assume once again that the supplier cannot prove that he was not responsible for the breach of contract. In that case, David can ask for compensation for the negative consequences of the defective application has on the other applications – 'remote operation TV recorder' and 'central heating system' – according to sections 249 et seq. Civil Code. It is not completely clear whether David had also suffered a financial loss due to the fact that the central heating thermostat had been set to 32 degrees Celsius all along (and that the consumption was higher than with a working central heating system application). If we assume that he did suffer a financial loss, this loss would be compensable under German law as it would pass the German equivalent of the English Law 'remoteness test' (which contains in a nutshell a three-step test: the so-called *Äquivalenztheorie, Adäquanztheorie* and *objektive Zurechnung*):[64] The defective app is conditio sine qua non for the higher consumption (Äquivalenztheorie), the loss is (based on the general life experience) not completely unlikely (Adäquanztheorie), and there are no reasons against the so-called objective attribution of the loss (objektive Zurechnung) to the supplier. Thus, under German law, this loss would not be too remote to be compensated.

(iii) Damage done to the Wi-Fi connector

Another kind of negative consequence caused by the defective application is to the hardware of David's tablet itself – more precisely to its Wi-Fi connector. Under German law, there would not be a difference to the just discussed damages done to the apps. In conclusion, David can ask for damages in addition to performance without the Nachfrist-procedure to claim for financial compensation for the damaged Wi-Fi connector.

V. Specific issues in Germany

Everything relevant for the German consumer sales law has already been mentioned respectively covered by this book chapter.

---

64 See e.g. Münchener Kommentar zum BGB/Oetker (C.H. Beck, 7th edition 2016), section 249 BGB no. 103 et seq. with further references.

4 Consumer sales law in Hong Kong

*Chen Lei and Geraint Howells**

I. The Hong Kong consumer market

Hong Kong has long been known as a shopping paradise. The retail sector is one of the major service sectors in Hong Kong in terms of transaction volumes and persons engaged. However, according to the Census and Statistics Department (C&SD) survey, sales and other receipts of the retail sector decreased at an average annual rate of 1.1% from 1995 to 2005.[1] Since around 2005, cross-border shopping from Mainland China has been an important part of the Hong Kong economy. Although Hong Kong has been considered to be the second most important place for Mainland Chinese to shop online (58%) after the United States,[2] there are signs that this is slumping given the relative stagnation in its economy and some tensions between Hong Kong and Mainland Chinese as well as indirect visa restrictions. While Hong Kong's economy expanded by 2% in real terms in 2016, the value of retail sales, in nominal terms, dropped by 1.3% year-on-year in January–March 2017, after the decline of 8.1% for 2016.[3] Many local smaller shops have been forced to close under pressure for retail outlets serving international tourists that can afford higher rents. This may be reversed as less tourists come from Mainland China and in particular as businesses move to online selling.

Complaints statistics

According to Complaints Statistics by the Consumer Council, the total number of complaints in 2014, 2015 and January–March 2016 are 31,048, 27,378 and 5,427, respectively.[4] While the complaints have dropped in number from 2014 to 2015 by 12%, they have nevertheless become increasingly more complicated

---

* Special thanks to Karen Choi Po Yan for her research assistance.
1 www.statistics.gov.hk/pub/B70707FC2007XXXXB0100.pdf.
2 See R. Fu, *Chinese Cross-Border Online Shoppers Insights*, www.chinainternetwatch.com/8625/cross-border-online-shoppers/.
3 Doris Fung, '*Economic and Trade Information on Hong Kong*' (HKTDC Research, 2016), http://www.hktdc.com/business-news/web/error/error_404.htm?LANGUAGE=en, accessed 20 January 2017.
4 Consumer Council, *Complaints Statistics for the Year From 2015 to 2017* (Consumer Council, 15 May 2017), www.consumer.org.hk/ws_en/statistics/complaints, accessed 21 May 2017.

in nature.[5] There has been rising travel complaints involving local residents in purchase of air tickets and hotel accommodation, and visiting tourists purchasing goods such as dried seafood. The Consumer Council is worried that if no remedial action is taken immediately, there will be long-term detriment to the tourism industry, one of the four pillar industries of the Hong Kong economy.

Telecommunication services and travel matters are the top two services/goods for complaints, receiving a total of 10,409 and 5,005 complaints respectively from January 2013 to March 2016.[6] Telecommunication services has remained at the very top of all complaint categories for 16 consecutive years, but there has been significant reduction in recent years due to improved billing and greater clarity by telecoms providers.[7] However, there are still issues with contract termination and overcharging.

There has also been increased complaints about beauty services and recreation/health clubs. Most complaints involved the use of coercive tactics to force consumers into purchasing highly priced treatment service. Several centres were prosecuted by the Customs and Excise Department in violation of the Trade Descriptions Ordinance.

II. Access to justice for consumers and enforcement of consumer law

This section will outline how consumers can enforce their legal rights, and how the compliance with consumer law and enforcement are handled by various public agencies in Hong Kong.

Venues for complaint

Consumer Council

Incorporated under the Consumer Council Ordinance (Cap. 216), the Consumer Council handles complaints from consumers and mediates between traders and consumers where there is a dispute. Where complaints cannot be resolved through negotiation between the trader or the industry association, the Council provides advice to consumers as to possible avenues of legal redress through private action.

However, it is not a law enforcement body unlike, for example, the Customs and Excise Department. It also has no authority to sue traders. It has no power

---

5 Consumer Council, *Overall Consumer Complaints Down 12% Amidst Travel Complaints Rising 41%* (Consumer Council, 2 February 2016), www.consumer.org.hk/ws_en/news/press/2015/yearender.html, accessed 21 May 2017.
6 Consumer Council, *Complaints Statistics for the Year From 2015 to 2017* (Consumer Council, 15 May 2017), www.consumer.org.hk/ws_en/statistics/complaints, accessed 21 May 2017.
7 Consumer Council, *Overall Consumer Complaints Down 12% Amidst Travel Complaints Rising 41%* (Consumer Council, 2 February 2016), www.consumer.org.hk/ws_en/news/press/2015/yearender.html, accessed 21 May 2017.

to apply on behalf of consumers to the court for an injunction to stop unfair business practices. Instead, the Council can censure trade malpractices by naming and publicising the traders concerned.

For cases that involve significant consumer interest, but cannot be resolved between the parties privately through mediation or negotiation, the complaint can make applications for assistance to the Consumer Legal Action Fund, which is run by the Council to assist consumers to pursue their matters in courts.[8]

Judiciary: Small Claims Tribunal

A small claims procedure in Hong Kong is handled in Small Claims Tribunal established under the Small Claims Tribunal Ordinance (Cap. 338). The Small Claims Tribunal provides an informal, quick and inexpensive means to deal with claims up to HK$50,000. No legal representation is allowed. The adjudicators are appointed by the Chief Executive (s.4). The main types of claims handled by the Tribunal include debts, services charge, damage to property, defective goods and other consumer claims.

If the consumer does not wish to submit the claim to the Small Claims Tribunal but to have it tried in the District Court or the High Court, he or she may apply for legal aid if certain conditions set out by the Legal Aid Department are satisfied.[9]

Consumer Council

The Consumer Council administers the Consumer Council Legal Action Fund. It is a trust fund set up to give 'greater consumer access to legal remedies by providing financial support and legal assistance'[10] for the benefit of consumers with similar grievances in cases involving significant public interest and injustice. It also aims to deter undesirable business practices and educate the public as to their existing consumer rights.

There is, however, no class action in Hong Kong. In May 2012, the Law Reform Commission proposed that a mechanism for class actions should be adopted in Hong Kong and recommended phasing its implementation by starting with consumer cases.[11] Under the existing law in Hong Kong, the sole machinery for dealing with multi-party proceedings is a rule on representative proceedings under Order 15 Rule 12 of the Rules of the High Court, which was criticised as restrictive and inadequate by the Chief Justice's Working Party on Civil Justice Reform in its Final Report in 2004.

---

8 For more information such as eligibility criteria, see www.consumer.org.hk/website/ws_en/legal_protection/consumer_legal_actions_fund/CLAFBriefPDF.pdf.
9 For more information such as eligibility criteria and different schemes offered by the Legal Aid Department, see www.lad.gov.hk/eng/las/overview.html.
10 Consumer Council, *Consumer Legal Action Fund* (Consumer Council, 2010), www.consumer.org.hk/ws_en/legal_protection/consumer_legal_actions_fund/clafinfo.html, accessed 21 May 2017.
11 The LRC's report is available in www.hkreform.gov.hk/en/docs/rclassactions_e.pdf.

Industry self-regulation bodies

There are various industry schemes on developing codes of practice and complaints mechanisms. For example, in the insurance industry, the Insurance Claims Complaints Bureau is set up to handle insurance claims complaints arising from all types of personal insurance policies with amounts not exceeding HK$1,000,000.[12] In the banking sector, one can find the regulator ensuring that the Code of Banking Practice enhances consumer confidence and regularly seeking the Council's views on ways to make the scheme more effective.

There are also avenues to seek redress from specific industry. For example, the Financial Dispute Resolution Centre provides consumers with an alternative avenue which is independent and affordable for resolving monetary disputes with the financial institution by way of 'mediation first and arbitration next'. The Customer Complaint Settlement Scheme for the Telecommunications Industry is a mediation scheme set up by the telecommunications industry aiming at resolving billing disputes in deadlock between the telecommunications service providers and their customers.

The Consumer Council launched a Code of Practice in collaboration with the Laundry Association of Hong Kong in 2015. This Code aims to enhance service quality and promote good trade practice in the laundry industry. An independent Complaint Review Committee will be established under the Code to handle complaints based on an established fair mechanism. It is expected that there will be more similar partnership schemes between the Council and different trade sectors.

Refund Protection Scheme (Registered Shops) for Inbound Tour Group Shoppers allows group visitors who patronise a registered shop arranged by the Travel Industry Council (TIC) members a full refund protection if they are dissatisfied with their purchases within 6 months (for mainland visitors) or 14 days (for overseas visitors) after purchase. Consumers seeking a full refund must produce the original receipt and return the purchased item. The item must be undamaged and with no wear and tear due to use. Registered shops must also honour a number of pledges made to the TIC. Registered shops in breach of any one of the pledges will be given a certain number of demerits by the Committee on Shopping-Related Practices. Their registration will be revoked if they have accumulated 30 demerits, and member agents will be forbidden to arrange for visitors to visit them.

Public enforcement

The Customs and Excise Department is the principal agency responsible for enforcing the Trade Description Ordinance (Cap. 362). In relation to claims connected to consumer protection, the Customs and Excise Department is responsible for conducting spot checks on the accuracy of measuring equipment and the compliance with the safety requirements for consumer goods, and investigating

---

12 Office of the Commissioner of Insurance, *The Role of the Office of the Commissioner of Insurance* (Office of the Commission of Insurance, 21 February 2017), www.oci.gov.hk/about/index08.html, accessed 21 May 2017.

complaints relating to short measures, unsafe consumer goods, false trade descriptions and unfair trade practices.[13] Concurrent jurisdiction is conferred on the Communications Authority, with the Office of the Communications Authority as its executive arm, to enforce the fair trading sections in the TDO in relation to the commercial practices of licensees under the Telecommunications Ordinance (Cap. 106) and the Broadcasting Ordinance (Cap. 562) that are directly connected with the provision of a telecommunications or broadcasting service under the relevant Ordinances. Under the TDO, a civil compliance-based mechanism is effected to encourage compliance by traders and curb unfair trade practices. As an alternative to prosecution, the authorised enforcement agencies are empowered to accept undertakings from a trader, whom the respective enforcement agency in-charge believes has involved in any conduct which constitutes an offence under the fair-trading sections.[14] The trader is obliged to undertake that he or she will not continue or repeat an offending conduct, or conduct of a substantially similar kind. Where necessary, the Customs and Excise Department and the Communications Authority[15] may apply to the Court for an injunction to order a trader not to continue or repeat or engage in the contravening conduct.[16]

The Court may grant an injunction if it is satisfied that a trader has engaged, is engaging or is likely to engage in conduct that constitutes an offence under the fair trading sections. The Court may also grant an interim injunction pending the determination of the application for an injunction if the Court considers it desirable to do so.[17] It is generally recognised that injunction, unlike damages or an account of profits which look to the past for compensating a plaintiff, looks to the future. Hence, the court will decide, even after an infringement has occurred, whether a future threat still exists.[18] It follows that the Court will usually refuse an injunction relief if it concludes that the infringement is only a one-off activity. For instance, in precedents which involve trademark infringement, Aldous LJ held that when a defendant has infringed a plaintiff's goods, the Court will normally assume that it is not a one-off activity, unless persuaded otherwise. It is then

13 The Government of Hong Kong Special Administrative Region, *The Estimates 2016–2017 – Head 031 Customs and Excise Department* (The Government of Hong Kong Special Administrative Region, 26 February 2016), www.budget.gov.hk/2016/eng/pdf/head031.pdf, accessed 6 June 2017.
14 S.30L of TDO.
15 The Customs and Excise Department is the principal agency responsible for enforcing the TDO. Concurrent jurisdiction is conferred on the Communications Authority, with the Office of the Communications Authority as its executive arm, to enforce the fair-trading sections in the TDO in relation to the commercial practices of licensees under the Telecommunications Ordinance (Cap. 106) and the Broadcasting Ordinance (Cap. 562) that are directly connected with the provision of a telecommunications or broadcasting service under the relevant Ordinances.
16 S.30P(1)(a) of TDO.
17 S.30Q of TDO.
18 *Creative Technology Limited v Videocom Technology Limited and Anor* HCA1434/2002 (unreported. 21st February 2003) para. 47.

up to the defendant to prove hardship and illustrate steps to be taken to avoid future infringement.[19]

III. The legal framework for consumer sales

Consumer contracts

Relevant rules on consumer contracts can be found under Sales of Goods Ordinance (Cap. 26) (SOGO), Control of Exemption Clauses Ordinance (Cap. 71) (CECO), Supply of Services (Implied Terms) Ordinance (Cap. 457) (SSO), and Unconscionable Contracts Ordinance (Cap. 458) (UCO).

SOGO s.2A, SSO s.4, CECO s.4 define 'dealing as consumer' as where:

1 the party neither makes the contract in the course of a business nor hold itself out as doing so;
2 the other party does make the contract in the course of a business; and
3 the services provided to the party under, or in pursuance of, the contract are of a type ordinarily supplied or provided for private consumption or benefit.

SOGO codifies the law relating to the sale of goods. 'Goods' are defined to include all chattels personal other than things in action and money.[20] From this definition, it seems that digital content supplied in tangible form subject to the rights and remedies in the sale of goods legislation, but digital content supplied in intangible form through downloads, streaming or other means may not subject to similar statutory regulation. However, the position remains unclear as unlike the United Kingdom there is no specific statutory regime for digital content. Some cases even went further to suggest that a distinction between the production of a 'bespoke' programme and the sale of a standard proprietary software should be made.[21]

SOGO has the following implied terms:

- implied condition that the seller has the right to sell (s.14(1)(a))
- implied warranty that the buyer shall have and enjoy quiet possession of the goods and that the goods shall be free from any charge or encumbrance (s.14(1)(b))
- implied condition that the goods shall correspond with the description (in the case of sale by description) and sample (in the case of sale by description and sample) (s.15(1))
- implied condition that
    - the bulk shall correspond with the sample in quality;

---

19 *Coflexip SA and Another v Stolt Comex Seaway Ms Limited and Another* [2001] RPC 9.
20 S.2(1) of SOGO (HK).
21 A summary of cases is discussed in detail in Robert Bradgate, "Beyond the Millennium – The Legal Issues: Sale of Goods Issues and the Millennium Bug" (1999) 2 *JILT*.

- the goods shall be free from any defect rendering them unmerchantable which would not be apparent on reasonable examination of the sample; and
- the buyer shall have a reasonable opportunity of comparing the bulk with the sample (s.17(2)).

- implied condition that the goods must be of merchantable quality where the seller sells goods in the course of a business (s.16(2)).

  S.2(5) lists out the criteria to be satisfied for goods to be of 'merchantable quality':

  (a) fit for the purpose(s) for which goods of that kind are commonly bought;
  (b) of such standard of appearance and finish;
  (c) free from defects (including minor ones);
  (d) safe; and
  (e) durable
  (f) as it is reasonable to expect.

  Regard must be had to the description applied to them, price and all the other relevant circumstances (s.2(5)).

- implied condition that, where the seller sells goods in the course of a business and the buyer, expressly or by implication, makes known to the seller any particular purpose for which the goods are being bought, the goods supplied under the contract are reasonably fit for that purpose (s.16(3)).

Where there is a breach of an *implied condition*, the buyer can repudiate the contract, reject the goods and sue for damages if any. Where the term breached by the seller is only an *implied warranty*, the buyer is only entitled to a claim for damages (s.13(2)).

SSO consolidates and amends the law with respect to the terms to be implied in contracts for the supply of services. It is implied in service contracts that:

- services should be carried out with reasonable care and skill (which generally means the services must meet the standard that a reasonable person would regard as satisfactory) (s.5);
- services should be performed within a reasonable time if the time of performance has not been fixed by the contract (s.6); and
- a reasonable charge should be paid if the charge has not been fixed by the contract (s.7).

If service suppliers fail to meet any one of the above conditions, they would be in breach of the service contract and liable for compensation to consumers. These implied terms cannot be excluded or restricted by reference to any contract term in the contract (s.8(1)).

CECO aims to limit the extent to which civil liability for breach of contract, or for negligence or other breach of duty, can be avoided by means of contract terms and otherwise; and to restrict the enforceability of arbitration agreements. Exemption clauses that exclude liability for death and personal injury are usually not effective.[22] Terms in consumer or standard form contracts that exclude liability or seek to allow a substantially different performance or no performance are subject to a 'reasonableness' test.[23] Schedule 2 sets out some guidelines on what may be considered 'reasonable', including the strength of relative bargaining positions of the parties. Significantly the implied terms as to title and relating to the quality of goods cannot be excluded in consumer contracts and can only be excluded if reasonable in other contexts.[24] Exemption clauses are also controlled by the rules of common law such as those on incorporation or the contra proferentum rule.

UCO empowers courts to give relief in certain contracts found to be unconscionable. 'Unconscionable' is not defined. The court refers to a non-exhaustive list in s.6(1) and common law definitions[25] which tend to focus on the totality of the circumstances and conduct that give rise to unfairness in the bargaining process. The court may (a) refuse to enforce the contract; (b) enforce the remainder of the contract without the unconscionable part; and (c) limit the application of, or revise or alter, any unconscionable part so as to avoid any unconscionable result.[26] Since coming into force 19 years ago, there have only been four successful challenges to unfair terms under UCO.[27] One possible reason suggested is that no enforcement body to pursue claims in a representative action.[28] An unfair term on its own may not be sufficient to make out a case for unconscionable contract.[29] In practice, UCO is ineffective in protecting consumers from unfair terms in standard form contracts, due to ineffectual legislation, lack of specific enforcement body and restrictions on accessing legal aid.[30] The Consumer Council has recommended the introduction of a legislation modelled on the UK Unfair Terms in Consumer Contracts Regulations 1999, with appropriate modifications in view of the differences in culture and marketplace.[31] The definition of unconscionability seems to have been more restrictively

---

22 S.7 of CECO.
23 S.8 and 3 of CECO.
24 Ss 11 and 12 of the CECO. S.3(1) of the CECO.
25 *Chitty on Contracts*(28th ed., 1999) Vol.1, p. 452 para.7–078 applied by *Shum Kit Ching v Caesar Beauty Centre Ltd.* [2003] 3 HKC 235.
26 S.5(1) of the UCO. See, e.g., *Cheung Kam Sing & Another v International Resort Developments Ltd.* [2003] 2 HKLRD 113 where the court refused to enforce an unconscionable contract.
27 L. Mason, *Hong Kong Consumers Deserve Fairer Deal in Goods and Services Contracts* (SCMP, 14 July 2014), www.scmp.com/comment/article/1553978/hong-kong-consumers-deserve-fairer-deal-goods-and-services-contracts, accessed 11 November 2014.
28 L. Mason, "Inadequacy and Ineffectuality: Hong Kong's Consumer Protection Regime Against Unfair Terms in Standard Form Contracts" (2014) 83 *HKLJ* 89, 90.
29 See, e.g., *Hang Seng Credit Card Ltd v Tsang Nga Lee* [2000] 3 HKC 269; *Shum Kit Ching v Caesar Beauty Centre Ltd.* [2003] 3 HKC 235.
30 L. Mason, "Inadequacy and Ineffectuality: Hong Kong's Consumer Protection Regime Against Unfair Terms in Standard Form Contracts" (2014) 83 *HKLJ* 93.
31 Consumer Council, *Unfair Terms in Standard Form Consumer Contract (Full Report)* (Consumer Council, April 2012), www.consumer.org.hk/website/ws_en/competition_issues/model_code/2012040301FullText.html, accessed 21 May 2017.

interpreted than the comparative Australian rules which are themselves subject to reform as many consider them to be too limited in scope to offer effective protection.

Consumer safety

Relevant rules on consumer safety can be found under Gas Safety Ordinance (Cap. 51), Pesticides Ordinance (Cap. 133), Electricity Ordinance (Cap. 406), Toys and Children's Products Safety Ordinance (Cap. 424), and Consumer Goods Safety Ordinance (Cap. 456).

Trade practices

Relevant rules on trade practices can be found in Money Changers Ordinance (Cap. 34), Weights and Measures Ordinance (Cap. 68), Travel Agents Ordinance (Cap. 218), Pyramid Schemes Prohibition Ordinance (Cap. 617), Trade Descriptions Ordinance (Cap. 362), Personal Data (Privacy) Ordinance (Cap. 486) and Estate Agents Ordinance (Cap. 511).

The Trade Descriptions Ordinance prohibits false trade descriptions for goods (s.7). It was amended by the Trade Descriptions (Unfair Trade Practices) (Amendment) Ordinance to extend to services (s.7A). These amendments, clearly influenced by the EU Unfair Commercial Practices Directive, introduced broader rules on unfair commercial practices that covered misleading omissions and aggressive practices. There were also some specific rules introduced on issues such as bait and switch tactics.

IV. Factual scenarios

Scenario 1

(i)(a) Brake and engine noise (new car)

Alison may have recourse against Billy on the grounds that

- the car is not of merchantable quality (s.16(2) SOGO); and
- the car is not fit for purpose (s.16(3) SOGO).

Although Hong Kong uses different terminology to the United Kingdom (merchantable quality versus satisfactory quality), in this type of circumstance similar issues are likely to determine whether the contract has been breached.

From the present facts, it appears that the car is unlikely to be of merchantable quality. The car started to show problems within 3 weeks, including the engine noise, and the sluggish brakes. Contrary to the manufacturer's advertising campaign referring to 'top reliability', these problems all show that the car was not durable, falling short of the criteria of 'merchantable' under s.2(5).

S.16(3) SOGO requires goods to be reasonably fit for purpose. It is an implied condition to a sale in the ordinary course of business. The particular purpose must be expressly implied or communicated to the seller by the buyer.

There must be reliance by the buyer on the seller's skill or judgement. The burden of proof is on the seller to show that there is absence of reliance or that the reliance was unreasonable in the circumstances. The reliance must be reasonable.

In the present facts, it appears that the car is unlikely to be fit for purpose. When Alison bought the car, she expressly explained to Billy that she needed the car for particular types of journey, being twice-daily 30-mile commute to and from work. Although she raised this primarily with regard to the car's fuel efficiency, it should also have been obvious to Billy that this particular purpose would be relevant to the car's general reliability. So if the brake problem and engine noise are caused because the car is only driven over relatively short distances, then Alison could additionally argue that the car was not fit for the purpose of being driven to and from work. It is arguable that she reasonably relied on the reassurance by Billy and bought the car.

The consequence of breaching implied conditions under s.16(2) and s.16(3) is that the buyer is entitled to reject the goods (s.13(2)). The consequence of rejection is that the buyer can decline to pay the price or recover the price if already paid. However, the buyer loses her right to reject where she accepted the goods, and acceptance is deemed where she retains the goods for a reasonable time without rejecting them (s.37(4)). 'Reasonable time' in this section has been held to be directed solely to what was a reasonably practical interval between the buyer receiving the goods and his ability to return them; it is not related to the opportunity to discover any particular defect, but refers to the opportunity to examine and try out the goods in general term.[32] It is arguable that Alison has accepted the goods after 3 weeks. If the remedy of rejection is not available, Alison may also claim damages for the breach of implied conditions. It is notable that the Hong Kong solution relies on old common law consumer case law which in the UK context has been replaced by a statutory short-term right to reject within the first 30 days.[33] It is possible, but not required, that the Hong Kong courts may take notice of this change when assessing what is a reasonable period for the purposes of acceptance. Damages will be available if rejection is not possible or could in any event be claimed as an alternative to rejection. Unlike the United Kingdom there are no formal remedies of repair or replacement, though these can of course be agreed to voluntarily.

(i)(b) Brake and engine noise (second-hand car)

Second-handed goods are not new and the standard expected of them is not the same as for new goods. The flexible definition of 'merchantable quality' accommodates second-hand goods.[34] S.2(5) SOGO allows the court to decide

---

32 *Bernstein v Pamson Motors (Golders Green) Ltd.* [1987] 2 All ER 220.
33 S.22 Consumer Rights Act 2015.
34 The Law Reform Commission of Hong Kong, *Report – Sale of Goods and Supply of Services [Topic 21]* (February 1990), www.hkreform.gov.hk/en/docs/rservices-e.doc; *Barlett v Sidney Marcus Ltd.*

what standard it is reasonable to expect having regard to the circumstances, including where the goods have been used for 3 years and where the goods may be of a lower price. It should also be noted that a buyer who knows that she is negotiating to buy a second-handed car will be more likely to examine it; if she does so, as regards defects which that examination ought to reveal, she will lose the implied term as to merchantable quality. In such case, Alison will have a higher hurdle to prove that the car is not of merchantable quality under s.16(2).

As for the requirement that the car would have to be fit for Alison's particular purpose, s.16(3) only requires the goods to be 'reasonably fit' for that purpose. If problems with the brakes and engine are caused by the second-hand nature of the car, then Alison will face a higher hurdle in proving reliance and that the car is not fit for purpose.

(ii) Higher-than-expected fuel consumption

The car is advertised as a car with 'low fuel consumption', and Alison expressly asked whether the car would maintain its low fuel consumption when used in the way she intended to use the car, that is, for her daily commute. After 3 weeks, the fuel consumption was significant by way of comparison with her previous car. The fact that another car has lower fuel consumption does not necessarily mean that Alison's new car cannot be said to be a low-fuel-consumption car. But assuming that the car does fail to live up to its low-fuel-consumption promise, Alison may have recourse against Billy on the grounds that:

- the car is not of merchantable quality (s.16(2) SOGO);
- the car is not fit for purpose (s.16(3) SOGO);
- Billy misrepresented to her in the sale.

In terms of merchantable quality, it can be argued that having regard to the description applied to the model of car and all relevant circumstances, such as the advertisement (s.2(5)), the low-fuel-consumption description is capable to raising the quality standard to be expected of the car. Although Hong Kong does not have a rule-making sellers liable for public statements of sellers, the fact that Alison sought confirmation from the seller may nevertheless make this a relevant factor. It will need to be decided whether the relevant comments on fuel consumption were specific enough to found liability. Looking at the actual quality of the car which consumed significantly more fuel, it is likely that the car is not of merchantable quality. As for fit for purpose, since Alison made her particular purpose known, it is likely that a car with high fuel consumption is not fit for daily commute and thus not reasonably fit for purpose. The same range of remedies regarding breach of implied conditions as discussed above would be available.

Alison may also have cause of action under Misrepresentation Ordinance. Under s.3(1) MO, where a party to a contract is induced to enter into that contract by a misrepresentation of a material fact made by the other party, liability may arise for the party who made the statement. In the present facts, Alison asked Billy whether the low fuel consumption would also show over short distances and was reassured that it would. Given his expertise, this would be taken as a statement of fact rather than mere opinion.[35] Alison was induced into entering into the contract. However the statement turned out to be false. It is likely that there is misrepresentation. The burden of proof is on Billy under the Ordinance to show that he has reasonable grounds to believe the car is one of low fuel consumption (s.3(1)). If the action is successful, Alison will be entitled to rescind the contract, unless it is barred by affirmation, lapse of time, impossibility to rescind, or where damages is a better remedy. Damages may also be granted if the misrepresentation was made fraudulently or negligently, but unlikely if made innocently.

Alison may also have recourse against Reliable on the grounds that the description of the car is false under Trade Description Ordinance. The Trade Descriptions Ordinance, in summary, requires vendors of goods to be honest in their descriptions of what they sell, such as in an advertisement. Criminal penalties can be imposed if the description is dishonest. Alison may be able to recover damages suffered as a result of the conduct of Reliance (s.36 TDO).

(iii) Failure to meet emissions standards

The car fails to meet emissions standards 'by a significant margin'. Assuming that the news reports are accurate, it is arguable that Alison may be able to have recourse against Billy and Reliable on the same grounds as (ii) (except for the ground on misrepresentation). Emissions are an important aspect of the expectations for the product and can even affect the ability to lawfully drive the car.

Scenario 2

The concerns of David centre around an application he purchased and downloaded onto his tablet computer. The issue to consider is the liability of a supplier of digital content (software) which does not seem to be of an appropriate level of quality and has caused a number of problems.

David has no recourse against Elizabeth under SOGO. Unlike the United Kingdom, despite the prevalence of the internet, Hong Kong does not have legislation like the Consumer Rights Act 2015, which applies to contracts for the supply of digital content. Due to the lack of tangibility, digital content such as 'application' in tablet computers does not fall into the definition of 'goods' in SOGO (s.2), and thus SOGO does not give buyers of digital goods the same legal protection as those who purchase physical goods, including implied conditions in relation to merchantable quality and fitness for purpose. The UK counterpart, Sales of Goods Act 1979, had the same problem, but the CRA 2015 has extended the protection and is applicable to contracts for the supply of digital content. Any remedy would

---

35 *Esso Petroleum Co Ltd* v *Mardon* [1976] EWCA Civ 4.

require Hong Kong court to give a broad definition to goods or apply similar rules of common law by analogy.

V. Specific issues in Hong Kong

Fitness centre chain malpractices

In April 2016, a fitness centre chain, California Fitness, was named and sanctioned by the Consumer Council for deploying intimidating and misleading sales practices to pressure consumers into purchasing membership and high-priced private lessons.[36] Existing members and new customers were all subjected to the heavy handed sales pressure of the centre, which resulted in their monetary loss and mental suffering. The past 3 years have seen consumer complaints against this fitness centre rising continuously from 227 cases in 2013 to 296 cases in 2015. This is the very first time that the Council publicly named and sanctioned a fitness centre for their malpractice.

There are other fitness centres deploying malpractices, but they are more willing to, upon the Consumer Council's intervention, provide full refund to the complainants. The Council stated that it was hoped that through this naming sanction, the industry will review their purchase. To further protect the interests and rights of consumers, the Council is also calling for legislation for the cooling-off period regime to safeguard consumers against prepayment transactions. Nevertheless, there had already been consultation in 2010 to combat unfair trade practices, in which the proposal of mandatory cooling-off periods was included, but the measures have not incorporated into the Trade Descriptions (Unfair Trade Practices) (Amendment) Bill 2012.[37] This was due to concerns expressed by the business sectors on the extensiveness of the applicability of the cooling-off periods.

---

36 Consumer Council, *Council Names California Fitness for Aggressive Sales Practices Calls for Cooling-off Period to Safeguard Consumer Rights* (Consumer Council, 26 April 2016), www.consumer.org.hk/ws_en/news/press/fitness.html, accessed 21 May 2017.
37 Commerce, Industry and Tourism Branch – Commerce & Economic Development Bureau, *LCQ7: Provision of a Cooling-off Period Clause in Consumer Contracts* (Commerce & Economic Development Bureau, 22 May 2013), www.cedb.gov.hk/citb/txt_en/Legco_Business/Replies_to_Legco_Questions/2013/P201305220637.html, accessed 4 June 2017.

5 Consumer sales law in People's Republic of China

Shiyuan Han

I. The China consumer market

Since 1979, China has been implementing its new policy to open up to the world and to reform its economic system. The reformation of the economic system is market-oriented and has been a big success. China has not only become a world factory with 'Made in China' being a familiar label, but it has also developed a big domestic market. Retail sales of consumer goods rose to 24.28428 trillion yuan in 2013, 27.18961 trillion Yuan in 2014 and 30.09308 trillion Yuan in 2015, according to the national data given by the National Bureau of Statistics (NBS) of China.[1]

As to the growth of the market, e-commerce occupies a remarkable share. According to the NBS, the online retail sale amount of 2014 is 27,898 hundred million Yuan, and that of 2015 is 38,773 hundred million Yuan.[2]

In 2012, the added value of service business occupied 45.5%, it has become the number one industry in the national economy of China. In 2015, the occupation of the added value of service business went up to 50.5%.[3]

Following the increasing growth of the market economy, the volume of consumer detriment in China is also remarkable. According to a report made by China Consumers Association (CCA) on the consumer complains of the first half of 2016, there are 258,555 consumer complaints to cars all over the country. Among the complaints, quality issues occupy 48.4%; after-sale service issues occupy 22.7%; contract problems occupy 11%; price issues occupy 4.5%; false advertising issues occupy 3%; safety issues occupy 2.1%; counterfeit issues occupy 1.7%; measure issues occupy 0.8%; and other issues occupy 5.8%.[4]

---

1 National Bureau of Statistics of China, *National Data*, http://data.stats.gov.cn/search.htm?s=社会消费品零售总额, accessed 30 May 2017.
2 www.stats.gov.cn/tjsj/sjjd/201603/t20160307_1327678.html, accessed 30 May 2017.
3 Ibid.
4 www.cca.org.cn/tsdh/detail/26871.html, accessed 30 May 2017.

II. Access to justice for consumers and enforcement of consumer law

A. Individual enforcement by consumers

Where any dispute over consumer rights and interests arises between business operators and consumers, consumers may settle the dispute by the following means:

(1) Conciliation with business operators through consultations.
(2) Requesting mediation by a consumer association or any other legally formed mediation organisation.
(3) Filing a complaint with the relevant administrative department.
(4) Applying to an arbitral institution for arbitration under an arbitral agreement with a business operator.
(5) Filing a lawsuit with a people's court.[5]

Where a consumer files a complaint with the relevant administrative department, the department shall, within 7 working days of the receipt of the complaint, process the complaint and inform the consumer.[6]

B. Public enforcement

1. Public state organs

In China, the State adopts the policy of consumer protection and has played an important role to in carrying out this policy. Consumer protection is carried out by many organs of the State.

Legislative organs of different levels have developed laws, regulations, rules and mandatory standards related to consumer rights and interests.[7]

The governments at all levels have the responsibility to strengthen their leadership, organise, coordinate and supervise the relevant administrative departments in satisfactorily protecting the lawful rights and interests of consumers, and to fulfil their duties in protecting the lawful rights and interests of consumers.[8] Among the administrative departments, the administrative departments for industry and commerce of the people's governments (the ADICs) at all levels and other relevant administrative departments have a function to protect the lawful rights and interests of consumers. The ADICs shall hear the opinions of consumers, consumer associations and other organisations on issues concerning the transactions of business operators and the qualities of commodities and services, and investigate

---

5 Art. 39 LPCRI.
6 Art. 46 LPCRI.
7 Art. 30 LPCRI.
8 Art. 31(1) LPCRI.

and address such issues in a timely manner.[9] The relevant administrative departments shall, within their respective functions, conduct spot check and inspection of the commodities and services provided by business operators on a regular or unscheduled basis, and publish the results thereof in a timely manner.[10] For example, General Administration of Quality Supervision, Inspection and Quarantine of the PR China (AQSIQ) is a ministerial administrative organ directly under the State Council in charge of national quality, metrology, entry–exit commodity inspection, entry–exit health quarantine, entry–exit animal and plant quarantine, import–export food safety, certification and accreditation, standardisation, as well as administrative law enforcement. China Food and Drug Administration (CFDA) has a function to formulate the investigation and enforcement system for food, drugs, medical devices and cosmetics, and organise their implementation; organise the investigation and punishment of major violations; establish recall and disposal system for defective products and supervise their implementation. Where the relevant administrative departments discover and determine that the commodities or services provided by business operators are defective and may endanger the personal or property safety, they shall immediately order the business operators to take measures such as cessation of sale, issuance of a warning, recall, harmless treatment, destruction, and cessation of production or service.[11]

Where a consumer files a complaint with the relevant administrative department, the department shall, within 7 working days of receipt of the complaint, process the complaint and inform the consumer.[12] The relevant state organs shall, in accordance with the provisions of laws and regulations, punish the illegal or criminal acts of business operators infringing upon the lawful rights and interests of consumers in providing commodities or services.[13] Public enforcement has its advantages, especially in a mass-damage case.

In the case of mass damage caused by defective product, remedies based on the contractual relationship show their limits as an effective remedy. One example in China is the 'Sanlu milk powder case'. In 2008, a lot of babies who had continuously drank Sanlu powder milk were found to be suffering from a kidney stone. Afterwards, it was found that melanine contained in from Sanlu milk powder. According to a report by the National Health and Family Planning Commission of the PRC on December 1, 2008, by November 27, 2008, there were more than 290,000 babies who had digested Sanlu powder milk or other defective powder milk and fallen ill with urinary system problems. About 51,900 babies had been hospitalised, among which 154 babies were gravely ill. Eleven babies died, and for six of them, it could not be excluded that problematic milk powder was a causative factor.[14]

---

9   Art. 32 LPCRI.
10 Art. 33(1) LPCRI.
11 Art. 33(2) LPCRI.
12 Art. 46 LPCRI.
13 Art. 34 LPCRI.
14 Yanbin Dong [董彦斌] and Zebin Wen [温泽彬] (eds.), *Zhongguo yingxiangxing susong shinian bai an 2003-2013* [*Impact Litigation in China 2003-2013* 中国影响性诉讼十年百案] (Beijing: 法律出版社, Law Press China, 2015), p. 296.

In the above-mentioned case, no one has chosen contract as the basis for its damages claim, since the producer is not a party of the consumer sales contract of the milk powder. The consumers have chosen the producer as the defendant by the consumers means that the case is based on product liability. However, most of the disputes are not resolved by courts. Actually, the Government of Shijiazhuang City supported by the central Government organised 22 relevant enterprises established a foundation in December of 2008. According to a press conference by the Government of Shijiazhuang City on December 25 of 2008, Sanlu Group as the producer borrowed 9.02 billion Yuan and trusted the Milk Product Association to pay compensation to the victims. The plan of compensation is divided into three categories: for death, 200,000 Yuan per person; for those gravely ill, 30,000 Yuan per person; for others, 2,000 Yuan per person.15 Following this scheme, most of the victims have agreed with the plan. There may be some victims who did not follow the above compensation plan and chose to engage in litigation. The author has not found any court judgement for such kind of litigation. Anyway, this is not a good route for remedy, because afterwards, the Sanlu Group filed and declared bankruptcy.

2. Consumer organisations

Consumer organisations also play a very important role in consumer protection. Consumer associations and other consumer organisations are social organisations legally formed to exercise social supervision over commodities and services and protect the lawful rights and interests of consumers.[16] Consumer associations have some public duties, including (a) accepting complaints of consumers and investigating or mediating complaints;[17] (b) for infringement upon the lawful rights and interests of consumers, supporting the victims in filing lawsuits or filing lawsuits in their own name.[18] For infringement upon the lawful rights and interests of a large number of consumers, the China Consumers' Association and the consumer associations formed in provinces, autonomous regions and municipalities directly under the Central Government may file lawsuits in the people's courts.[19] According to Article 55 of the Civil Procedure Law of the PRC (2012 Amendment), for conduct that infringes upon the lawful rights and interests of a large number of consumers or otherwise damages the public interest, an authority or relevant organisation as prescribed by law may institute an action in a people's court. On July 1, 2016, China Consumers' Association has filed a lawsuit against Lovol Heavy Industry Co., LTD. in the 4th Beijing Medium People's Court. In this case, the plaintiff claimed that the motor tricycle products by the defendant did not conform with the mandatory national standards of China. This is the first

---

15 Ge Wu [吴革] (ed.), *Zhongguo yingxiangxing susong: yingxiang Zhongguo de shi da ming an* [*Impact Litigation in China: Ten Famous Cases during 2008 to 2010* 中国影响性诉讼 – 影响中国的十大名案2008－2010] (Beijing: 法律出版社, Law Press China, 2015), p. 20.
16 Art. 36 LPCRI.
17 Art. 37(5) LPCRI.
18 Art. 37(7) LPCRI.
19 Art. 47 LPCRI.

case of public benefit lawsuit initiated by the China Consumers Association since the 2013 amendment of the LPCRI.[20]

III. The legal framework for consumer sales

A. *Contract law and consumer law*

In China, consumer sales is a kind of consumer contract. As for the relevant rules on consumer sales, firstly, there is the *Contract Law* (1999, CCL), which does not distinguish between commercial contracts or consumer contracts, but provide general rules and principles for both kinds of contracts.

Secondly, there is the *Law of the PRC on the Protection of Consumer Rights and Interests* (2013 Amendment, LPCRI). The LPCRI provides some special rules on consumer contracts, including punitive damages.

Thirdly, there is the *Food Safety Law of the PRC* (2015 Amendment, FSL). The FSL also provides some special rules on consumer contracts, including punitive damages.

In addition to the above laws, judicial interpretations made by the Supreme People's Court (SPC) of the PRC an important sources of law in China.[21] Among them, *Interpretation of the SPC on Issues Concerning the Application of Law for the Trial of Cases of Disputes over Sales Contracts* (Interpretation no. 8 (2012) is very important to the topic of this chapter.

B. *Remedies for non-conformity: a unified approach*

Under traditional civil law, there is a set of special rules on warranty of the quality or title of the goods sold. It is a Roman law tradition. If the goods sold has latent defects, the buyer may claim either price reduction or the termination of the contract. The remedies are special on the point that fault of the seller is not a precondition, while for damages for non-performance such a fault is required, even though the fault is presumed. Before the *Contract Law 1999*, China followed a similar approach. As to the warranty liability, there is a system called '*San-bao*' under Chinese laws of that period. *San-bao* means three kinds of warranties, namely warranty of repair, warranty of replacement and warranty of return of the subject matter (3Rs). *San-bao* is not exactly the same thing from the Roman law tradition; it is only a special set of rules adopted by Chinese law makers before the *Contract Law 1999*. Now Article 111 of the *Contract Law 1999* has integrated *San-bao* with other remedies for non-conformity. The Chinese law has adopted a unified approach to non-conformity.

---

20 www.cca.org.cn/zxsd/detail/26882.html, accessed 30 May 2017.
21 For more information, see Shiyuan Han, "A Snapshot of Chinese Contract Law From an Historical and Comparative Perspective" in Lei Chen and C.H. (Remco) van Rhee (eds.), *Towards a Chinese Civil Code* (Netherlands: Martinus Nijhoff Publishers, 2012), p. 248 ff.

C. Compensatory damages and punitive damages

At the beginning of 1990s, Chinese legislature prepared to draft the LPCRI. As a response to the issue of fraudulent transaction practice, some people suggested for the Law to adopt a rule of punitive damages. When the Law was enacted in the year 1993, Article 49 of the Law really adopted a rule of punitive damages. It reads:

> Business operators engaged in fraudulent activities in supplying commodities or services shall, on the demand of the consumers, increase the compensations for victims' losses; the increased amount of the compensations shall be one time the costs that the consumers paid for the commodities purchased or services received.

Some suggest that the Article is inspired by American law. Actually American law on punitive damages are mainly tort law rules, such as those of product liability. However, the Chinese rule here is a rule of contract law and not a rule of tort law. Someone said the Chinese rule comes from Chinese customs, such as 'one fake, ten times as punishment'.[22] This saying is much more reliable.

The LPCRI has been amended in 2013. The original Article 49 has become a new article, namely Article 55. It reads:

> Business operators which fraudulently provide commodities or services shall, as required by consumers, increase the compensation for consumers' losses, and the increase in compensation shall be three times the payment made by a consumer for the commodity purchased or the service received or be 500 yuan if the increase as calculated before is less than 500 yuan, except as otherwise provided *for by the law*. . . .
>
> Where business operators knowingly provide consumers with defective commodities or services, causing death or serious damage to the heath of consumers or other victims, the victims shall have the right to require business operators to compensate them for losses in accordance with Articles 49 and 51 of this Law and other provisions of laws, and have the right to claim punitive compensation of not more than two times the amount of losses incurred.

IV. Factual Scenarios

Scenario 1

In this scenario, Alison (A) has a contract of sale with Billy (B), so we may discuss relevant questions from this perspective. Since R is the manufacturer of the car

---

22 See Shan He [河山], *Xiaofeizhe quanyi baohu fa quanshi* [*Law on Consumers' Rights and Interests* 消费者权益保护法诠释], (China: Law Press China, 2014), Preface.

and has no contractual relationship with A, if A wants to find any recourse against R, the only possibility left is a tort one (e.g. product liability).

For consumers of a new car, *Provisions on the Liability for the Repair, Replacement and Return of Household Automotive Products* (the 3Rs Provisions) issued by State Administration of Quality Supervision, Inspection & Quarantine on December 29, 2012, is very important, and the Provisions have come into force on October 1, 2013. It provides detailed rules and standards on remedies for non-conformity of a car bought by a consumer.

(i)(a) Brake and engine noise (new car)

According to the 3Rs Provisions, the warranty period of the repair of household automotive products shall not be less than 3 years or a mileage of 60,000 km, whichever is earlier; and the validity term of 3Rs for household automotive products shall not be less 2 years or a mileage of 50,000 km, whichever is earlier. The warranty period and the validity term of 3Rs for a household automotive product shall commence from the date of issuance of the purchase invoice by the seller.[23]

Where there is any product quality problem with a household automotive product during the warranty period of the household automotive product, the product shall be repaired free of charge (including hourly charges and cost of material) by the repairer provided that the consumer presents the 3R voucher.[24] So A may claim the seller as a 4 S (*Sale, Spare Part, Service* and *Survey*) to *repair* the car, at least for the brake.

Where there is any product quality problem with a main part of the engine or transmission of a household automotive product within 60 days from the date of issuance of the purchase invoice by the seller or within the mileage of 3,000 km (whichever is earlier), the consumer may choose to replace the engine or transmission free of charge.[25] As to the engine noise problem, if it is a product quality problem with a main part of the engine, A may claim to *replace* the engine free of charge.

Where, during the warranty period of a household automotive product, the time of each repair (including time of waiting for the spare parts for repair) for a product quality problem is more than 5 days, the consumer shall be provided with a spare vehicle or reasonable compensations for travel expenses.[26]

Where there is a failure of the steering system, a failure of the braking system, a body cracking or a leakage of fuel of a household automotive product within 60 days from the date of issuance of the purchase invoice by the seller or within the

---

23 Art. 17 the 3R Provisions.
24 Art. 18(1) the 3R Provisions.
25 Art. 18(2) the 3R Provisions. The scope of types of the main parts of engines and transmissions shall be explicitly stated by the producer in the 3R voucher in compliance with the relevant national standards or provisions, and the provisions on the specific requirements shall be issued separately by the AQSIQ.
26 Art. 19(1) the 3R Provisions.

mileage of 3,000 km (whichever is earlier), if the consumer chooses to replace or *return* the household automotive product, the seller shall be responsible for the replacement or return free of charge.[27] In this case, if the brake problem is getting worse and becomes a failure of the braking system, then A may return the car.

Where the engine or transmission still cannot work normally after it has been replaced twice cumulatively or after the same main part of the engine or transmission has been replaced twice cumulatively for a quality problem (the replacements of the engine, transmission and their main parts shall not be counted repeatedly), or where the same main part of the steering system, the braking system, the suspension system, the front or rear axle or the body still cannot work normally after it has been replaced twice cumulatively for a quality problem, and it is during the validity term of 3Rs for a household automotive product, the consumer chooses to replace or return the household automotive product, the seller shall be responsible for the replacement or return.[28]

(i)(b) Brake and engine noise (second-hand car)

If the car is second-hand and 3-years-old, the 3Rs Provisions do not apply to the case. The relevant rules can be found from the *Business Criterion for Second-Hand Vehicle* (the BCSV).[29] If B is a second-hand distributing enterprise, and when selling the automobile that the period for use is within 3 years or the travelling mileage is within 60,000 km (take which reaching first as standard, except for the commercial vehicle), it shall provide the consumers with quality guarantee of no less than 3 months or 5,000 km (take which reaching first as standard). The quality guarantee includes engine system, steering system, transmission system, brake system, and suspension system.[30] However, when the second-hand car is 3-years-old, there is no mandatory standard for quality guarantee, and it depends on the agreement between the parties of the second-hand car sells contract. And the general rules in the Contract Law (1999) may be used when there is a fraud, duress, or mistake, etc. In practice, it is generally accepted that a second-hand car has been used and may have some defects, including both obvious and covert defects. Therefore, in this kind of transactions, except especially agreed by the parties, it is a general rule that the second-hand car is sold according to status in quo.[31] If B is an auctioneer, it has a duty to make defects of the objects of auction known to bidders.[32] If the auctioneer or client fails to make clear defects of the objects of auction and thus causes losses to the vendee, the vendee shall have the

---

27 Art. 20(2) the 3R Provisions.
28 Art. 20(3).(2)(3) the 3R Provisions.
29 Announcement No. 22 [2006] of Ministry of Commerce.
30 Art. 16 BCSV.
31 Zhang Youjun vs. Wuhan Yongshun Auto Consulting Service Co. Ltd., Civil judgement of Hubei Province Wuhan Intermediate People's Court, (2016) Er 01 min zhong No.1040 [湖北省武汉市中级人民法院民事判决书（2016）鄂01民终1040号].
32 Art. 18(2) the Auction Law (2004 Amendment).

right to claim compensation from the auctioneer; where the client is responsible for the loss, the auctioneer shall have the right of recourse against the client. Where an auctioneer and client declare, prior to the auction sale, that they cannot guarantee the genuineness or quality of an object of auction, they shall not be liable for the guaranty of the object.[33] If B is a natural person and sells the used car to A, the quality standard is up to them to agree upon. The two parties have a duty to fill in relevant information according to the terms in their contract and shall bear corresponding legal liability.[34]

(ii) Higher-than-expected fuel consumption

In *Tang Hong-bo v Zhuzhou City Yida Auto Co. Ltd and Dandong Huanghai Auto Co. Ltd*,[35] the plaintiff (X) bought a car from the first defendant (Y1) in June 2009. Y1 handed over the car with a certificate of conformity to X. From the certificate of conformity, it is shown that the emission standard of the car is GB18352.3–2005 National III, GB3847–2005. Afterwards X felt the fuel consumption was higher than expectation, since the average cost of the same kind car was 0.3 to 0.6 Yuan per kilometre and that of his car was 0.6 to 1.1 Yuan per kilometre. When the car was used for 151,761 kilometres, X trusted a designated Station of Automobile Product Quality Supervision and Inspection. An outcome was given in March 2015, showing that the engine of the car is conformed only to National II standard. It is not a National III standard engine. In the lawsuit X claimed: (1) replacement of a National III standard engine by the two plaintiffs, and for them to bear costs to make a re-registration; (2) compensation for the loss of more fuel consumption; (3) inspection costs; (4) costs of the lawsuit. Finally, all the claims of X were supported by the court.

In this case, it is a question of whether higher-than-expected fuel consumption constitutes a breach. As a reason of the higher-than-expected fuel consumption, it was proved that the engine of the car was not conformed to the National III standard, as agreed upon by the contract. And this constitutes a breach of contract.

If we focus only on higher-than-expected fuel consumption, the advertisement 'low fuel consumption', even it was made by R, will still be treated as a part of the of the agreement of A and B. So the key issue will be what the standard for fuel consumption is. Have the parties agreed a standard, no matter it is a subjective one or an objective one? If A and B have agreed that the fuel consumption of the car is no more than 7 litres per hundred kilometres, it is a subjective standard of the fuel consumption. In the given case, A asked B whether the low fuel consumption would also be shown over short distances and was reassured that it would. This does not constitute a concrete subjective standard of fuel consumption. So the

---

33 Art. 61(1) the Auction Law (2004 Amendment).
34 Art. 38 BCSV.
35 Civil Judgement of Hunan Province Zhuzhou City Hetang District People's Court, (2015) Zhu he fa min er chu zi No. 118. [湖南省株洲市荷塘区人民法院民事判决书（2015）株荷法民二初字第118号].

issue has to be decided according to an objective standard, namely a standard of contemplation by a reasonable man. For a daily commute from home to work, a distance of 30 miles, for a judge as a reasonable man, 7–10 litres per hundred kilometres will be acceptable. If it becomes 12–15 litres per hundred kilometres, it will be unacceptable.

(iii) Failure to meet emissions standards

As in *Tang Hong-bo v Zhuzhou City Yida Auto Co. Ltd and Dandong Huanghai Auto Co. Ltd*, if the failure to meet emissions standards has been proved, this is a serious breach of the contract. As a general rule, if a car does not conform with the mandatory standard of emissions, it will not pass annual inspection of cars by administrative authority and will not be permitted to drive on the road. In that case, as remedy, X can claim a replacement of a new and conformed engine. Otherwise, it is a good reason to terminate the contract according to Article 94(4) of the Contract Law and reject the car.

Scenario 2

The issue in scenario 2 concerns the liability of a supplier of digital content (software) which fails to function properly and has caused trouble to the consumer. There is no explicit rule on this issue in China, so the possible remedies will be analyzed following general rules both in contract and tort.

(i) Failure of the app and failure to patch the problem

Since David (D) bought and downloaded the sports application onto his tablet and paid $15, there is a contract between D and the app-shop (S). This contract is a consumer contract.

Since the 2013 amendment of the LPCRI, the law has adopted a rule of 'cooling-off'. Accordingly, where business operators sell commodities on the Internet, on television, over the telephone or by mail order, among others, consumers shall have the right to return the commodities within 7 days of receipt of them without cause.[36] However, the rule of cooling-off has four exceptions, the third of which concerns 'audio-visual recordings, computer software, and other digital commodities downloaded online or unpacked by consumers'. So D may not return the sports app to S on the ground of cooling-off of the LPCRI.

In the Contract Law (CCL), Chapter 9 is on the contract of sale, which is defined as a contract whereby the seller transfers the ownership of the subject matter to the buyer, and the buyer pays the price.[37] This means the subject matter is a thing, either a moveable thing or an immoveable thing. A downloaded app, as a

36 Art. 25(1) LPCRI.
37 Art. 130 CCL.

piece of software, is not such a thing, and the buyer of it does not really obtain the ownership of the software. However, the contract to buy software, as a non-gratuitous contract, can apply the rules on sales contract by analogy.[38] So D may seek possible remedies from rules on sales contract.

As a statutory obligation, the seller shall deliver the subject matter in accordance with the agreed quality requirement. If the seller provides a description of the quality of the subject matter, the delivered subject matter shall conform to the quality requirement contained in the description.[39] If the subject matter delivered by the seller does not conform to the quality requirement, the buyer may demand the seller to bear liabilities for breach of contract pursuant to Article 111 of the CCL.[40] This means, as a general default rule, the aggrieved party may, according to the nature of the subject matter and the extent of his loss, choose to reasonably demand the other party to bear such liability for breach of contract as making repairs, replacement, redoing, return of the goods and reduction of the price or remuneration.[41] In addition, where a party commits a breach of contract, making it impossible to accomplish the purpose of the contract, the other party may terminate the contract.[42] After a contract is terminated, the unperformed part ceases to be performed. In regard to the performed part, a party may, depending upon the circumstances of performance and the nature of the contract, demand restoration of *status quo ante*, resort to other remedial measures and have the right to claim damages.[43]

In this case, since the company failed to patch the app problem and stopped trying to solve the problem 6 months later, and since the app malfunctions and the purpose of D to use the app to connect his smartwatch and keeps track of where he has been running, his heart rate and made extensive use of the new application has been impossible to accomplish, following the above rules, it is possible for D to terminate the contract by giving S a notice. The contract shall be terminated when the notice reaches S.[44] According to the circumstances of performance and the nature of the contract, D may delete downloaded app and claim S to refund the price.

(ii) Interference with other apps/(iii) damage done to the Wi-Fi connector

Unlike the UK Consumer Rights Act 2015 (CRA), Chinese law does not make a difference between the above two situations and give them different remedies. Under Chinese law, for the above two kinds of damage, two questions will be

---

38 Art. 174 CCL.
39 Art. 153 CCL.
40 Art. 155 CCL.
41 Art. 111 CCL.
42 Art. 94(4) CCL.
43 Art. 97 CCL.
44 Art. 96 CCL.

tackled here. First, may a remedy or remedies be found on a contractual ground according to the CCL? Second, may a remedy or remedies be found on a tort ground according to the Tort Law 2009 (CTL) or any other Chinese laws?

Under the CCL, even the contract has been terminated by D, he may still claim damages according to Article 97. The damages here are damages for breach. It can be damages for expectation interest with a limitation of foreseeability rule,[45] but not limited to expectation interest. If a party fails to perform his or her contractual obligations or where his or her performance of the performance of the contractual obligations is not in conformity with the agreement, and if, after performing the obligations or taking remedial measures, the other party still has 'other losses', damages shall be paid.[46] It is not clear whether or not the damages here still follow the foreseeability rule, but it is clear that damages for breach of contract is not limited to expectation interests, it may include losses to a party's inherent interests. In the given case, losses suffered both from interference with other apps and damage done to the Wi-Fi connector may be classified as losses to inherent interests. If damages for losses to inherent interests follow the foreseeability rule, the losses result from interference with other apps and the damages done to the Wi-Fi connector may be classified as foreseeable at the time of the conclusion of the contract, and costs necessary to repair other apps and the Wi-Fi connector may be claimed. However, the additional energy costs will be too remote to recover. If damages for losses to inherent interests do not follow the foreseeability rule, but a rule similar to tort law rule, possible result will be analyzed in next paragraph.

If we think the problem from a tort law approach, the key issue would be whether a piece of software may be classified as a 'product' and to apply product law rules. Relevant rules may be found out from Product Quality Law of the People's Republic of China (2009 Amendment, PQL) and the Tort Law of the People's Republic of China (2009, CTL). Under the PQL, products are referred to products processed and manufactured for the purpose of marketing.[47] It is not limited to a tangible 'thing', so software, although with some objections from scholars,[48] may be classified as a product and apply product law rules. In practice, there is a case, both courts of the first instance and second instance adopted affirmative position.[49] If D claim damages on product liability ground, the damages will be a summation of compensation for different loss items. Instead of the foreseeability rule in contract

---

45 Art. 113(1) CCL.
46 Art. 112 CCL.
47 Art. 2(2) PQL.
48 Xiao Cheng [程啸], *Qinquan zeren fa* [*Tort Law*侵权责任法], 2nd ed. (China: Law Press China, 2015), p. 492.
49 Beijing Beixinyuan zidonghua jishu youxian gongsi, Shanghai Linhao wangluo jishu youxian gongsi su Jinxin zhengquan youxian zeren gongsi Dongyan wu ning xilu zhengquan yingyebu chanpin zeren jiufen kangsu an [北京北信源自动化技术有限公司、上海林皓网络技术有限公司诉金信证券有限责任公司东阳吴宁西路证券营业部产品责任纠纷抗诉案], Supreme People's Procuratorate Motion of Protest of Civil Matters, Gao jian min kang (2004) No.12, March 24, 2004.

case, causation rule will be the basic rule to define the margin of damages.[50] In practice, a theory of direct causation is now gradually displaced by a theory of adequacy, as a result of influence of German civil law theories. As a result, damages here may be similar to that of damages on the ground of contract relation, the additional energy costs will be too remote to be recovered, reasonable costs to repair other apps and the Wi-Fi connector may be claimed.

V. Specific issues in China: 'knowing the fake and buying the fake'

Since the rule on punitive damages comes into effect, there emerges an interesting problem called 'Wang Hai Phenomenon', or 'knowing the fake and buying the fake'. In this case, Mr. Wang Hai bought from a shopping mall in Beijing two sets of Sony earphones, which he afterwards identified as fake. Then he bought ten other sets of the same earphones and successfully claimed punitive damages according to Article 49 of the LPCRI. The case inspired Mr. Wang to use Article 49 of the LPCRI to earn money. Even though Mr. Wang does not win every case, he has won quite a lot of cases and earned a lot of money. Until now, Mr. Wang still use the rule of punitive damages as a new profession. The Wang Hai Phenomenon has raised a lot of debates. Is it immoral knowing the fake, buying the fake and claim punitive damages? Should Mr. Wang be treated as a consumer? Is there a fraud in legal meaning? In August 2016, the State Administration for Industry & Commerce of the PRC has prepared a draft of Implementing Regulations of the LPCRI and submitted for public comment. Since the draft seems to adopt a negative position to 'knowing the fake and buying the fake', it causes a heated debate in society.[51]

---

50 Arts. 41 and 43(1) CTL.
51 http://news.hexun.com/2016-08-22/185627406.html, accessed 30 May 2017.

6 Consumer sales law in New Zealand

Chris Nicoll

I. The New Zealand consumer market

New Zealand has a diverse and globally connected consumer market. Importantly, consumer spending has increased off the back of rising gross domestic product (GDP) growth, employment and household incomes. Data analysed in an annual report released by the New Zealand Commerce Commission has identified the composition of consumer spending in respect of transaction media (i.e. internet and in-store purchases) and industries. The report also identifies potential problems facing consumers and the incidence, and nature, of consumer complaints under consumer legislation.[1]

In the most recent year of data, the Commission received 5,073[2] complaints from consumers under the Fair Trading Act 1986, an increase of 15% from the 2014 report.[3] It is believed that this increase has come about in part due to increased publicity and improved awareness of avenues for consumer redress.[4] Indeed, such publicity also coincided with visits to the Ministry of Business, Innovation and Employment's fact sheet on the Consumer Guarantees Act 1993 (the CGA).[5] Interestingly, patterns of consumer complaints suggest that many of these issues are trader-specific, with 25% of the complaints received by the Commission generated by 21 traders.[6]

NZ consumers exhibit high use of social media, and many purchasing decisions are now found in the online sphere. This has been identified as a key risk

---

1 Commerce Commission, *Consumer Issues 2016* (Commerce Commission, 27 September 2016), www.comcom.govt.nz/the-commission/consumer-reports/consumer-issues-report/, accessed 18 June 2017. The Commerce Commission primarily deals with complaints under the Fair Trading Act 1986, which deals with unfair or misleading conduct among other things.
2 This includes only those problems which are reported to the Commerce Commission and may therefore understate the true scale of the problem.
3 The 2014 report indicated that there were 4,377 complaints.
4 The Commerce Commission is a widely known body. Such causes are also promoted by way of mainstream television programming on consumer issues.
5 Commerce Commission, *Consumer Issues 2015* (Commerce Commission, 24 September 2015), www.comcom.govt.nz/the-commission/consumer-reports/consumer-issues-report/, accessed 29 August 2016, at 30.
6 A similar figure was observed in 2014 which saw 24 organisations generate 25% of complaints.

to consumers. Indeed, the data indicate that most consumer complainants claim to have been misled through the media of online purchases (34% of complaints), with contracts and invoices close behind (30% of complaints), and in-store purchasing generating less concern (14% of complaints).[7]

New Zealand has seen recent changes to consumer law, the most notable concerning unfair contract terms in standard form agreements.[8] This allows the Commission to apply to court, on behalf of the public, for a declaration that a term in a standard form agreement is unfair. This legislation has the potential to carry industry-wide consequences, with respect to many oppressive terms readily used by multiple traders. This legislation is discussed in more detail in Part V.

Particular risks identified by the Commission include the prevalence of mobile traders,[9] the disproportionate number of complaints arising from disputes with a small number of traders, the telecommunications industry and consumers' growing reliance on it, and domestic appliance retailers.[10]

Goods vs services

As has been noted, 25% of complaints made to the Commission under the Fair Trading Act 1986 (the FTA) were in respect of only 21 traders. Telecommunications (providers and carriers) is the most complained about industry (9%) with the two traders generating the most complaints overall operating in that industry.[11]

Domestic appliance providers (including electronics and phones) shared the top position as an industry with Telecommunications, although the data suggest that consumer complaints are trader-specific and indicate very little in respect of wider industry practices. A practice noted by the Commission was that of charging non-refundable deposits on goods returned to the retailer for warranty repairs. Moreover, many appliance wholesalers have sought to limit responsibility by referring consumers to the manufacturer, often a more difficult avenue for redress for the consumer.[12] Similarly, motor vehicle sales were in third position with 6% of all complaints generated by that industry.[13]

One risk factor identified by the Commission in 2014, in the separate category of consumer finance, was the prevalence of mobile traders (truck shops) in poor communities. Such traders are often found in lower socio-economic communities exhibiting heavy reliance on high-interest debt. Other risks identified include the use of subscriptions, particularly online subscriptions,[14] which carry the risk of subjecting consumers to oppressive terms, and misrepresentations of products,

---

7 Commerce Commission, at 15 above, n 1.
8 Fair Trading Act 1986, s 26A.
9 A survey of 32 mobile traders found that only one was operating within the law (see Commerce Commission, at 25 above, n 5).
10 Commerce Commission, at 44 above, n 5.
11 Commerce Commission, at 17 above, n 1.
12 Commerce Commission, at 33 above, n 5.
13 Commerce Commission, at 17 above, n 1.
14 See Commerce Commission, at 47 above, n 5, where the term 'subscription traps' is used.

both in terms of quality and place of origin.[15] It should be noted, however, that complaints in this category decreased in 2015 from 34 to 14.[16]

Online vs offline

Online trading grew by around 16% from February 2016 to February 2017. This is equivalent to 7.4% of all retail spending over the same period.[17] The Commerce Commission has noted that, although there are measures in place to deal with offshore traders, these are often ineffective due to communication issues.[18] As a result, consumers face a great deal of risk when making online purchases from offshore traders.

Online transaction-based challenges are likely to persist in the future with a growing number of consumers relying on internet-based intermediaries for goods and services. Seventy-four per cent of New Zealanders now use smartphones to research products online, with 33% of them following through to purchase the product.[19] With the rise of online services such as Netflix, which often require subscriptions subject to long terms and conditions, consumers are progressively going to find themselves facing more risk – particularly in respect of unfair clauses and a less direct path to redress.

II. Access to justice for consumers and enforcement of consumer law

This section will outline how consumers can enforce their legal rights, and also how compliance with consumer law and enforcement is handled by various public agencies in New Zealand.

Individual enforcement by consumers

Individual enforcement is the Achilles' heel of New Zealand consumer law. There is no requirement for suppliers or manufacturers to adopt any particular standards or procedures for dealing with customer complaints and the cost of taking action in the Courts is prohibitive given the lack of a properly funded legal aid system for civil actions. Legal aid is only available to those earning less than the average wage and, for civil as opposed to criminal matters, only the poorest members of society qualify for assistance. Yet they are the ones least likely to be educated to a level where they are aware of their rights and have the practical skills to enforce them.

The most effective way for an individual to enforce legal rights is to bring a claim under the Disputes Tribunals Act 1988. Disputes Tribunals have simplified

---

15 Commerce Commission, at 46 above, n 5.
16 Commerce Commission, at 33 above, n 1.
17 Bank of New Zealand, *New Zealand Online Retail Sales Monthly Update for January 2017* (28 February 2017), http://img.scoop.co.nz/media/pdfs/1702/NZ_Online_Retail_Sales_in_January_2017_20170228_FINAL.pdf.
18 Commerce Commission, at 16 above, n 5.
19 Commerce Commission, at 21 above, n 5.

procedure, are presided over by referees who may adopt an inquisitorial approach and who are not bound by rules of evidence and the Tribunals have an upper limit in jurisdiction of $15,000. However, if the claim exceeds $15,000, but falls short of $20,000, then the Tribunal may hear the case if both parties agree in writing by filing a form to extend the financial limit. Referees primarily seek to facilitate settlements between the parties who are not entitled to be represented by legal counsel and their judgements, where such are made failing a negotiated settlement, are not subject to appeal apart from on the grounds of procedural unfairness. They may not have their decisions overturned for errors of law.

The Disputes Tribunals have jurisdiction over disputes in contract and tort, among other things, and have jurisdiction under the FTA, CGA and Contractual Remedies Act 1979 (the CRA).[20] There are some specialised tribunals but, apart from the Motor Vehicle Disputes Tribunal, these do not deal with the sale of goods. The Motor Vehicle Disputes Tribunal deals with disputes between motor vehicle traders and consumers where the amount involved does not exceed $100,000 and its jurisdiction, apart from the upper monetary limit, is concurrent with that of the Disputes Tribunal in cases involving FTA, CGA and CRA. Unlike the Disputes Tribunal referees, the adjudicator in the Motor Vehicle Disputes Tribunal must be a lawyer of no less than 5 years in practice.

Disputes Tribunals have a wide discretion in respect of granting orders where the FTA has been contravened. A Tribunal, on the application of any person who has suffered, or is likely to suffer, loss by way of a contravention of the FTA, may make one or more orders of the following nature:[21]

- A declaration that a contract between the buyer and seller is void (the Tribunal has retrospective powers to void the contract from a prior date)
- A variation of the contract or arrangement
- A refund or return of property
- Payment of the corresponding loss suffered
- Repair of, or provision of parts for, goods that have been supplied
- Supply of specified goods

For the 12-month period ending 30 June 2015, there were 14,263 new claims filed nationally with a Disputes Tribunal. There were 14,737 claims withdrawn or settled by the parties, or settled by the Tribunal or sent to the District Court, and 3,142 cases were awaiting a hearing or awaiting final judgement.[22] The fees to bring a claim in the Disputes Tribunal are modest.[23]

20 The Contractual Remedies Act 1979 has now been consolidated into the Contract and Commercial Law Act 2017 which came into force on 1 September 2017.
21 Fair Trading Act, ss 43(1) and 43(2).
22 See Courts of New Zealand, *Statistics* (Courts of New Zealand, 30 June 2015), www.courtsofnz.govt.nz/from/statistics/annual-statistics/june-2015/specialist-courts-and-tribunals/disputes-tribunal-claim-workload-statistics-for-the-12-months-ending-30-june-2015, accessed 29 August 2016.
23 $45.00 NZD for a claim under $2,000; $90.00 for a claim between $2,000 and $5,000; $180.00 NZD for a claim over $5,000. An application for appeal costs $200.00 NZD.

However, avenues for redress outside the Tribunal process remain unaffordable and troublesome for most NZ consumers. In 2006, an empirical study was carried out in which New Zealanders were asked to identify types of problems they had had with the law over the past year. Consumer-related problems were the most common non-trivial problem, with 10.4% of respondents indicating that they had experienced such a problem.[24] It is widely agreed that the court process is out of reach for many ordinary consumers.[25]

Public enforcement

The only area where there is the potential for significant public enforcement is under FTA. The Commerce Commission has exclusive power to take action with respect to unfair standard form contracts and unsubstantiated representations. There are also a number of provisions under this Act which give rise to criminal liability, and these actions are begun by the Commission, although s 9 (misleading and deceptive conduct) is not one of them and gives rise solely to civil liability.

However, apart from the foregoing qualifications, any person may bring a civil action for breach of the Act (including s 9), and this provides a way for the Commerce Commission to initiate proceedings and secure compensation for a person or class otherwise unlikely to take direct action themselves.

The Commerce Commission receives around 10,000 calls and e-mails annually. Accordingly, the Commission is required to determine whether a particular complaint justifies an investigation, and subsequent court action, if the damage caused by the contravention is widespread. Following an investigation, the Commission may be able to provide financial redress for affected consumers. The Commission considers the extent of the detriment, the seriousness of the conduct, and the public interest concern regarding the conduct.[26] In many cases, complaints pertain to few specific traders with respect to whom the Commission may initiate proceedings. A brief search through a NZ case database[27] shows that, from December 2014 until April 2016, the Commerce Commission was involved in litigation with at least ten organisations, with one case reaching the Supreme Court, New Zealand's highest appellate court.

---

24 Ignite Research (Report commissioned by the Legal Services Agency) Report on the 2006 national survey of unmet legal needs and access to services (2006) as cited in S. Righarts and M. Henaghan, "Public Perception of the New Zealand Court System: An Empirical Approach to Law Reform" (2010) 12(2) *OLR* 329, 330.
25 In Righarts and Henaghan, at 336–337 above, n 19, an empirical analysis indicated that over 50% of respondents disagreed with the proposition that the average New Zealander could afford to take a case to court. Over 40% of respondents disagreed that their case would be resolved in a reasonable time if they took it to court.
26 The Commerce Commission website outlines a structured process by which a complaint is considered for further action.
27 LexisNexis NZ.

III. The legal framework for consumer sales

Introduction

New Zealand consumer law is neither consolidated nor codified. It is to be found in a range of statutes and in parts of the common law touching on exclusion clauses and the principle of fairness although some statutes relevant to contract and commercial law have recently been collected together into the Contract and Commercial Law Act 2017.[28] Sales law was for many years governed exclusively by the Sale of Goods Act 1908 (SOGA) which is still little changed from Chalmer's original formulation.[29] The provisions of this Act are now to be found in the 2017 Act. The SOGA implied conditions of merchantability, fitness for purpose etc., still apply to consumer sales but are seldom used in this context because the Consumer Guarantees Act 1993 (CGA) now offers richer rights and remedies. These extend to services, include dispositions of a possessory interest in goods such as a lease, and cover intangible personal property such as computer software.

In addition to the CGA, there are a number of statutes and regulations which are industry-specific although, except in the case of motor vehicles, these govern the supply of services rather than the supply of goods alone. Instances are the supply of gas,[30] electricity, telecommunications, financial services, the provision of consumer credit, health and disability services, and real estate agency services.

Relevant New Zealand law can be separated broadly into pre- and post-contractual requirements and obligations.

Pre-contract

Pre-contract law governs inducements to contract including misrepresentations and advertising. The general law of contractual misrepresentation was codified by the Contractual Remedies Act 1979 (the provisions of which are now to be found in Part 2 Subpart 3 of the Contract and Commercial Law Act 2017) but, of more significance in the consumer setting, by s 9 of the Fair Trading Act 1986[31] (FTA),

---

28 *Interfoto Picture Library Ltd v Stiletto Visual Programmes Ltd.* [1989] Q.B. 433. In particular the judgement of Bingham L.J. at 439 who likened the civil law principle of good faith to 'playing fair', 'coming clean' or 'putting one's cards face upwards on the table'. And then went on to say, in the context of an onerous exclusion clause: 'The tendency of the English authorities has, I think, been to look at the nature of the transaction in question and the character of the parties to it; to consider what notice the party alleged to be bound was given of the particular condition said to bind him; and to resolve whether in all the circumstances it is fair to hold him bound by the condition in question. This may yield a result not very different from the civil law principle of good faith, at any rate so far as the formation of the contract is concerned'.
29 International sale of goods is governed by the Vienna Convention on the International Sale of Goods 1980 which is part of New Zealand's domestic law by virtue of Part 3 Subpart 7 of the Contract and Commercial Law Act 2017.
30 Non-reticulated gas is covered by the CGA.
31 The Fair Trading Act 1986 marks the first step taken by the New Zealand legislature on the road to a developed law for the protection of consumers. It came into force on 1 March 1987 and was modelled on the Australian Trade Practices Act 1974 (Cth).

which prohibits misleading and deceptive conduct 'in trade'.[32] Wider than the Contractual Remedies Act 1979 (the CRA), it includes misrepresentations of law and, because it defines conduct to include an omission to act, it may include silence although probably not going so far as to impose a duty of disclosure.[33]

The relief available for breach of s 9 is not restricted to damages but may include the following orders: to direct the person in default to repair or provide parts for faulty goods; to refund money or return goods; and to vary the contract or arrangement or to declare the contract void. Where damages are awarded, they are not a right (as they are for breach of contract), but depend on the discretion of the court which may order a sum to put the complainant in the same position as if the representation had been true (the contract measure) or in the same position as if the representation had not been made (the tort measure) or without direct reliance on either measure.

Probably the most important difference between s 9 and the common law is that anyone may recover damages and other relief for misleading or deceptive conduct notwithstanding lack of privity of the (or any) contract and whether or not the conduct was negligent.

Also in the pre-contract category, the FTA prohibits particular types of inappropriate conduct in trade,[34] promotes safety of goods and services and provides for disclosure of consumer information concerning goods and services.

In addition, the advertising industry moderates advertising through the Advertising Standards Authority, which maintains a number of codes including a code of ethics and various specific codes of practices governing particular areas of industry such as tobacco, food, gambling, vehicles and weight management, and

---

32 Section 9 provides: 'No person shall, in trade, engage in conduct that is misleading or deceptive or is likely to mislead or deceive'. '[T]rade' by s 2 means: 'any trade, business, industry, profession, occupation, activity of commerce, or undertaking relating to the supply or acquisition of goods or services or to the disposition or acquisition of any interest in land'. 'Business' under s 2 means: 'any undertaking –

(a) That is carried on whether for gain or reward or not; or
(b) In the course of which –

  i   Goods or services are acquired or supplied; or
  ii Any interest in land is acquired or disposed of

whether free of charge or not'.

33 Notwithstanding this liberalising feature, New Zealand and Australian authorities have tended to restrict the application of s 9 to 'half-truths'. On the cusp or, arguably an exception, is the case of *Hieber v Barfoot and Thompson Ltd.* [1996] 5 NZBLC 104 at 179 where the plaintiff purchased a beachfront property with an expansive view of the Waitemata Harbour in Auckland including an unobstructed view of Rangitoto (an extinct volcanic cone). He inspected the property with an estate agent and had an opportunity to inspect the view himself. It had been described in the Defendant's pamphlet as having 'magnificent sea views'. The agent was found liable because it had not volunteered the information that a yacht club was to move its club house and so obstruct the view (which would have maintained its magnificence even with this obstruction). The case was put by Kerr J. partly on the ground that the plaintiff had a reasonable expectation the disclosure would be made.

34 For example, 'bait' advertising, s 19 and pyramid selling schemes, s 24.

particular ethical questions such as advertising to children and comparative advertising. An advertisement which is found by the Advertising Standards Complaints Board to have contravened a code will be prohibited from further exposure.

The marketing of products in some industries is regulated directly by statute. For example, the Smoke-Free Environments Act 1990 bans advertising and sponsorship of tobacco; the Sale and Supply of Alcohol Act 2012 prohibits advertising which encourages the excessive consumption of alcohol and the Medicines Act 1981 forbids advertising of products which claim to cure certain diseases or conditions.

Finally, it should be noted that the Fair Trading Amendment Act 2013[35] prohibits representations in trade which are unsubstantiated. This is so irrespective of whether they are misleading or deceptive. An unsubstantiated representation is one for which, at the time it is made, there was no reasonable evidence. However, claims for unsubstantiated representations in trade must be taken by The Commerce Commission; there is no direct recourse by the consumer.

Post-contract

Once the contract for disposition of goods or for mixed goods and services has been made, the position in New Zealand is largely governed by the CGA, although, since 17 March 2015, a new unfair contract terms law was introduced through the FTA. This is covered below in section V, although it is of limited effect; applying only to standard form contracts and withholding direct recourse by consumers to its remedies as applications under its terms must be made by The Commerce Commission. It appears to straddle both the pre- and post-contract stages in that it covers unfairness in presentation (pre-contract) and unfairness in a substantive sense (post-contract). However, how these aspects work together is unclear given the way the relevant sections of the FTA have been drafted.

The CGA came into effect after the FTA and built upon the implied conditions provided by the SOGA, namely, the need for the goods to comply with their description in the contract along with their need to be fit for purpose and of merchantable quality. The supplementary obligations in the CGA are called 'guarantees', the change in terminology marking the fact that, unlike the implied conditions, they cannot be contracted out of. It is unlawful to purport to 'contract out' of the CGA, except for limited situations expressly catered for in the legislation, and a supplier or manufacturer liable for doing so faces a fine of up to $200,000 in the case of an individual and $600,000 in the case of a body corporate.[36]

The guarantees are only available to a consumer. A consumer is defined as a person who acquires goods or services of a kind *ordinarily* acquired for personal, domestic or household use or consumption and who does not hold out as

---

35 Section 12A.
36 Under Fair Trading Act 1986, s 13(i).

acquiring them for resupply in trade, consumption by processing or (in the case of goods) using them for treatment or repair of other goods in trade.[37] So, for example, the purchase of a large coffee maker usually used in a restaurant would not be covered by the Act even though intended by the purchaser to be used at home. This is because such machines are not 'ordinarily' acquired for domestic use. In contrast, a domestic coffee maker would be covered even if purchased by a business, for example, for use in the tearoom. It is the article purchased or the service provided which is the main indicator of coverage subject to the exceptions of resupply, processing, repair or treatment. Additionally, the goods or services must be supplied 'in trade'. A supplier includes an agent[38] and 'trade' has the same meaning as in the FTA, except it relates only to goods and services and not to land or goods attached to real property.

As for the guarantees themselves, the Act provides guarantees for title and description which are similar, but not identical to those in the SOGA. It also provides useful safeguards for manufacturers' guarantees so that, while the guarantee must be given with the express or apparent authority of the manufacturer, this will be presumed (subject to evidence to the contrary) if the guarantee is in a document relating to the goods which appears to come from the manufacturer. It is not necessary for the consumer to prove that it was induced by the guarantee to enter into the contract.

As far as the 'fitness for purpose' guarantee is concerned, the consumer does not in every case have to make it known to the supplier the particular purpose for which the goods are required. If the consumer does expressly or impliedly make known a particular use and the supplier replies affirmatively, s 8(1)(a) protects (as in SOGA). However, if the supplier *volunteers* assertions of fitness for purpose, these will be binding by virtue of a new guarantee under s 8(1)(b). Moreover, if a consumer acquires goods, it will be impliedly made known that they are acquired for their *common* or *usual* purpose. Reliance on express or implied assertions by the supplier is required by SOGA and by CGA; otherwise the fitness for purpose implied condition or guarantee will be ineffective. However, 'reliance will in general be inferred from the fact that the buyer goes to the shop in the confidence that the tradesman has selected his stock with skill and judgement'.[39] Finally, it should be noted that goods must only be 'reasonably' fit for purpose.

With respect to 'acceptable quality', the guarantee applies at time of receipt by the consumer,[40] and it differs from the SOGA equivalent because it requires the goods to be 'fit for *all* purposes for which goods of the type in question are commonly supplied'; the warranty of merchantable quality is satisfied if the goods were saleable for just one purpose for which they are commonly supplied.[41]

---

37 Section 2(1).
38 Catching estate agents, insurance brokers and the like.
39 *Grant v Australian Knitting Mills Ltd.* [1936] AC 85 (PC).
40 Section 2(3).
41 *Nesbit v Porter* [2000] 2 NZLR 465 (CA).

Additionally, the goods must, to comply with this guarantee, be

(b) acceptable in appearance and finish; and
(c) free from minor defects; and
(d) safe; and
(e) durable; . . .

These four attributes are judged according to the standard a reasonable consumer would regard as acceptable assuming he or she is 'fully acquainted with the state and condition of the goods, including any hidden defects' having regard to

(f) the nature of the goods;
(g) the price (where relevant);
(h) any statements made about the goods on any packaging or label on the goods;

[(ha) the nature of the supplier and the context in which the supplier supplies the goods];[42]

(i) any representation made about the goods by the supplier or the manufacturer;
(j) all other relevant circumstances of the supply of the goods.

The remedies for breach of the guarantees may be separated into those pursued against the supplier or retailer and those pursued against the manufacturer.

With suppliers, the first question to be resolved is whether the breach is capable of being remedied. If it is, the supplier must be given the opportunity to do so within a reasonable time and this will involve either repair or replacement at the supplier's option. If the breach is not capable of remedy, the consumer has an option: either to require replacement or a refund. However, the foregoing is subject also to the question whether the failure to comply with the guarantee is 'of a substantial character' as defined. If goods fall into this category, the consumer may, at its option, call for replacement or refund or repair (with repair obviously only an option if the defect is capable of being remedied). If the consumer has an option to reject the goods, this must be exercised within a 'reasonable' time.

Failure is of a substantial character if

1 A reasonable consumer would not have acquired the goods if it had known the nature or extent of the defect
2 In a sale by description the goods fail to meet the description in one or more significant respects
3 The goods are substantially unfit for purpose
4 The goods are not of acceptable quality because they are unsafe.

---

42 Inserted by the Consumer Guarantees Amendment Act 2013 which came into force on 17 June 2014.

In addition to these remedies, the consumer may claim consequential loss or damage provided it is reasonably foreseeable. So, for example, in a case where a defective electric blanket caused a fire to break out in the house, the fire damage was recoverable along with a sum to compensate for distress and inconvenience.[43] But it should be noted that The Court of Appeal in *Cox & Coxton Ltd v Leipst*[44] has held that 'loss or damage' does not include 'loss of a bargain'. This is the usual contract measure and is calculated by taking the difference between the price and the market value of goods having the characteristics bargained for.

With respect to manufacturers, the remedies differ as there are two exceptions to liability where the guarantee is of quality or description: (a) The manufacturer will not be liable if the fault is caused only by something outside human control once it has left the manufacturer's control; (b) in the case of the quality guarantee, the manufacturer will not be liable where the fault is caused only by the representation, act or omission of someone other than the manufacturer, its agent or servant and, in the case of the description guarantee, the manufacturer will not be liable where the fault is caused by the act or omission of the manufacturer, its agent or servant.

Manufacturers are defined to include people in the business of processing, producing or assembling goods, anyone holding itself out as a manufacturer, anyone putting its brand or mark on goods or a component of goods and, where the manufacturer has no presence in New Zealand, the importer or distributor.

IV. Factual scenarios

Scenario 1

In this scenario, it will be assumed that Reliable has a place of business in New Zealand, so it would be regarded as a manufacturer within the meaning of CGA.

(i)(a) Brake and engine noise (new car)

Engine noise manifesting itself over 3 weeks or a similar period in the case of a new car would contravene the guarantee of acceptable quality. Sluggish brake response or even a noticeable deterioration in brake response over a period of 3 weeks would have the same consequences, but more markedly so because this defect goes to safety. It is also likely the car would contravene the guarantee that it be fit for purpose regardless of whether there is a causative link between the defects and the fact that the expressed purpose was to commute a distance of 30 miles. This is because it is a common or usual purpose for a modern vehicle to be used for commuting.

---

43 Hosking v The Warehouse Ltd., unreported District Court, Auckland NP1476/97, 5 October 1998.
44 [1999] 2 NZLR 15.

The test is whether a reasonable consumer would regard the car as acceptable in quality. Given that it is new, even minor defects but especially defects relevant to safety would not satisfy the objective test. For the same reasons and in both cases of brake deterioration and engine noise, the defect would be of a substantial nature as no reasonable consumer knowing the car would develop these faults after such a short time would have completed the purchase.

Consequently, Alison would have recourse against Billy. She would have the choice of returning the car with a full refund of the price or she could demand a replacement. As it is likely the defects would be repairable, she would also, subject to one qualification, have a repair option. She would have to make an election of repair preventing her from later seeking to have the car replaced. However the qualification is that her election must have been a properly informed one. So, for instance, if the defects are, to the supplier's knowledge, of a serious nature and the consumer is not so informed and elects to repair, she may yet be able to reject the vehicle on discovering the true situation.[45]

As there are no acts, omissions, defaults or misrepresentations by anyone apart from the manufacturer under this heading, Reliable would also be liable in the same way and to the same extent as the supplier and both would have to bear responsibility for consequential loss such as the foreseeable need for Alison to hire a replacement vehicle.

(i)(b) Brake and engine noise (second-hand car)

If the car's brake and engine issues occurred after 3 years, the same test as the foregoing would be applied. However, the state of the vehicle after that period would be measured against what a reasonable consumer would expect from a vehicle of that age assuming regular maintenance had occurred. For example, a vehicle purchased new in 1997 came with a manufacturer's recommendation to service the transmission after 50,000 km. This was not done and in 2002, after 100,000 km, the transmission failed. The consumer was not entitled to redress.[46]

The case would turn on the expert evidence: what were the causes of the faults and were they perhaps symptomatic of a more serious mechanical problem? Also are the problems capable of repair? A car which is 3 years old is not old by any means, and the manufacturer's advertising would lead the average consumer to believe that it is more reliable than similar vehicles.

Consequently, assuming the vehicle is capable of repair, it has been properly maintained and the faults give rise to no suspicion of more fundamental issues and taking into consideration the manufacturer's advertising which one assumes is supported by reasonable evidence, a reasonable consumer would not regard the

---

45 *Stephens v Chevron Motor Court Ltd.* [1996] DCR 1.
46 *Marella-Wolfe v Crestview Chrysler Dodge Ltd.* [2003] SKPC 64 (Provincial Court), a case decided under the Consumer Protection Act 1996 (Saskatchewan, Canada).

car as being of acceptable quality. Neither would it be unfit for purpose given the element of 'reasonableness' in the test.

However, in light of the car's age and the assumed fact that repair would be carried out successfully, it is unlikely the defects would be held to be of substantial character and the consumer would not be entitled to reject. The remedy would in all probability be restricted to repair and both manufacturer and supplier could be called upon, by way of consequential compensation, to provide a replacement vehicle whilst repairs are effected although, obviously, the consumer could not receive double compensation under this head.

(ii) Higher-than-expected fuel consumption

The starting point for this enquiry is the manufacturer's advertisements that the R1 Reliable is 'Low Fuel Consumption, Best for the Environment' and that it depicts a family setting off on a holiday and travelling the entire length of the United Kingdom without stopping to refuel. This is because the advertising sets the scene and provides the context for possible breaches of guarantee under CGA and may give rise to remedies under the FTA.

Recent amendments to FTA now demand that advertising is capable of being substantiated by reasonable evidence although, apparently to avoid penalties for what is a clear 'puff', the Act does not require substantiating evidence where a reasonable person would not so expect. Consequently, if it is unbelievable that a vehicle could travel from one end of the United Kingdom to the other without refuelling, this aspect of the advertising would be innocuous. The relevant section[47] provides that 'A person must not, in trade, make an unsubstantiated representation'. This is then disapplied by s12A (3) which provides: 'This section does not apply to a representation that a reasonable person would not expect to be substantiated'. It would therefore appear that the initial burden would be to prove that the representation was made and that a reasonable person would not expect it to be substantiated before the advertiser would need to substantiate the representation.

Of more weight is the representation that the vehicle has 'Low Fuel Consumption'. This is a relative statement: *low* compared to *what?* In the context of the wider advertising campaign, it could be interpreted as a representation relative to cars of a similar size and engine type, and this becomes a more credible argument when the particular purpose for the car is explained by the customer, namely, to commute 30 miles per day and the question posed whether the low fuel consumption will persist on journeys of this nature.

All things considered, it is likely Alison would have a remedy under the fitness for purpose guarantee against the supplier. She may also successfully maintain the argument against the manufacturer that the advertising campaign was misleading and deceptive, and the Commerce Commission may also strike on the grounds that the advertising cannot be substantiated.

---

47 Section 12A.

As the purpose was made known to the supplier and the question of fuel consumption was raised in this context, it is likely that the vehicle would be found substantially unfit for purpose, provided the fuel consumption was higher than that of a comparable vehicle. This proviso is important as we do not know what sort of vehicle Alison had previously. If substantially unfit for purpose, the car may be rejected and a refund obtained as long as this option is exercised within a reasonable time.

(iii) Failure to meet emissions standards

The R1 was sold pursuant to the manufacturer's advertising campaign in which it was claimed the vehicle was 'Best for the Environment'. A news story breaks after purchase, which suggests cars of this manufacturer fail to meet emissions standards by a significant margin. If it is proven that the R1 purchased by Alison falls into this category, the advertising claim, which is clearly not a puff, will not be substantiated. Hence, the car was purchased in partial reliance on a misleading and deceptive statement, which will give the Court power to order that it may be returned and a full refund obtained.[48] The manufacturer may also be fined, and action may be taken by the Commerce Commission for the unsubstantiated representation.

In addition, the guarantee of acceptable quality will be breached giving rise to the remedy of rejection; as a car not meeting emission standards presents a failure of substantial character in that a reasonable consumer would not have acquired it knowing the nature or extent of the defect. Assuming the car is not roadworthy in this condition, it will not be of merchantable quality under SOGA and may be subject to compulsory product recall under FTA.

Scenario 2

This scenario is centred on new computer software sold bundled with hardware, a new tablet computer. New Zealand law treats software as a good. Hence, CGA and its guarantees make no distinction between hardware and software whether sold individually or in a package. It is presumed that Elizabeth is manufacturer and supplier. However, the software at fault is supplied by a third party who has a separate contract with David and whom, it is assumed, is both manufacturer and supplier. This third-party app (TPA) is not in any way connected with the software provided by Elizabeth except to the extent that, one assumes, it was supplied to work with David's operating system. This assumption is reasonable as consumers are requested to specify their operating systems, for example, Windows, Linux etc. before purchase. It is also assumed that David provided the correct information. The computer consultant has confirmed the TPA is at fault, so this excludes the possibility of applications supplied by Elizabeth (as opposed to the operating system) in any way contributing to the problem.

---

48 Section 43 Fair Trading Act 1986.

(i) Failure of the app and failure to patch the problem

The TPA monitors route, heart rate and blood pressure while David is running. This functionality would have been claimed by the third party as part of its specifications for the software otherwise David would have made his purchase with no or only vague knowledge of what it would do; and this is most unlikely.

It is possible or even likely this application is not unique and that David would have had a choice of other applications which achieve the same three objects at a similar price. If this is so, it is relevant because each feature would be essential to a reasonable consumer; the reasoning being that if one has a choice to buy an application which does three things, why would one be satisfied with an application which only does two things, all else being equal? This reasoning may also hold good if the particular consumer was not, at the time of purchase, particularly interested in one of the three functions.

The failure under this heading could be said to break s 9 CGA and s 15 SOGA in that the goods do not match their description. While s 15 would require the customer to have relied on the description when buying the goods, there is no such requirement under s 9. In addition, breach of the guarantee allows the consumer to take advantage of the more extensive remedies afforded by the CGA. But counter to this argument, it could equally be claimed that, because the blood pressure reporting did function for a short while, the goods met their specification and, rather, their fault was one of quality.

Nevertheless, there is a clear breach of the guarantee of acceptable quality, and it is strongly arguable this is of a substantial nature in that, particularly if there was a wide choice of apps with these functions, no reasonable consumer would have made the purchase knowing the extent of the defect.

David would be entitled under the CGA to reject the goods and obtain a refund. If he has lost the opportunity to buy similar goods at the same price, he may also be able to claim consequential damages, but it is unlikely that opportunity would have been lost.

The third party has, however, supplied a patch to fix the defect. Does this affect David's right to reject? If he called for a patch, the supplier is entitled to exercise an option to repair, but having failed to do so within a reasonable time, David's right of rejection is renewed. If the supplier supplied the patch without being prompted to do so, its failure to remedy within a reasonable time would have the same result.

(ii) Interference with other apps

Under CGA the consumer is entitled to consequential loss or loss which is 'reasonably foreseeable'. The precise boundaries of this remedy have not yet been delineated. However, as far as the measure of damages is concerned (how they are calculated), it is clear that the consumer cannot obtain expected gains under the contract of sale or, in other words, damages for 'loss of a bargain'[49] although

---

49 *Cox & Coxton Ltd v Leipst* [1999] 2 NZLR 15 (CA).

much the same result may be reached if the claim is formulated as one of damages for loss of an opportunity or chance, and that opportunity has truly been lost.

As far as remoteness of damage is concerned, the foreseeability aspect, it appears that neither the tort nor the contract test of remoteness will necessarily be applied. The key question is one of fact and whether 'the particular damage claimed is sufficiently linked to the breach of the particular duty to merit recovery in all the circumstances'.[50] The Courts appear unwilling to commit to a formulaic approach and wish to retain discretion to do justice in the particular circumstances.

With the present state of the law, the question under this heading could produce widely differing opinions. Given the supplier's presumed ignorance of the apps on David's computer and therefore of the damage interference with them could cause, it is unlikely damages for excessive power usage would be recoverable. However, damages for inconvenience may be awarded for failure to record his TV programmes.

(iii) Damage done to the Wi-Fi connector

This form of damage is subject to the same principles discussed under the previous subheading and would likely depend on expert evidence. For example, is the damage to the Wi-Fi hardware damage of a type that can be repaired by reinstalling the firmware (software) which runs the hardware, or has it caused damage to the hardware itself by, perhaps, causing a surge of electricity or something of that nature? The likelihood of the latter type of damage is probably more remote than the former, but this is something on which only a technical expert could venture a useful opinion. If the hardware is capable of repair by a firmware reinstall, it is likely that this part of the claim would only serve to uplift the distress and inconvenience damages under the previous subheading.

V. Specific issues in New Zealand

New Zealand's recent unfair contracts law was introduced in 2015 under FTA and only applies to standard form contracts. It addresses two distinct types of unfairness. First, 'substantive' unfairness, in other words, unfairness in the substance of the contract when it is read objectively according to recognised canons of construction and, secondly, 'presentational' unfairness, or the way a standard form contract is presented to consumers. For example, a contract may be unfair in its presentation if it is expressed in 'legalese', if it is illegible or if it incorporates other terms and conditions which are difficult although not impossible to find.

The question raised by the new law is whether a standard form contract can be unfair because of the way it is presented when it is substantively fair.[51]

---

50   *McElroy Milne v Commercial Electronics Ltd.* [1993] 1 NZLR 39, 41 (CA).
51   It is clear it cannot be saved from substantive *unfairness* no matter how fairly it is presented.

Resolution of the question whether a contract term is unfair depends on the interpretation of s 46L(1) and (2) read together. The meaning of these provisions is not entirely clear.

Section 46L(1) provides:

A term in a consumer contract is unfair if the court is satisfied that the term

(a) would cause a significant imbalance in the parties' rights and obligations arising under the contract; *and*
(b) is not reasonably necessary in order to protect the legitimate interests of the party who would be advantaged by the term; *and*
(c) would cause detriment (whether financial or otherwise) to a party if it were applied, enforced or relied on [emphasis added].

Requirements (a) and (b) are concerned only with inequality. Requirement (a) necessarily requires interpretation of the contract as a whole according to established legal principles. If there is a significant imbalance to the contract as a result of the individual term in question, then requirement (b) becomes relevant because the imbalance may be justified to protect legitimate interests of the proferor. For example, a term may, at first glance, seem excessively to favour the proferor but if, as a result of inserting the term, the proferor is able to offer the goods or services at a much lower price than otherwise, a legitimate interest may be established. But both of these requirements are concerned with imbalance on an objective interpretation of the contract as it stands. Requirement (c) seems capable of easy determination because, once (a) and (b) are established, detriment naturally follows. It may be financial or it may be some other detriment such as inconvenience or lost time.

If the legislation is only there to protect against substantive unfairness arising just from the nature of the contract itself, then there would appear to have been no need to go any further than s 46L(1).

However, s 46L(2) goes on to speak in terms of presentational unfairness. It provides that 'in determining whether a term . . . is unfair, the court may take into account any matters it thinks relevant, but must take into account "the extent the term is "transparent" and consider the "contract as a whole"'. The Fair Trading Act 1986, s 2 defines as transparent a term which

(a) is expressed in reasonably plain language; and
(b) is legible; and
(c) is presented clearly; and
(d) is readily available to any party affected by the term.

So any additional enquiry under s 46L(2) must involve itself with presentational unfairness which is what transparency is all about. But how is transparency relevant to requirements (a) and (b) in s 46L(1)? The answer is that it cannot be relevant because an objective interpretation of the contract does not depend on how transparent the wording is. Is it relevant to 'detriment' in requirement (c)? Possibly it is, as a party may suffer disappointment, inconvenience or surprise because he or she has not appreciated the true nature of the term owing to its expression in 'legal' rather than 'plain' English (for example). Nevertheless, no contract under the reformed law may be unfair unless all three requirements of s 46L(1) are satisfied.

It would seem therefore, and this may not have been intended by the reformers, that the question posed above must be answered in the negative: A contract which is objectively fair cannot be rendered unfair no matter how lacking in transparency its presentation was.

7 Singapore consumer law

Gary Low[1]

I. The Singapore consumer market

Singapore has a highly developed free market economy, with a large manufacturing base, but also increasingly important high-tech as well as services sectors. It has a population of over 5 million, and a gross domestic product (GDP) per capita of over USD 52,000 as of 2015,[2] being second in Asia with Japan being first. It is classified by the United Nations as a developed nation, with all the commercial infrastructure of Western developed economies. About half its population belong to the middle and upper classes, and thus, taken as a whole, it has a considerable spending power.[3] The country capitalises on its historic geographical position as a port of transhipment and is a major facilitator of entrepot trade in the region. It is one of the freest economies in the world, and has concluded FTAs with the United States, the European Union (EU) and China, just to name a few. The upshot of all this is an increasingly affluent Singapore consumer with an ever-expanding range of products and services to consume from.

Household internet penetration rate is about 88% and growing.[4] Nine in every ten households owns a mobile device.[5] An estimated 49% shop online at least once a month. Major international online retailers have in recent years established a local presence as a result of growth potential here and regionally.[6] The government has been actively encouraging local and foreign businesses to do so

---

1 G. Low, Assistant Professor of Law at the Singapore Management University.
2 World Bank: Doing Business in Singapore, http://data.worldbank.org/country/singapore, accessed 14 May 2016.
3 DP Credit Bureau News Release: New Insight Reveals the Nine Faces of Singapore Credit Consumer Behaviour, www.dpgroup.com.sg/Attachments/98_DP%20Mosaic%20Release%20FNL.pdf, accessed 14 May 2016.
4 According to 2014 Statistics by the Infocomm Development Authority (IDA) of Singapore, www.ida.gov.sg/Tech-Scene-News/Facts-and-Figures/Infocomm-Usage-Households-and-Individuals, accessed 14 May 2016.
5 CBRE APAC Consumer Survey 2014: Singapore, www.cbre.com/research-and-reports/apac-consumer-survey-2014-singapore, accessed 14 May 2016, at p. 4.
6 Regionally, Singapore's share of the e-commerce pie is larger than that of its immediate neighbours Malaysia and Indonesia: A.T. Kearney, *Lifting Barriers to E-Commerce in ASEAN* (Kuala Lumpur, Malaysia: CIMB ASEAN Research Institute, 2015).

through a variety of initiatives and subsidies, seeing e-commerce as contributing to economic growth and job creation.[7] E-commerce in Singapore is developing apace, with cross-border online shopping set to balloon,[8] with predictions that the value of online spending will outstrip offline shopping by 2020.[9]

That having been said, the present paints a different picture. A 2015 government survey notes that online purchases account for a mere 4% of overall consumer spending.[10] Fifty-six per cent of Singaporeans are estimated to shop offline as their main mode of purchase, with between a third and a quarter expected to increase the proportion of offline spending within the next 2 years, with this being especially true for those in the 18–34 age group. The persistence of offline spending can be attributed to Singapore consumers exhibiting a 'mall culture',[11] and malls responding to the threat posed by e-commerce by sharpening their competitive edge through a 'retailtainment' strategy, hoping to turn what would otherwise be a mundane visit to a mall into an entertaining experience.[12] Another factor affecting the size of the domestic e-commerce pie is that consumers tend to prefer shopping offline for more expensive products than offline, and vice versa.[13] This behaviour appears quite rational, since inter alia the risk (of defect) is mitigated when inspection prior to purchase is possible. For many businesses, though, these different modes of selling are seen to be complementary. Indeed, an increasing number of traditionally brick-and-mortar retainers are adopting an omnichannel market strategy, thus enabling shoppers the opportunity of a look-and-feel before deciding whether to buy a product (online).[14]

With more participants in the market and an increase in the value and number of transactions, there is bound to be a concomitant growth in the number of consumer-related problems. The government does not appear to track this, although the Consumers Association of Singapore (CASE) – the main non-governmental consumer advocacy group – periodically releases media statements on problematic sectors or Consumer-related issues, based on regularly collected and collated data from consumer complaints registered with the organisation.[15]

---

7   See for instance, Spring Singapore's Innovation and Capability Voucher scheme and their Capability Development Grant, IDA's iSPRINT grant, and tax allowances and credits under IRAS's PIC grant; and Mindy Tan, "Government to Launch E-Commerce and HR Platform for SMEs", *Business Times* (10 March 2015).
8   "Singapore Leads in APAC Online Buying: Report", *Channel News Asia* (14 January 2016).
9   "More Singaporeans Turn to Virtual Stores for Shopping", *Business Times* (22 September 2014).
10 J. Lim, "Households Not Big on Buying Online", *Straits Times* (7 April 2015).
11 K. Paterson, "Mall Culture Puts Singapore Ahead of the Global Ecommerce Game", *Digital Market Asia* (14 November 2014).
12 Supra fn 5 at pp. 6–7.
13 Ibid.
14 Ibid.
15 Bi-monthly statistics from July 2015 to July 2016 are kept on file with the author. For CASE's statistics on complaints for the year 2015, see www.case.org.sg/consumer_guides_statistics.aspx, accessed 20 July 2016.

With regard to contracts for the sale of goods, the largest proportion of complaints relate to defective goods. Many of the claims related to second-hand cars, as can be expected due to the nature of the good, arise from complaints of *latent* defects. Regarding both beauty and travel, many complaints were with regard to substandard or total failure in provision of the agreed services. (At this juncture, the reader would do well to be aware of the possible reason why: that the number of complaints in these sectors spiked due to the recent and unexpected closure of a small number of large spas or salons or travel agencies, leaving customers who have prepaid in the undesirable position of being unsecured creditors, and with one of their remedial measures being an immediate registering of a complaint with the police as well as with CASE. Through self and co-regulatory measures in place in these sectors, as well as the presence of the current legislative framework, risk exposure to a majority of consumers is well mitigated.)

Across both goods and services, other significant issues relate to false or misleading claims, as well as pressure selling leading to duress or undue influence. In the recent past, complaints related to timeshare contracts featured prominently, but legislation allowing for withdrawal rights for such contracts as well as the outlawing of pressure selling appear to have nipped the problem in the bud. These days, the major culprit appears to be from vendors of electrical and electronic goods. Indeed, whilst this has probably been the trend for some time, it is only recently – due largely to increasing ease and reliance on social media – that these problems which consumers otherwise perennially face have attracted the attention of society at large as well as the relevant authorities.

II. Access to justice and enforcement issues

Caveat emptor remains the backbone of the consumer protection and enforcement framework in Singapore. Consumers are expected to take personal responsibility not only for deciding whether to enter into a transaction, but also in seeking redress should problems arise. The majority of remedies listed in the main consumer protection legislation – the Consumer Protection (Fair Trading) Act (CPFTA)[16] – are therefore private in nature, whether addressed through self-help or with assistance from the courts.

Many consumers do in fact seek redress directly with the traders involved. As the sums involved tend to be modest, virtually all consumer disputes fall within the monetary jurisdiction of the State Courts[17] (formerly the Subordinate Courts of Singapore) rather than that of the Supreme Court (which deals with disputes of a value of at least S$250,000).[18] Within the State Courts structure, the majority of disputes are dealt with in the Small Claims Tribunal (SCT, which deals with

---

16 Consumer Protection (Fair Trading) Act, Cap 52A, 2009 Rev Ed.
17 Section 2, Small Claims Tribunal Act, Cap 208, 1998 Rev Ed.
18 Section 2, State Courts Act, Cap 3212007 Rev Ed.

disputes of a value of up to S$10,000).[19] A concerted effort has been made, over the last three decades, to streamline the judicial process and to attempt to ensure costs are not inhibitive. The result is a fast-tracked and relatively cheap procedure, at least insofar as the SCT is concerned. Thus, consumer disputes within the value of S$5000 require only a lodgement fee of S$10, and S$20 for between that and S$10,000. Information on how to commence claims and to enforce judgements is readily available in electronic and hardcopy format. Most if not all are adjudicated without legal representation, thus keeping costs down.

A key approach to domestic dispute resolution in Singapore, perhaps in a nod to Confucian influences, is to encourage mediation rather than litigation.[20] As such, once a claim is lodged, and it is one that does not involve personal injury (as the run-of-the-mill consumer disputes tend not to be), action is stayed in favour of state-supported mediation. Mediation typically occurs within 14 days of a claim being lodged, and if it is not resolved before the State-appointed mediator, is thereafter fixed for a hearing within 10 days of the failed mediation session.

As tourism is a major contributor to the Singapore economy, an even faster-track is put in place for tourist disputes. Mediation and/or a hearing may be fixed within 24 hours of a claim being lodged. Hearings before the SCT are largely documentary affairs, and although formally a court procedure, the SCT Referee usually conducts matters as informally as possible; and as a matter of judicial policy, encourages parties to settle their dispute amicably, and steps in to adjudicate only as a last resort. Decisions of the SCT are enforceable as court orders, and claimants may avail themselves of general enforcement mechanisms like writs of seizure and sale, garnishee orders or examination of judgement debtors. Problems related to debt enforcement appear a growing concern in Singapore. Like any other country, sometimes the costs of enforcement vis-à-vis the value of the debt dissuade (would-be) creditors from going down this route: this is especially true of many consumer disputes since the values tend to be small.

Insofar as the financial sector is concerned, Singapore's de facto Central Bank – the Monetary Authority of Singapore – worked together with stakeholder banks and other financial institutions to set up the Financial Industries Dispute Resolution Centre (FIDReC).[21] FIDReC, in operation since 2003, offers a fast-track arbitration process to deal with complaints between consumers (often retail investors) and financial institutions. FIDReC's attractiveness lay in the fact that it offered something for everyone – defendants got the confidentiality they wanted, and both parties could avail of a speedy process. Its caseload ballooned in the

---

19 This sum can, by consent of parties to the dispute, be increased to a maximum of S$20,000: supra fn 17 section 5(4).
20 See for instance Joel Lee and Teh Hwee Hwee (eds.), *An Asian Perspective on Mediation* (Singapore: Academic Publishing, 2009), pp. 54, 55; S. Menon, *Building Sustainable Mediation Programmes: A Singapore Perspective* (Singapore: Academy Publishing, 14 February 2015), keynote address at the Asia-Pacific International Mediation Summit (Singapore Mediation Centre's Asian Journal on Mediation, 2015).
21 See www.fidrec.com.sg/website/background.html, accessed 10 June 2016.

wake of the 2008 global financial crisis, especially since a sizeable number of consumers purchased instruments linked to the now-defunct Lehman Brothers.

An important *facilitator* of the private enforcement of consumer rights is CASE. The organisation is many-tentacled. It conducts post-market regulation[22] and surveillance,[23] is heavily involved in consumer outreach and education,[24] and runs an independent legal advisory and mediation service.[25] CASE cannot represent consumers in private actions against firms, but can and often uses its clout to attempt to reach an amicable agreement. Like many of its counterparts across the developed world, CASE is non-governmental and membership based. Akin, for example, to the UK's Which? and the Dutch *consumentenbond*, its articles of association restrict its capacity to act in consumer disputes to those on its membership. Due in part to buy-in from the national labour movement, it must be said, it does represent a large swathe and cross-section of the domestic consumer population. Furthermore, to get around this formality, membership fees for individuals are kept deliberately affordable: non-members who approach CASE regarding their disputes may enrol for a pittance to take advantage of CASE's professional expertise and leverage with the trading community, or otherwise, pay a fraction of that for CASE to assist in drafting preliminary correspondence with the trader in question to commence negotiations over redress.

The CPFTA names CASE, together with the Singapore Tourism Board, as 'specified bodies' to advance the interests of consumers and tourists to the country.[26] As specified bodies' under the Act, CASE and STB are empowered to negotiate with firms who are or appear to be engaging in unfair trading practices with a view to changing their behaviour. If an agreement is reached, it can be concretised in a Voluntary Compliance Agreement (VCA), and which amongst others may contain a commitment from the firm to compensate consumers who have already suffered a loss as a result of the firm's behaviour and to refrain from such conduct in the future.

Prior to changes to the CPFTA which entered into force in December 2016, if an errant firm is unwilling to enter into a VCA or breaches it, the specified body may, on approval from the Injunctions Proposals Review Panel (as appointed by the Minster for Trade and Industry), make an application before the courts for an injunction on pain of contempt of court to restrain the firm in question from

---

22 Notably through the CASETrust accreditation initiative, which encourages voluntary industry-wide best practices and audits participating firms in a wide range of sectors.
23 Through the Consumer Standards and Products Testing committee, whose members are experts in their respective fields of testing, and of which this author chairs. The committee is involved in advising product standards and best practices in for example supply chains, although its main activity is to ensure consumer products operate as claimed, and against health and safety standards.
24 It has a publication and media arm, as well as a separate committee which runs regular talks at schools as well as suburban residential estates.
25 CASE employs staff officers to deal with the day-to-day advisory operations, but also enjoys support from a body of legally qualified volunteers who administer its mediation scheme.
26 Supra fn 16, s 8(10) CPFTA.

persisting in its behaviour.[27] This ability of specified bodies to apply for an injunction provides a legal incentive for errant firms to conform. That being the case, CASE has not often invoked its right to pursue injunctive relief, and, where it has, it has encountered mixed success. First, the costs incurred are inevitably not recovered – either because the law rarely allows recovery on a complete indemnity basis, or because of impecuniosity of the defendant firm – and therefore the decisions on whether to proceed with injunction invariably involve questions of where the scarce resources of a not-for-profit organisation ought best to be employed. Second, the facilitative efficiency of Singapore's company laws means that a firm that is or is about to be injuncted can simply wind-up, and the errant trader can swiftly set up a new company in order to circumvent the order. Most disputes are therefore resolved through the signing of VCAs, direct legal action by consumers, or invoking extra-legal reputational sanctions like naming-and-shaming on (social) media.

The situation has of course, as mentioned, changed. The apparent reason for this legislative initiative is the recent spate of negative publicity due to errant behaviour by a handful of traders. In terms of legislative changes, CASE and STB no longer have the power to initiate injunction proceedings. This is instead allocated to a new department within SPRING Singapore, a statutory board under the purview of MTI and which is currently the standard setter and regulator for weights and measures. In addition, SPRING now has powers of entry and arrest in order to investigate possible breaches of the CPFTA.[28]

On the one hand, this is to be commended since in the present context, powers of entry and arrest could only be exercised by the police, and which would only be invoked on suspicion of breaches of the Penal Code, for example incidences of intimidation or cheating.[29] SPRING is the right choice for empowerment since it already has both experience and expertise in investigating and prosecuting breaches of the Weights and Measures Act. On the other hand, taking away CASE's right to apply for injunction, or where SPRING exercises its investigative and injunctive powers without seeking CASE's views, may undercut its ability to negotiate with errant traders as regards the undertaking of VCAs. This may be mitigated by establishing a cooperation protocol between CASE and SPRING on information sharing and consultation. Neither the proposed bill nor its accompanying explanatory notes indicate that such a protocol will be explored or encouraged, but some form of cooperation can be expected. Officers of SPRING are regularly appointed to CASE's central committee and its sub-committee on Product Standards and Testing, allowing, informally, for professional relationships between the two entities to be nurtured. The concern is as regards turnover of key personnel in either organisation, leading to a possible loss of relationship and knowledge unless these processes are institutionalised. The

---

27 Ibid. s 10 CPFTA.
28 The wording is in pari materia with the like sections of the Competition Act.
29 Ss 417, 420, and 506 of the Penal Code, Cap 224, 1985 Rev Ed.

two entities would do well to take note of the like situation in the Netherlands, where the *consumentenbond* (Dutch consumer association) and the *Autoriteit Consument en Markt* (Dutch Competition and Consumer Authority) inked a *samenwerkingsprotocol* (legally binding memorandum of cooperation), obliging information sharing and consultation.[30]

Merely looking at the legislative framework provides an incomplete picture of the remedial and enforcement mechanisms in Singapore, however. A pantheon of governmental and quasi-governmental agencies regulates market entry of consumer goods and services either by actual inspection or the formulation of standards, as well as conducting post-entry surveillance. An equally large number of specific pieces of legislation target particular sectors or types of goods, like electronic or electrical goods[31] or cosmetics or goods with medicinal qualities[32] or fisheries and food.[33] Likewise, as mentioned previously, CASE complements these tasks by themselves encouraging sectoral self-regulation, providing standard setting through accreditation, and conducting their own post-market surveillance.

III. The legal framework for consumer sales

Any discussion on Singapore's consumer protection framework must start with the obvious historical observation that, together with its common law tradition, a number of its important statutes are derived from its erstwhile colonial master – the United Kingdom.

It is therefore unsurprising that a key plank in protecting consumers in the marketplace remains the Sale of Goods Act (Cap 393),[34] which for all intents and purposes mirrors the UK's Sale of Goods Act 1979 from which it is derived. Applicable to all, and not only consumer contracts, that Act protects consumers as purchasers of goods in that it has provisions obliging sellers to take into account the description s 13, quality s 14, purpose and title of the goods so sold s 14. Liability is strict, not fault based. Another important part of its English heritage is the Unfair Contract Terms Act (Cap 396), which is derived from the UK Unfair Contract Terms Act 1977.[35] The English lawyer will therefore be

---

30 *Samenwerkingsprotocol tussen Autoriteit Consument en Markt en de Consumentenbond* (10 December 2015, Staatscourant Jaargang 2015 no 44660). See https://zoek.officielebekendmakingen.nl/stcrt-2015-44660.html, accessed 30 July 2016.
31 The Standards Productivity and Innovation Board of Singapore, an agency of the Ministry of Trade and Industry.
32 The Health Sciences Authority, a statutory board of the Ministry of Health.
33 The Agri-Food and Veterinary Authority of Singapore, an agency of the Ministry of National Development.
34 The Sale of Goods Act, Cap 393, 1999 Rev Ed (originally enacted from the UK Sale of Goods Act 1979 c 54) See also the Supply of Goods and Services Act, Cap 394, 1999 Rev Ed, taken also from the UK Supply of Goods and Services Act 1982, c 29.
35 The Unfair Contract Terms Act, Cap 396, 1994 Rev Ed. Taken from the UK Unfair Contract Terms Act 1977, c 50.

unsurprised in that Singapore consumer contracts may not exclude or restrict liability for death or personal injury, whereas other contractual terms limiting or exempting liability on the part of the seller are subject to a judicial control of reasonableness. The prototypical consumer protection legislation in Singapore is its Consumer Protection (Trade Descriptions and Safety Requirements) Act of 1975,[36] and one might find parallels in its counterparts in the United Kingdom[37] and Malaysia,[38] from which it drew inspiration.

From a legislative perspective, status quo ante persisted for decades: that is, until the passage in late 2003 of the Consumer Protection (Fair Trading) Act (CPFTA), through the successful lobbying of CASE.[39] What undergirded CASE in its lobbying for a consumer-specific – and, indeed, centric – piece of legislation, was their noticing a growing trend of sharp business practices, including aggressive and unethical sales tactics, across different market segments, but also across different modes of sale. The occasion for the CPFTA was a root-and-branch overview commencing in 2001 by the Ministry of Trade and Industry (MTI) of the legislative framework for consumer protection and which precipitated negotiation for and the signing of a Free Trade Agreement with the United States in 2003 (which also led to the introduction of Singapore's first antitrust regime).

Growing confidence and influence from the legal autochthony movement probably resulted in a move away from traditional English legislative influence, and the CPFTA was the product of other commonwealth jurisdictions, most notably Sasketchewan in Canada and New South Wales in Australia.[40] A further update was done in 2008 in order to introduce a greater range of remedies and raise the standard of consumer protection to that of the EU.[41]

Akin to the legislative method employed in the EU's Unfair Terms in Consumer Contracts Regulation (UTCCR), the CPFTA provides a list of 20 specific practices deemed unfair, and many of which find counterparts in the UTCCR, such as the concealment of onerous or material terms in small print, and the warranting to consumers that a particular good has a quality or grade that is known not to have. The CPFTA provided, for the first time, civil remedies like damages for consumers aggrieved or injured by unfair business practices.[42] Since 2008, available remedies include a general right to cure or price reduction, as well as a right of withdrawal for certain types of contracts, like those concluded via colpor-

---

36 Act 10 of 1975.
37 Trade Descriptions Act 1968 c 29.
38 Trade Descriptions Act 1972.
39 The association was set up in 1971 as a formal arrangement between academia and trade unions who sought, as was then the trend globally, to organise the consumer movement in Singapore.
40 R. Chandran, "Consumer Protection (Fair Trading) Act" (2004) *Singapore Journal of Legal Studies* 6.
41 Singapore Parliamentary Debates, vol. 88 (9 March 2012) (Mr Teo Ser Luck, Mr Lim Biow Chuan).
42 See Loo Wee Ling et al., "Award of Damages Under the Singapore Consumer Protection (Fair Trading) Act" (2007) 9 *The Australian Journal of Asian Law* 66.

tage, and also timeshare contracts, both of which attracted scrutiny for the use of pressure tactics to close deals.[43] Furthermore, there is a presumption of non-conformity of goods at the time of sale or delivery where defects are uncovered within 6 months of sale or delivery.[44]

Certain types of contracts remain outside the ambit of the CPFTA. These include the sale of immoveable goods as well as employment contracts, indicating that the main purpose of the CPFTA, like the Sale of Goods Act, is to regulate the everyday exchange of goods in the marketplace.[45] Contracts involving financial instruments or services were initially excluded from the application of the CPFTA, since these were regulated by way of specific legislation. Since the recent global financial crisis gave rise to many complaints regarding the behaviour of financial institutions in the marketing of such products and the rendering of advice, the government felt the need to safeguard the interests of retail investors. This resulted – speedily, one might add – in an important amendment in 2008 to the CPFTA to extend it to financial products and services insofar as financial institutions committed unfair practices, specifically including the application of undue influence or unconscionable conduct.[46]

A final observation regarding market regulation must be made. Legislative initiative and policy-making in the realm of consumer protection falls on the shoulders of the Ministry of Trade and Industry. The fundamental government approach to consumer policy remains that of caveat emptor, with specific exceptions carved out by the various aforementioned pieces of legislation. What this means is that the onus remains on the consumer to be reasonably well informed regarding the transaction he or she wishes to enter into, and to assess his or her risks accordingly. Where in the context of consumer contracts the seller has acted unfairly or performed his obligations imperfectly, likewise, the onus is on the consumer to rectify the problem via a specified set of self-help remedies or to seek recourse through the courts. Enforcement costs are therefore largely borne by consumers themselves.

There are several theoretical and practical reasons explaining the apparent laissez-faire attitude of Singapore's erstwhile consumer policy and its legal framework. Given that consumer policy is within the remit of MTI, it is subservient to the prevailing philosophical attitude towards the management of the wider economy: neo-liberalism. There appears to be a firm belief in the efficiency of the market; that given the rationality of actors, Adam Smith's invisible hand will eventually correct any deficiencies that may occasionally plague marketplace transactions. This explains why, for instance, the primary regulator for financial products consistently insists that '[c]onsumers bear the primary responsibility for protecting their interests. They should exercise due care in their selection of . . .

---

43 Supra fn 37.
44 Supra fn 16, s12B(3) CPFTA.
45 Ibid. s 2 CPFTA.
46 Consumer Protection (Fair Trading) Amendment Act 2008, s 2.

products and service providers'.[47] It also explains the preference for rules improving market competition *rather than* protecting consumers per se:

> [t]he emphasis in Singapore has been on encouraging competitive processes and raising consumer awareness . . . as active competition policy is seen as a more efficient way to deliver benefits . . . to end-user consumers . . . [and] business consumers.[48]

This explains why, under the Singapore regime, mandatory information disclosure regarding description and quality of goods are regulated under the Sale of Goods Act as well as the CPFTA (for misleading or false statements), and under pointilistic subsidiary legislation for rights of withdrawal. Disclosure of information is seen as paramount policy objective since it enables consumers to make informed decisions in a competitive market as to which product best enhances their welfare.

IV. Factual scenarios

Scenario 1

There are three problems raised in the scenario: sluggish brakes and engine noise, higher fuel consumption, and the failure to meet emissions standards. The possible solutions to Alison's woes are set out as follows.

(i)(a) Brake and engine noise (new car)

The first point is that of the sluggish brake and engine noise, as well as higher than anticipated fuel consumption. The brake and engine problems were first noticed 3 weeks after purchase, and no explanation is given for the observed sluggishness or noise. Alison's – and indeed, most consumers' – legal point of reference remain the SOGA and CPFTA: section 12B(1)(b) of the CPFTA provides Alison with a list of possible remedies 'if the goods do not conform to the applicable contract at the time of delivery'. 'Conformity' as referred to in the CPFTA bears the same meaning in SOGA in that goods sold need to fit with their description and be of satisfactory quality. As to the latter requirement, the law

---

[47] Monetary Authority of Singapore, Objectives and Principles of Financial Supervision in Singapore (April 2004, revised April 2013) at p. 9.
[48] The Competition Commission of Singapore, *The Interface Between Competition and Consumer Policies – Contribution From Singapore* (Organisation for Economic Co-operation and Development, Directorate for Financial and Enterprise Affairs, 21 February 2008) DAF/COMP/GF/WD(2008)(3) at p. 3. This is underscored by the fact that there is an independent state regulator – the Competition Commission of Singapore (CCS) – with dedicated resources to ensure a competitive market, but none specifically for the furtherance of consumers' interests.

requires that the following factors must be included in assessing whether the car is of satisfactory quality: It must be fit for purpose, have the appearance and finish of the standard of other like cars, be free of minor defects, and be durable and safe.[49] In other words, the legal requirements are largely the same as that under English law. To avoid unnecessary repetition, the reader would do well to refer to the elucidation on the matter in the chapter by Twigg-Flesner.

I will merely offer some further observations based on variations or departures under Singapore case law. Alison will have to establish that the sluggish brakes and engine noise are of such extent that she may invoke the above-mentioned s 14(2B) of SOGA. This means, amongst others, that it is incumbent on Alison to prove that they are of such a degree to render the car unfit for purpose, or not a minor defect, or are a safety hazard. The factual scenario does not hint at the cause or the extent of the problem, and so one is left to speculate. In other words, Alison must have the car inspected to reveal whether the brakes render the car road unworthy, and whether the cause of the engine noise for example is due to a faulty gear transmission system giving rise to a risk of a runaway car on the highway. Failure to do so means Alison would not have proven the car is of unsatisfactory quality in that it is unfit for purpose (since it is still roadworthy and *in that sense* not a major defect).

(ii) Higher-than-expected fuel consumption

What of the advertisement that the car is of 'top reliability' or of low fuel consumption? Here one notes a possible departure from the English position. An uncannily similar position faced by Alison was dealt with in *Koh Wee Meng v Trans Eurokars Pte Ltd*.[50] In that case, the consumer purchased a Rolls-Royce Phantom, which was marketed on the basis of its 'waftability' and driving experience as a 'magic carpet ride'. The consumer alleged a 'loud moaning noise' and significant vibration from the steering wheel whenever he turned the car, and sued the dealership on the basis that the car was of unsatisfactory quality taking into account what was represented in its advertisements. That part of the claim was dismissed by the learned judge on the basis that those terms were in law mere puffs, and no reasonable consumer could rely on such statements to the extent that the manufacturer did not and could not promise absolute silence.[51] On the other hand, that case could be distinguished from the present in that 'top reliability' does not mean absolute reliability, and that the presence and extent of sluggish brakes and loud engine noises detract from a standard the manufacturer held itself to. It is, arguably, likely, especially given high fuel and car prices in Singapore, that far from being a mere puff not to be relied on, a claim on fuel consumption would be material to a consumer's purchasing decision.

---

49 S 14 SOGA, especially subsection 2B.
50 [2014] SGHC 104.
51 At para 116.

Alison mentioned the particular purpose of the purchase, which is short daily commutes to work, and which ties in with the need for low fuel consumption. The position under Singapore law is the same as in English, and again I defer to the English advice rendered elsewhere in the book.

(i)(b) Brake and engine noise (second-hand car)

The above-described position under Singapore law is *largely* unchanged even if the car sold is second-hand and 3 years old. This is since s 12B(3) of the CPFTA states that defects arising within 6 months of purchase are presumed to have been present at the time of purchase. This rule covers both new and second-hand goods. While the presumption is a rebuttable one, it shifts the burden of proving otherwise to the seller. Such a seller will have a hard time defending Alison's claim if detailed inspections were not made *at the time of sale*.[52] That having been said, complaints arising from defects from second-hand cars are consistently at the top of the list of problematic sectors, with many disputes failing to be resolved through mediation. Resistance to amicable solutions could possibly be due to the following: an unwillingness by sellers to assume risk of defects (and therefore the cost of remedy) due to this being a high volume low margin sector, and a difference in opinion between buyers and sellers of what constitutes a 'defect' and ordinary wear-and-tear. If the car has high mileage, then wear-and-tear might contribute to sluggishness due to the wearing out of the brake discs or pads, and a Singapore court would not rule in favour of Alison: see *Speedo Motoring v Ong Gek Seng* (upholding the ruling of the Small Claims Tribunal referee on this point).[53]

That having been said, a further three points need to be made.

First, in most cases, those who purchase brand new cars directly from manufacturers in Singapore need not seek recourse to the consumer protection framework as industry practice is to supply the car with a warranty of 2 to 3 years.[54] Second, the situation is wholly different for those who purchase from parallel importers, and who may not offer warranties, or may not offer warranties as extensive as those from manufacturers. In such cases, consumers may seek recourse as Alison is advised to do. Third, a trend especially with second-hand car dealerships in

---

52 This also means, concomitantly, that if the consumer discovers a defect 6 months after the purchase, the burden of proving the defect existed at the time of purchase is reversed onto him or her, and he or she will likely struggle to overcome this evidential obstacle. Note that under the CPFTA, the shifting of the burden does not apply to (perishable) goods which are not intended to last longer than 6 months.
53 [2014] SGHC 71.
54 Ibid. A consumer purchased a second-hand hybrid car from a dealership, and obtained a discount off the purchase price in return for waiving the usual warranty to correct defects. The battery became defective after 2 months. The consumer sued, and the dealership refused to correct the defects, relying on the waiver. The court held that the rules of the CPTFA are mandatory and cannot be opted out of, and therefore required the dealership to make good on the battery.

Singapore is to sell on a consignment basis – that is the dealership acts not as principal, but agent for a private second-hand car seller. Such arrangements are properly c2c contracts and therefore fall outside the scope of the CPFTA, which regulate only b2c contracts: If this is the case, Alison can avail herself only of the SOGA framework and does not benefit from the favourable list of remedies under the CPFTA nor the presumption of defects within the 6-month framework.

Assuming Alison is successful in prosecuting her claim, she is entitled to the following. She may elect to have the defects in the car repaired or replaced at the seller's cost and within a reasonable period of time.[55] Alison's right to elect her remedy of choice is limited only insofar as such remedy is impossible or is disproportionate in cost, and the seller must not cause significant inconvenience to Alison.[56] The meaning of proportionality is hotly contested in the car industry. As mentioned, if the consumer deals directly with the manufacturer, he probably need not fret. The manufacturer usually has a ready stock of parts as well as an in-house servicing workshop. For reasons of cost as well as reputation, defects are therefore usually resolved without an inkling of dispute. If such is not the case, car dealers may be resistant to honour the consumer's election of repair or replacement on the basis of any arrangement it may have with workshops relative to manufacturer or third-party spare part suppliers.

What is reasonable time[57] is of course context-dependent, and factors may include the seriousness of the defects, as well as availability of spare parts, but also the inconvenience to Alison to make alternative daily travel arrangements. The CPFTA does not oblige the seller to provide a courtesy car during the period the remedy is effected, and the resultant inconvenience might shorten what might otherwise be a lengthier time for the seller to resolve the matter. Taking that into account, if Alison is not satisfied within a reasonable period of time, she may require the seller to reduce the price of the defective car, or to refund her the purchase price.[58] These rights and remedies may be enforced without recourse to the judicial system, except of course in the case of errant sellers.

(iii) Failure to meet emissions standards

As to the last point on the failure to meet regulatory emissions standards, the position is once again the same as under English law. Two additional points may be made. The first is that Alison could possibly and in addition claim under the common law against the seller for negligent or fraudulent misrepresentation, and have damages assessed on the basis of diminution of value. That having been said, the preferred route would be to claim under the CPFTA since it offers her the same and wider set of remedies. The second point to raise is that the result might

---

55 Supra fn 16, s 12C(1) CPFTA.
56 Ibid. s 12C(2), (3) and (4) CPFTA.
57 Ibid. s 12C(5) CPFTA.
58 Ibid. s 12D read with s 12E CPFTA.

be different if the claim was made by the manufacturer, but not Billy, or if done on a consignment basis, in that recourse might be had only if a warranty is in place, or where Alison had specifically intimated she wanted an environmentally friendly car (and therefore the car was not fit for purpose).

Scenario 2

Once again, recourse is to be had with the CPFTA. While there is no mention of digital goods or services in that statute, the interpretation section of the Act does state that goods can be intangible, and the definition of services is non-exhaustive and therefore does not exclude those provided in digital format or over the internet.[59] The provisions of the CPFTA are therefore prima facie applicable.

(i) Failure of the app and failure to patch the problem

Is the sports app of satisfactory quality? Arguably not. Its high price relative to other similar apps is perhaps indicative of the quality of service provision to be expected. The fact that it does not take his blood pressure is itself proof that it is not fit for purpose. Fitness for purpose in these types of situations must imply that the app does not compromise the functionality of other programmes, and this is clearly not the case here.

The issue is as regards the available remedies. Regardless of whether the update was requested for or pushed by the developer, it does not work as it should. In other words, repair is ineffective, and no further attempt is made by the developer to rectify the situation. Although David has the right to elect for replacement, this type of legal remedy is wholly irrelevant in the digital context (unless of course a corruption of the underlying code occurred during the downloading or installation process, by which a simple deletion and reinstallation ought to do the trick, without any fuss from the developer). Perhaps David could ask for a reduction in price, since although it does not take his blood pressure, it does monitor his heart rate. This seems the unlikely route since using this app does mean he cannot use other apps in his internet of things. Thus, it is open for David to request a refund from the developer for the full sum paid.

(ii) Interference with other apps/(iii) damage done to the Wi-Fi connector

That may leave David unsatisfied, given the loss and inconvenience he has suffered regarding his remote digital recording and central heating. Unfortunately, and unlike the recent English position, Singapore's statutory framework does not regulate the loss caused to other digital or non-digital goods and services by digital goods or services, like the other apps on the tablet as well as the Wi-Fi router.

---

59 Ibid. s 2 CPFTA.

The legal route open to David is to sue under the generally established common law rules on damages for breach of contract, subject to the rules on foreseeability and remoteness.

V. Recent issues in Singapore

Recent and sudden closures in the wellness,[60] travel,[61] bridal[62] and fitness[63] sectors, leaving hundreds of customers in a lurch, have also cast a bad light on the current state of consumer protection. The primary issue being the lack of protection for prepayment of packaged services in the event of the firm's liquidation. There has been discussion on protecting such consumers by requiring banks to relax their chargeback rules and assume the risk of liquidation as well as failures by traders to provide goods or services, akin to s 75 of the UK's Consumer Credit Act.[64] Given the current approach to consumer protection remains caveat emptor, and the government's concern not to overburden businesses, it is unlikely that Singapore will follow the UK's suit. Indeed, the government's response is to continue to emphasise consumer education as to the possible risks of transacting in the market.[65] One can expect, instead, encouragement of industry self- and co-regulation with CASE, and protecting prepayments through tried-and-tested devices like insurance, performance bonds and escrow accounts.[66]

---

60 Jessica Lim, "Bridal Salon's Sudden Closure: Packages of Disappointment", *Straits Times* (13 October 2015), and also Carolyn Quek, "Spa's Sudden Closure: 240 Turn to CASE", *Straits Times* (12 November 2009).
61 "Over 500 Complaints on Sudden Closure of Travel Agencies Since 2012: CASE", *Todayonline* (31 July 2015), www.todayonline.com/singapore/over-500-complaints-sudden-closure-travel-agencies-2012-case, accessed 20 May 2016.
62 Aw Cheng Wei and Janice Tai, "76 Couples Hit by Abrupt Closure of Bridal Salon", *Straits Times* (13 October 2015).
63 Kelly Ng, "MPs Lawyers Call for More Safeguards for Consumers Buying Prepaid Deals", *Todayonline* (23 July 2016) and "Banks' Credit Card Scheme Could Help California Fitness Client Get Refunds", *Todayonline* (24 July 2016), www.todayonline.com/singapore/mps-lawyers-call-more-safeguards-consumers-buying-prepaid-deals and www.todayonline.com/singapore/hope-some-california-fitness-members-who-want-money-back, accessed 24 July 2016.
64 UK Consumer Credit Act 1974, c39.
65 Cindy Keng for MTI, "Ministry CASE to Enhance Consumer Awareness of Prepayment Risks", Forum reply to the *Straits Times* (1 August 2016), www.straitstimes.com/forum/letters-in-print/ministry-case-to-enhance-consumer-awareness-of-prepayment-risks, accessed 1 August 2016.
66 Ibid.

8 Consumer sales law in the United Kingdom

Christian Twigg-Flesner

I. The UK consumer market

The United Kingdom has a buoyant consumer market, both with regard to face-to-face and online purchases of goods, services and digital content. The most recent statistics about consumer markets were the results of a survey published by the Department for Business, Innovation and Skills (BIS) in 2014.[1] The findings of this survey provide data about how consumers participate in the market, and the extent to which they encounter problems ('detriment').

With regard to the volume of consumer detriment, these statistics suggest the following: in 2014, there were approximately 18.7 million instances of consumer problems with goods and services, affecting just over one-fifth of consumers.[2] Most of these problems appear to be defective goods or poor service quality. BIS cautiously estimates that the overall value of consumer detriment in 2014 was in the region of £4.15 billion,[3] but it is also interesting to note that only about one-third of problems involved costs of more than £20 to a consumer (with an average financial loss of £223).[4] More recently, research for Citizens Advice[5] suggested that in 2015, there were 123 million incidents of consumer detriment,[6] with a total cost of at least £22.9 billion.[7] These figures are significantly higher than those in the BIS survey;[8] possible reasons identified by the researchers conducting the Citizen Advice survey included questions on how frequently a particular type of problem occurred.[9] However, it is also plausible that there has been a steady increase in instance of consumer detriment,[10] a possibility reinforced

---

1 BIS, *Consumer Engagement and Detriment Survey 2014*,
2 Ibid., p. 5.
3 Ibid.
4 Ibid.
5 Oxford Economics, *Consumer Detriment – Counting the Cost of Consumer Problems* (London: Citizens Advice, September 2016), p. 3.
6 The definition of 'consumer detriment' for the purposes of this survey was 'an incident that the survey respondent regarded as worthy of complaint'" (ibid., p. 7).
7 Ibid., p. 3.
8 A point noted in the Citizen Advice survey, e.g., at p. 12.
9 Ibid., p. 56/7.
10 Ibid., p. 57.

by the statistics presented by Ombudsman Services.[11] Their statistics suggest that consumers made 55 million complaints in 2016 (an increase of 3 million), with a further 75 million issues ignored as consumers thought complaining would be too burdensome.[12] This suggests that there is a continuing rise in consumer detriment issues, although the underlying reasons seem difficult to identify.

Goods vs services

The BIS survey findings suggest that one-third of consumers reporting problems had encountered a service-related issue (22% complaining about poor quality, and 10% stating that the trader had not performed the service at all).[13] Similarly, a further one-third of consumers reported problems with faulty or insufficiently durable goods. The largest proportion of goods-related problems related to household fittings and appliances.[14] The findings of the Citizens Advice Bueraux (CAB) research on consumer challenges[15] suggest that problems with second-hand cars are also a significant problem. The Oxford Economics report indicates that almost half of consumer detriment is caused by substandard services (41.8 million instances), followed by poor quality goods (18.2 million instances).[16]

Online vs offline

Online purchases of goods are now very popular, and this has also resulted in an increase in the volume of consumer problems with online purchases. The CAB statistics suggest that between 2004 and 2013, there has been a decline in the proportion of problems based on in-store purchases, but a rapid increase in the proportion of problems with online purchases.[17] More specifically, there are particular problems caused by the rise of online marketplaces and the so-called peer-to-peer economy (consumers selling goods to other consumers via online platforms such as eBay).[18]

II. Access to justice for consumers and enforcement of consumer law

This section will outline how consumers can enforce their legal rights, and also how the compliance with consumer law and enforcement is handled by various public agencies in the United Kingdom.

---

11 See Ombudsman Services, *Consumer Action Monitor* (January 2017).
12 Ibid., p. 1 and p. 10.
13 BIS, *Consumer Engagement and Detriment Survey*, p. 27.
14 Ibid., p. 29.
15 A. Pardoe and J. Plunkett, *Consumer Challenges 2015* (London: Citizens Advice, 2015).
16 Oxford Economics, *Consumer Detriment – Counting the Cost of Consumer Problems* (Citizens Advice, September 2016), p. 18.
17 A. Pardoe and J. Plunkett, *Consumer Challenges 2015* (London: Citizens Advice, 2015), p. 62.
18 Ibid., p. 64.

Individual enforcement by consumers

Research for Citizens Advice suggests that the majority of consumers who have encountered some detriment do not take any steps towards seeking redress at all,[19] with the Ombudsman Services report suggesting that only 37% of consumers raised a complaint.[20] Reasons why consumers choose not to take any kind of action include a feeling that the problem was not serious enough (22%), that it would take too long or be too complicated (11%), or that no positive outcome was expected (31%);[21] or that it was not worth the hassle.[22]

Both reports confirm that the majority of consumers who take action do so by contacting the relevant trader directly. In many cases, this informal approach will provide a solution which is acceptable to a consumer, and most businesses offer a clear customer complaints procedure through their overall policies.[23] However, if this fails, the consumer may wish to pursue additional steps. A trader who has failed to resolve a consumer complaint is now required to advise the consumer of the availability of an alternative dispute resolution mechanism which could consider their dispute,[24] as well as the EU's Online Dispute Resolution (ODR) platform.[25] Some trade associations provide such ADR schemes for their members, and the trader will have to comply with the trade association's obligations with regard to ADR procedures. If the trader is not a member of a trade association, then the trader needs to inform the consumer of an ADR body competent to deal with the consumer's complaint. However, there is no obligation on a trader (other than through the terms of his trade association membership) to use an ADR body.

Instead of using an ADR or ODR procedure, a consumer may wish to enforce their rights through the civil courts. If they wish to pursue their claim in court, the vast majority of consumer claims will be dealt with in the County Court, the lowest civil court in the English legal system, and assigned to the 'small claims track'. This is the usual track for claims with a value of up to £10,000. In order to start a claim, it is necessary to complete a claims form.[26] If the consumer has a claim for a fixed sum of money, this can be filed online.[27] If the claim is

---

19 Oxford Economics, *Consumer Detriment – Counting the Cost of Consumer Problems* (London: Citizens Advice, September 2016), p. 43, putting that figure at 55%.
20 Ombudsman Services, *Consumer Action Monitor* (January 2017), p. 2.
21 Oxford Economics, *Consumer Detriment – Counting the Cost of Consumer Problems* (London: Citizens Advice, September 2016), p. 46.
22 Ombudsman Services, *Consumer Action Monitor* (January 2017), p. 2 suggests that 44% thought it 'was not worth the hassle', and 28% 'could not be bothered' to complain.
23 There is an international standard on complaints handling and customer satisfaction: ISO 10002 (2014 version).
24 See Reg.19 of the Alternative Dispute Resolution for Consumer Disputes (Competent Authorities and Information) Regulations 2015 S.I. 2015/542, which implement Directive 2013/11/EU on alternative dispute resolution for consumer disputes.
25 Reg.19A, S.I. 2015/542. The ODR platform is based on Regulation 524/2013/EU on online dispute resolution for consumer disputes.
26 Available electronically at http://hmctsformfinder.justice.gov.uk/HMCTS/GetForm.do?court_forms_id=338.
27 Via www.moneyclaim.gov.uk/web/mcol/welcome.

defended, then the case is allocated to the small claims track and a hearing is fixed.[28] Although the hearing itself is a formal court hearing, it will be conducted in a more informal manner and the strict rules for hearings, presentation of cases and rules of evidence applicable in the High Court and above do not apply.[29] The judge in a small claims hearing takes quite an active role – he determines how to conduct the particular hearing fairly and may question witnesses directly.[30] Parties may be represented by a lawyer but this is not required, and the costs of legal representation cannot normally be recovered. A consumer who wins their case will receive back the court fee, and other expenses might also be recoverable. Should the consumer lose, they will not receive back the court fee but they will not usually be required to cover the costs incurred by the defendant except for items specified in CPR 27.14, including court fees paid by the defendant, as well as the cost of attending the hearing (CPR 27.14(2)(e)) and any expert fees (CPR 27.14(2)(f)).[31] In addition, if the claim was one for specific performance, a sum for legal advice may be recovered.[32] This could be significant if a consumer requests a remedy such as repair or replacement of faulty goods (see discussion of the relevant law below) as this is, in effect, a request for specific performance.

However, figures suggest that few consumers who complain about a problem in the first place will ultimately take court action: Citizens Advice put the figure at around 3%,[33] whereas the figures put forward by the Ombudsman Services suggest that 7% of those who complain go to the small claims track, and 3% to the High Court.[34]

Public enforcement

In addition to individual consumers asserting their rights in an informal or formal setting, the United Kingdom has a strong legal framework for the enforcement of consumer legislation by public bodies, as well as the private Consumers' Association ('Which?'). The rules for the enforcement of consumer law are found in Part 8 of the Enterprise Act 2002. There are 'general enforcers' (the Competition and Markets Authority and every local weights and measures authority,[35] usually

---

28 For an informative, if now dated, study of the small claims process, see J. Baldwin, *Small Claims in County Courts in England and Wales: The Bargain Basement of Civil Justice?* (Oxford: Clarendon Press, 1997).
29 The detailed rules for the small claims procedure are found in Part 27 of the Civil Procedure Rules (CPR), www.justice.gov.uk/courts/procedure-rules/civil/rules/part27, accessed 29 March 2016.
30 See CPR 27.8 on 'conduct of the hearing'.
31 The maximum amounts recoverable are fixed in Practice Direction 27: The daily rate for court attendance is capped at £95, and the maximum sum in respect of each expert is fixed at £750 (see paras 7.1–7.3 of the Practice Direction).
32 CPR 27.14(2)(b). The maximum amount is fixed at £260 (Practice Direction 27, para 7.2).
33 Oxford Economics,*Consumer Detriment – Counting the Cost of Consumer Problems* (London: Citizens Advice, September 2016), p. 44.
34 Ombudsman Services, *Consumer Action Monitor* (January 2017), p. 10.
35 S.213 Enterprise Act 2002.

known as 'Trading Standards Departments'), as well as designated enforcers. The focus of the enforcement scheme is to ensure compliance with consumer protection legislation in the first instance, but if this is not successful, an enforcer can take steps towards formal enforcement action, with the ultimate outcome being an enforcement order,[36] possibly combined with a requirement to take an 'enhanced consumer measure'.[37] However, a prior step will usually be for a trader subject to enforcement action to give an undertaking that the trader will cease any infringement of consumer protection legislation. Such undertakings may also be given to a court during enforcement proceedings.[38] Undertakings or enforcement orders are designed to stop a trader from engaging in conduct which would be an infringement of consumer protection rules, as well as not to continue or repeat an infringement already established. Since the enactment of the Consumer Rights Act 2015, an enforcement order can be accompanied by an enhanced consumer measure. There are three types of these measures: (1) redress (offering compensation or redress to consumers affected by an infringement),[39] (2) compliance (to prevent the risk/reduce the risk of occurrence or repetition of the infringement),[40] and (3) choice (measures to enable consumers to choose more effectively between different suppliers).[41] Enforcers are given extensive investigatory powers, now found in Schedule 5 of the Consumer Rights Act 2015.

III. The legal framework for consumer sales

In March 2015, the UK Parliament enacted the Consumer Rights Act 2015 (CRA), which is a major consolidation and simplification of some aspects of consumer law, including consumer sales law. Prior to the CRA, the legal rules dealing with consumer sales transactions were found in the Sale of Goods Act 1979, as amended, and other transactions for the supply of goods were governed by the Supply of Goods (Implied Terms) Act 1973 (for hire-purchase) and the Supply of Goods and Services Act 1982 (for hire and other supply transactions such as barter). The provisions on the quality and fitness requirements for goods ('conformity with the contract' requirements) and the associated remedies are now all found in chapter 2 of Part 1 of the CRA. This chapter applies to[42] (1) sales contracts (including contracts for goods to be manufactured or produced),[43] (2) contracts of hire,[44] (3) hire-purchase agreements[45] and (4) contracts for the

---

36 S.217 Enterprise Act 2002.
37 See ss.219A to 219C of the Enterprise Act 2002, inserted by the Consumer Rights Act 2015.
38 S.217(9) Enterprise Act 2002.
39 S.219A(2) Enterprise Act 2002.
40 S.219A(3) Enterprise Act 2002.
41 S.219A(4) Enterprise Act 2002.
42 S.3(2) CRA.
43 Further defined in s.5 CRA.
44 S.6 CRA.
45 S.7 CRA.

transfer of goods.[46] There is a separate chapter dealing with 'digital content' (Chapter 3), but if goods include digital content and there is a problem with that, then this is treated as an issue affecting the goods themselves.[47]

A contract must be between a trader ('a person acting for purposes relating to that person's trade, business, craft or profession, whether acting personally or through another person acting in the trader's name or on the trader's behalf'[48]) and a consumer ('an individual acting for purposes that are wholly or mainly outside that individual's trade, business, craft or profession'[49]).

Every contract to which Chapter 2 applies is 'to be treated as including a term' that the goods are of satisfactory quality,[50] fit for any particular purpose,[51] and that the goods correspond with any description.[52] Goods are of satisfactory quality if 'they meet the standard that a reasonable person would consider satisfactory, taking account of (a) any description of the goods, (b) the price or other consideration for the goods (if relevant), and (c) all the other relevant circumstances'.[53] These relevant circumstances include the state and condition of the goods, as well as (a) fitness for all the purposes for which goods of that kind are usually supplied; (b) appearance and finish; (c) freedom from minor defects; (d) safety; and (e) durability,[54] although other matters might also be relevant.[55] This does not cover any problems with the goods specifically drawn to the consumer's attention or, where the consumer examines the goods, which he ought to have discovered during that examination, in both cases before concluding the contract.[56] Finally, the relevant circumstances also include public statements made by the trader, the producer or their represensentatives, particularly in advertising or labelling.[57]

---

46 S.8 CRA. These contracts are primarily those where the consideration provided by the consumer is something other than payment of the price (primarily contracts of barter), but s.8(b) refers to a contract which 'for any other reason [is] not a sales contract or a hire-purchase agreement', which could apply to other contracts under which a trader transfers ownership in goods to a consumer.
47 S.16 CRA.
48 S.2(2) CRA.
49 S.2(3) CRA.
50 S.9 CRA.
51 S.10 CRA.
52 S.11 CRA.
53 S.9(2) CRA.
54 S.9(3) CRA.
55 Case law under the equivalent provisions of the Sale of Goods Act 1979 (which used to apply to consumer sales until 1 October 2015) had covered such factors as inaccurate or misleading instructions (*Wormell v R.H.M. Agriculture (East) Ltd.* [1987] 1 WLR 1091), compliance with technical standards (*Messer UK v Britvic* [2002] 2 Lloyd's Rep. 368) and energy efficiency ratings (*Jewson Ltd v Boyhan* [2004] 1 Lloyd's Rep. 505).
56 S.9(4)(a) and (b) CRA. S.9(4)(c) contains a similar exclusion in respect of problems apparent from a sample of the goods if this had been shown to the consumer before concluding the contract.
57 S.9(5)/(6) CRA. Exclusionary provisions for this are found in s.9(7) CRA.

If the consumer makes known to the trader any particular purpose for which the consumer requires the goods, then the goods must be reasonably fit for that purpose, even if this is not a purpose for which the goods are usually supplied.[58] However, this requirement does not apply where the consumer did not rely on the skill or judgement of the trader.[59]

Furthermore, goods must match any description and/or sample of the goods where the goods are sold by that description and/or sample.[60] In addition, all the pre-contractual information requirements under the Consumer Contracts (Information, Cancellation and Additional Charges) Regulations 2013, are also treated as included as a term of the contract.[61]

There are further provisions requiring correspondence of the goods supplied with any sample[62] or model[63] which the consumer has examined before concluding the contract.

There are three other requirements of note here: first, goods are deemed not to be in conformity with the contract where installation is part of the contract and the trader has installed the goods, but done so incorrectly.[64] Secondly, if goods include digital content and the digital content is not in conformity with the contract as required by Chapter 3 of Part 1 (the provisions of which are similar to those applicable to goods), then the goods themselves are treated as not being in conformity with the contract.[65] Finally, there is a requirement that the trader has the right to sell the goods (or transfer possession if the contract is one of hire) and that the goods are free from any charge or encumbrance.[66]

If the goods are not in conformity with the contract, there are a range of remedies available to a consumer, but different remedies are available for different instances of non-conformity, as summarised in table 8.1.[67]

In addition, a consumer can seek other remedies not provided for in the Act, including damages, but not to the extent that doing so would mean that the consumer would recover twice in respect of the same loss.[68]

First, there are three rights to reject the goods:[69] the 'short-term' right to reject within 30 days (see below), the 'final' right to reject, and right to reject for breach of the term included in the contract by s.17(1). There are no formal requirements for rejecting the goods, as long as it is sufficiently clear to the

---

58 S.10(1)–(3) CRA.
59 S.10(4) CRA.
60 S.11(1)–(3) CRA.
61 S.11(4) CRA and s.12(2) CRA.
62 S.13 CRA.
63 S.14 CRA.
64 S.15 CRA.
65 S.16 CRA.
66 S.17 CRA.
67 See C. Twigg-Flesner, R. Canavan and H. MacQueen, *Atiyah and Adams' Sale of Goods*, 13th ed. (London: Pearson, 2016), ch.22 p. 506.
68 S.19(11) CRA.
69 See s.20 CRA.

Table 8.1 Remedies in respect of goods

Non-conformity due to breach of	Rights (remedies)
• satisfactory quality (s.9) • fitness for particular purpose (s.10) • matching description (s.11) • matching sample (s.13) • matching model (s.14) • non-conformity of digital content (s.16)	Short-term right to reject Repair or replacement Price reduction Final right to reject (s.19(3))
• incorrect installation (s.15) • other contractual requirement	Repair or replacement Price reduction Final right to reject (s.19(4))
• pre-contractual information duties (s.12)	Recovery from trader amount of any costs incurred by consumer as a result of breach, up to the amount of price paid or value of other consideration given (s.19(5))
• right to supply (s.17(1))	Right to reject (not restricted by time limits) (s.19(6))

trader that the consumer is rejecting the goods.[70] A trader then has to give the consumer a refund,[71] which has to be done 'without undue delay', and no later than 14 days from when the trader agrees that the consumer is entitled to a refund.[72] After rejecting the goods, the consumer has to make the goods available for collection by the trader, or to return them if this has been agreed,[73] with the trader covering any reasonable costs of returning the goods. The time limit for the short-term right of rejection ends 30 days after the date of delivery. However, if a consumer asks for repair or replacement of the goods within the 30-day period, the countdown stops on that day and a 'waiting period' starts,[74] and this ends on the day the consumer receives back the repaired goods or a replacement.[75]

As an alternative to rejection, a consumer may be entitled to request a repair or replacement. However, the trader cannot be required to repair or replace an item if that is impossible, or if the remedy the consumer has requested is disproportionate to compared the other of those remedies (i.e. if repair was requested, the comparison is with replacement).[76] A remedy is disproportionate if it would

70 S.20(4)-(6) CRA.
71 S.20(7)(a) CRA.
72 S.20(15) CRA.
73 S.20(7)(b) CRA.
74 S.22(8)(a) CRA.
75 S.22(8)(b) CRA.
76 S.23(3) CRA.

impose unreasonable costs on the trader, taking into account (a) the value which the goods would have if they conformed to the contract, (b) the significance of the lack of conformity and (c) whether the other remedy could be effected without significant inconvenience to the consumer.[77] A remedy must be provided within a reasonable time and without significant inconvenience to the consumer.[78] The trader has to cover the relevant costs of providing the chosen remedy, including postage, materials and labour.[79]

A consumer is entitled to request a price reduction, or exercise the final right to reject (although not both) where[80]

1. The goods do not conform to the contract after *one* repair or replacement. This requires that the consumer has requested or agreed to repair or replacement, and the trader has delivered or made available goods to the consumer in response.[81]
2. The consumer is neither entitled to repair nor replacement (as per s.23(3)).
3. The trader is in breach of the requirement to provide the repair or replacement requested within a reasonable time and without significant inconvenience to the consumer.

'Price reduction' means that the price payable is reduced by an 'appropriate amount' including a reduction to zero.[82] If the consumer exercises the final right to reject, the trader has to provide a full refund, but after more than 6 months from delivery, a deduction from that refund may be made to reflect the period of time during which the consumer was able to use the goods.[83] However, in respect of motor vehicles, a deduction for use may be made at any point in time.

IV. Factual scenarios

Scenario 1

In this scenario, the contract of sale is between Billy (the trader) and Alison (the consumer). There are three distinct grounds for complaint for Alison, and this discussion will look at each of these separately. It must however be noted that in a situation such as this, all these complaints would be taken together to establish whether Alison has a claim against Billy, and what remedies Billy would have to provide.

---

77 S.23(4) CRA.
78 S.23(2)(a) CRA.
79 S.23(2)(b) CRA.
80 S.24(5) CRA.
81 If repair is carried out at the consumer's premises, this will be once the trader indicates that repairs are finished (s.24(6)(b)).
82 S.24(2).
83 S.24(8)–(10).

(i)(a) Brake and engine noise (new car)

The first complaint essentially relates to mechanical problems. The brakes have become more sluggish, and there is an unusual engine noise (although nothing is said about its potential cause). For Alison to have any recourse against Billy, there has to be a breach of at least one of the requirements as to goods under the CRA 2015. As explained above, s.9 CRA requires goods to be of satisfactory quality, and so it needs to be considered whether a reasonable person would regard this car as satisfactory. Bearing in mind the description of the goods ('a new car'),[84] the existence of what is at least one and probably two 'minor defects' (sluggish breaks and engine noise)[85] and the lack of durability as far as the brakes are concerned,[86] there is strong argument that the car is not of satisfactory quality. Moreover, the manufacturer's advertising campaign referred to 'top reliability', which should be taken into account as part of the overall assessment of whether the car is of satisfactory quality[87] – and even with such a general statement, a reasonable person would not accept quite a significant problem such as sluggish brakes – indeed, this could also raise safety concerns.[88] All of these factors taken together point towards the conclusion that the car is not of satisfactory quality, and that Alison should be entitled to a remedy in accordance with s.19 CRA.

Although it is likely that the car will not be of satisfactory quality which on its own would be sufficient to entitle Alison to the various remedies under the CRA, she also explained that she needed the car for particular types of journey, that is twice-daily 30-mile commute to and from work. Although she raised this primarily with regard to the car's fuel efficiency, it should also have been obvious to Billy that this particular purpose would be relevant to the car's general reliability. So if the brake problem and engine noise are caused because the car is only driven over relatively short distances, then Alison could additionally argue that the car was not reasonably fit for the particular purpose of being driven to and from work.[89]

From the foregoing, Alison should have little difficulty in establishing that the car was not in conformity with the contract as it was a 'new car', and (lack of satisfactory quality, and not reasonably fit for her particular purpose), so she will be entitled to one of the remedies under the CRA. The initial choice for Alison would be between the short-term right to reject, repair of the car or replacement.[90] As only 3 weeks have passed since the contract was made (and therefore since the date of delivery), the 30-day period during which the short-term right to reject is available has not yet expired, and Alison would be able to return the car for a full refund. Alternatively, Alison could consider having the car repaired

---

84 Cf. s.9(2) CRA.
85 Cf. s.9(3)(c) CRA.
86 Cf. s.9(3)(e) CRA.
87 Cf. s.9(5)/(6) CRA.
88 Cf. s.9(3)(d) CRA.
89 Cf. s.10 CRA.
90 S.19(3) CRA.

or replaced. A pre-condition to either remedy is that it must be 'possible'.[91] Replacement of a new car with another new unit of the same model would be possible. Repair of the faults in question would probably also be possible – the brakes might require adjustment and the engine noise might be the result of problem with the transmission system. Assuming that both remedies are possible, it also needs to be considered whether one would be regarded as disproportionate compared to the other. Billy, the trader, would no doubt seek to argue that it would be disproportionate to replace the car instead of repairing it, assuming that (i) the car has not dropped significantly in value merely because of the non-conformity, the non-conformities are easily repairable, and (ii) the repair could be effected without causing significant inconvenience to Alison (she could be provided with a courtesy car of the same make and model whilst her car is undergoing repairs). It would probably be significantly cheaper to repair the car then to supply Alison with a replacement, bearing in mind the rapid depreciation in value of any new car as soon as it has been brought into use.

So Alison could request repair initially. As only 3 weeks (21 days) have elapsed since the car was delivered, this request would mean that the 30-day period for the short-term right of rejection stops, and the so-called waiting period commences.[92] This period stops time running for the 30-day period whilst the car is being repaired, and it will restart once Alison receives back her car after repairs. At that point, the period will restart, with 9 days left to run – so if during those 9 days, it transpires that the repair has not solved the problem, then Alison could still exercise her short-term right of rejection. Had there only been fewer than 7 days of the 30-day period left when Alison requested repair, then she would have had a period of 7 days during which the short-term right to reject would have remained active. Had the non-conformity occurred after more than 30 days, then the short-term right of rejection would not have been available at all.

Alternatively, if Alison has requested a repair but this has not been carried out within a reasonable period of time or caused significant inconvenience to her, then she could move to the second-stage remedies of price reduction and the final right of rejection. The same would be possible if after one repair (or replacement), the car still was not in conformity with the contract.[93] Determining whether the repair was done within a reasonable period of time and without causing significant inconvenience requires taking account of the nature of the goods and the purposes for which the goods were acquired.[94] So if it took several weeks for Billy to repair the car and Alison was not provided with a courtesy car in the meantime (requiring her to rely on public transport, if available), then that would allow Alison to move to the second-stage remedies. On the facts given, Alison would, of course, have retained her short-term right of rejection until

---

91 S.23(3) CRA.
92 S.19(6) and (8) CRA.
93 S.24(5) CRA.
94 S.23(5) CRA.

after completion of the repairs, but if it is assumed that she did not have this right anymore when she requested a repair, the option of moving to the second-stage remedies is important. Once a reasonable period of time has passed and/or significant inconvenience caused, Alison could either ask for an appropriate reduction in the price or exercise the long-term right of rejection, presumably even if Billy eventually repairs the car (and that repair has cured the non-conformity). Although the CRA does not explicitly state this, the amount by which the price is reduced would probably be the same irrespective of whether repair has been effected eventually or not, and be a proportionate reduction of the price based on the actual value of the non-conforming goods as against the value of conforming goods.[95] On the other hand, if Alison chooses to exercise the long-term right of rejection, she will have to return the car but any refund she would be entitled to from Billy would be subject to a deduction for use to take into account the use she has had of the car[96] – and as noted earlier, in the case of a motor vehicle, such a deduction can be made at any time.[97]

Finally, in addition to any remedies claimed under the CRA, should Alison occur any additional losses as a result of the non-conformity, she might be able to claim damages under the relevant common law principles.[98]

(i)(b) Brake and engine noise (second-hand car)

The analysis described above would be different if the car was a second-hand car and 3 years old. The same legal principles set out above would apply, but their application might lead to a different outcome.

First, in applying the satisfactory quality test, account would be taken of the fact that the car in question is a second-hand car and 3 years old. Under the law in force prior to the CRA, it had already been established that with a second-hand car, it would be reasonable to make allowances for some minor defects, and therefore the overall expectations as to quality would be lower.[99] It might be necessary to produce evidence as to the likely faults which might arise with second-hand cars of that age: such cars are more likely to show signs of wear and tear and might more readily require repairs – something which a consumer might have to anticipate.[100] It is possible that this might mean that, despite having problems which would render a new car as unsatisfactory, the position would be different with a used car of this age. If that were so, it might be concluded that the car was

---

95 This point has not yet arisen before the English courts, nor has this issue been referred to the CJEU from another jurisdiction for a preliminary ruling on the interpretation of Art.3 of Directive 99/44/EC, to which these provisions in the CRA give effect.
96 S.24(8) CRA.
97 S.24(10)(a) and (12)–(13) CRA.
98 S.19(11) CRA. However, any common law right of termination for breach of condition would not be available in respect of any non-conformities as defined in the CRA.
99 See e.g. *Millars of Falkirk v Turpie* (1976) SLT 66 and *Thain v Anniesland* (1997) SLT Sh Ct 102.
100 Cf. *Thain v Anniesland* (1997) SLT Sh Ct 102.

of satisfactory quality despite the problems and that Alison would therefore not be entitled to a remedy.

As for the requirement that the car would have to be fit for Alison's particular purpose, s.10 CRA only requires that goods must be 'reasonably fit' for that purpose. If the problems are due to the car's age and second-hand nature, then it seems likely that that car would be regarded as reasonably fit for Alison's particular purpose, despite the problems.

It would therefore be more difficult for Alison to establish that the car is not in conformity with the contract, although it would not necessarily be impossible to do so.

If it is established that the second-hand car is not of satisfactory quality and/or not fit for purpose, then the remedies under the CRA would be available as outlined above. However, as the car is now a second-hand car, the remedy of 'replacement' would very probably not be available as it is generally assumed that this kind of remedy is not available with regard to second-hand goods.[101] However, the short-term right of rejection as well as repair and the other remedies would be available in the same way as explained above.

(ii) Higher-than-expected fuel consumption

A second complaint is that the car's fuel consumption is higher than expected. It would need to be considered whether this would also mean that the car is not in conformity with the contract. As explained earlier, each complaint is considered on its own terms; however, with a case such as this, all of these complaints would be taken together to establish whether the car was in conformity with the contract, and if not, then the remedies as discussed would be available (although there might be a different outcome than suggested in respect of the mechanical faults focused on above).

There are two key points to note: first, the car is advertised as a car with 'low fuel consumption', and secondly, Alison expressly asked whether the car would maintain its low fuel consumption when used in the way she intended to use the car, that is, for her daily commute. Also, Alison raises her concerns about fuel consumption by way of comparison with her previous car, but the fact that another car has lower fuel consumption would not inevitably mean that Alison's new car cannot be said to be a low-fuel-consumption car. But assuming that the Reliable R1 car does indeed fail to live up to its low-fuel-consumption promise, would this allow Alison to argue that the car is not in conformity with the contract?

Starting with satisfactory quality, the main reference to low fuel consumption is the producer's advertising campaign. This would be a public statement which could be taken into account in establishing whether a reasonable person would regard the car as satisfactory.[102] Billy might try to argue that Alison's decision

---

101 Cf. Recital 16 of the Consumer Sales Directive (99/44/EC), which states that 'Whereas the specific nature of second-hand goods makes it generally impossible to replace them; whereas therefore the consumer's right of replacement is generally not available for these goods'.
102 Cf. s.9(2) and(6) CRA.

to buy the car could not have been influenced by the advertising.[103] However, whilst it would be unrealistic to expect any car to use so little fuel that it could be driven the entire length of the United Kingdom, the claim that the car is a low-fuel-consumption car is likely to have been a relevant consideration, and there is no reason to treat that statement as a 'mere puff'. So, it would seem possible to argue that the car is not of satisfactory quality.

Alison also made her particular purpose known.[104] On the one hand, the car could be said to be reasonably fit for the purpose of being used for the daily commute (ignoring the mechanical faults), but it would seem to be taking too narrow a view of fitness for purpose if the high fuel consumption was not taken into account. It seems plausible to suggest that a car with a high fuel consumption for what is not an unusual purpose would not be reasonably fit for purpose. So on balance, it seems that Alison could establish a non-conformity on the basis of this complaint alone.

In terms of remedies, the same range of remedies as discussed above would be available, starting with the short-term right of rejection. However, for other remedies, it needs to be established whether the fuel consumption issue affects only Alison's car, or whether this is a general problem with this model. If it affects only Alison's car, then the cause of the problem would need to be identified. Doing so would determine whether repair or replacement would be possible, that is, whether the car could be modified to ensure low fuel consumption, or, if not, whether a replacement might be better (subject to the proportionality criterion discussed above). However, if this is a problem affecting this particular model of car, then Alison should exercise her short-term right of rejection. Were this not to be available (i.e. had this issue only arisen after more than 30 days since delivery), then the long-term right of rejection would seem to be the most appropriate remedy, subject to a deduction from any refund to reflect the period of use had. In such a situation, it might need to be considered whether Alison would have a claim for damages to reflect the additional fuel costs she incurred, and whether this could be set-off against any deduction Billy might wish to make.

(iii) Failure to meet emissions standards

The final complaint is that the car fails to meet emissions standards 'by a significant margin' (assuming that the news reports reflect accurate facts). It may be assumed that there is a general expectation that new cars would comply with the relevant emission standards, and so a reasonable person is unlikely to regard a new car which significantly fails to do so to be of satisfactory quality.[105] Such a

---

103 Cf. s.9(7)(c) CRA.
104 Cf.s.11 CRA.
105 Contrast this with *Jewson Ltd v Boyhan* [2004] 1 Lloyd's Rep. 505, a case decided under s.14(2) of the Sale of Goods Act 1979 which is a near-identical provision to s.9 CRA. In this case, heating boilers installed in a particular building failed to provide acceptable energy efficiency readings, but did so in other buildings, so there was no intrinsic problem

problem is presumably not easily rectifiable, so the only sensible remedy would be to reject the goods and terminate the contract, as previously discussed.

Scenario 2

The focus of David's complaints all centre around an application he bought and downloaded onto his tablet computer. The issue to consider here therefore concerns the liability of a supplier of digital content (software), which does not seem to be of an appropriate level of quality and has caused a number of problems.

The CRA introduced specific provisions on the quality and fitness for purpose of digital content and remedies into UK Law for the first time. These provisions are in Chapter 3 of Part 1 of the CRA and apply to contracts for the supply of digital content ('data which are produced and supplied in digital form'[106]) supplied for a price paid by the consumer.[107] There are then requirements that digital content must be of satisfactory quality,[108] fit for a particular purpose[109] and as described[110] comparable to the provisions for goods outlined above. Remedies are also similar, but are limited to repair and replacement,[111] as well price reduction,[112] but there is no right to reject.[113]

As David has paid for the app, his contract with the supplier is subject to the rules in Chapter 3. Their application to his various complaints will now be considered.

(i) Failure of the app and failure to patch the problem

The first issue focuses on the quality of the app itself and the fact that the patch (update) did not seem to solve the problem. Applying the satisfactory quality test, a reasonable person might regard this app as not being of satisfactory quality for the following reasons: first, the price would suggest that the application is of a certain level of quality which should at the very least ensure the uninterrupted functionality of its main features, but the blood pressure readings have failed.[114] Secondly, the purpose for which an app of this kind is usually supplied would be to transfer and record relevant health measurements from a device such as David's smartwatch to a tablet computer, but the failure to transfer blood

---

with those boilers. In our scenario, the emissions problem would be such an intrinsic problem.
106 S.2(9) CRA.
107 S.33(1) CRA.
108 S.34 CRA.
109 S.35 CRA.
110 S.36 CRA.
111 S.43 CRA.
112 S.44 CRA.
113 A full refund is available under s.45 CRA if the trader is in breach of the requirement that he must have the right to supply the content (s.41 CRA).
114 Cf. s.34(2)(b) CRA.

pressure readings would suggest that the app is not fit for such a purpose.[115] So David should be able to establish that the app/digital content was not of satisfactory quality. It is not entirely clear whether the update was sent at David's request (and could therefore be treated as a remedy provided to cure a non-conformity) or whether this was an automatic update. If the latter, then there is a requirement that updated ('modified') content also has to be in conformity with the contract, but the update has not solved the problem. If the initial update was provided at David's request, then this could be regarded as a 'repair' of the non-conformity[116] which has not resolved the problem – indeed, the problem continues to exist 6 months after it first occurred. This triggers David's right to a price reduction, because the trader has failed to repair the digital content within a reasonable period of time.[117] The price should therefore be reduced by an appropriate amount[118] (which can be up to the full amount of the price paid[119]).

(ii) Interference with other apps

The non-conforming app also seems to have affected the way other applications work, including the remote operation of his digital TV recorder and central heating system. The CRA contains a specific provision on damage caused by digital content to other digital content belonging to the consumer.[120] From the evidence provided, it seems that the sports app has indeed damaged the remote recording and central heating applications belonging to David.[121] David might be entitled to a remedy as a result, but this also requires David to establish that this damage is 'of a kind that would not have occurred if the trader had exercised reasonable care and skill'.[122] This provision is potentially problematic: the trader who supplied the app to David might not be the same business which created the app – for example, if this app was purchased from an online intermediary seller. In that case, there might be no room to argue that the intermediary had failed to exercise reasonable care and skill. However, assuming that the contract of supply is with the trader who created the app, the question of whether reasonable care and skill had been exercised can be considered. Here, it would seem to be a fairly strong argument to suggest that an application which interferes with other apps in this way had not been created with reasonable care and skill. If so, the available remedies are either repair of the damage within a reasonable period of time and without causing significant inconvenience,[123] or compensation for the damage

---

115 Cf. s.34(3)(a) CRA.
116 Cf. s.43 CRA.
117 Cf. s.44(3)(b) CRA.
118 S.44(1) CRA.
119 S.44(2) CRA.
120 S.46 CRA.
121 S.46(1)(b) and (c) CRA.
122 S.46(1)(d) CRA.
123 Cf. s.46(2)(a), (3) and (4) CRA.

with an 'appropriate payment'.[124] There is no guidance as to what issues this compensation payment might cover, and, indeed, whether the damages would follow a contract-based measure or a tort-law-based measure (bearing in mind that the test as to whether the trader is liable for damage effectively adopts a tort law standard akin to negligence), or be treated as a new type of compensation not based on either measure. As this provision is still very new (it took effect on 1 October 2015), there is as yet no reported case law on this section. In particular, it is unclear whether it might be possible to recover for the additional energy costs which David incurred due to the high setting of the thermostat on his central heating setting, or whether this loss would be regarded as too remote. If the measure of damages is contractual,[125] then the loss would have to

> fairly and reasonably be considered either arising naturally, i.e. according to the usual course of things, from such breach of contract itself, or such as may reasonably be supposed to have been in the contemplation of both parties, at the time they made the contract, as the probable result of the breach of it.

On that test, it seems unlikely that David would be able to recover for this additional loss, as this is neither naturally arising or reasonably foreseeable. If the measure is tort-based, then the principles of remoteness pertaining to pure economic loss could equally mean that David would not be able to recover.[126] However, if this form of compensation is treated as a statutory form of compensation, then it remains to be seen whether a more generous remoteness test might develop.

(iii) Damage done to the Wi-Fi connector

The second type of damage caused by the application is to the hardware on which the app was installed, that is David's tablet computer. This is damage which also falls within s.46 CRA (discussed in the previous section), for which a remedy may be available. According to s.46(2) CRA, the trader must either repair the damage or compensate the consumer with an appropriate payment. So, it would need to be established whether the Wi-Fi connector can be repaired – if this is possible, then it will be the trader's obligation to do so; otherwise, the trader has to pay compensation. If the Wi-Fi connector has been damaged permanently, then the tablet will have lost much of its functionality, so compensation might extend to the cost of a replacement tablet. However, as noted above, the scope of the remedies in this section remains unexplored at the time of writing.

---

124   S.46(2)(b) CRA.
125   On the basis of *Hadley v Baxendale* (1854) 9 Exch. 541 and related case law.
126   The additional costs would be regarded as 'pure economic loss' and therefore not be recoverable: *Spartan Steel & Alloys Ltd v Martin & Co (Contractors) Ltd.* [1973] 1 QB 27; *Murphy v Brentwood District Council* [1991] 1 AC 398.

V. Specific issues in the United Kingdom

The UK's legislation to protect consumers against poor quality goods, services and digital content and the associated remedies is robust on paper and covers most eventualities that might arise. Nevertheless, the volume of consumer detriment and the number of complaints seems to be increasing steadily. The reasons for this are yet to be probed fully – it is noteworthy that Ombudsman Services reported that 41% of consumers who took action voiced their displeasure via social media.[127] The UK's main concern, therefore, is not the quality of its consumer protection legislation; rather, the level of compliance by traders and the associated difficulties consumers face in enforcing their rights would seem to be of particular concern. Despite improvements made to the enforcement infrastructure and the range of avenues open to consumers wishing to seek redress, the number of unresolved consumer problems seems surprisingly high. As noted, the United Kingdom has strong enforcement powers for its regulators and enforcers, but the extent to which these are utilised successfully remains unclear.

---

127 Ombudsman Services, *Consumer Action Monitor* (January 2017), p. 10.

9 Consumer sales law in the United States

Larry A. DiMatteo

Introduction

United States (US) consumer sales law will be examined to provide a descriptive review, as well as providing some normative thoughts. The chapter concludes the following: (1) The US does not have a separate, holistic consumer sales law regime, but the answer is a bit more nuanced in that consumers are given protective status through a mix of laws and regulations despite the lack of a specialised consumer sales law. (2) Consumers are protected by implied warranties, but they are easily disclaimable, and sellers generally impose rigid notification of defect requirements that are generally enforced. Certification of non-use of child or prison labour and environmental compliance are left to non-legal market sanctions, such as 'watchdog' groups. (3) Generally, the remedial regime offered by the Uniform Commercial Code and common law of contracts has proven sufficient in the consumer realm. However, due to the high cost of litigation, additional protections, such as statutory penalties are necessary as an alternative means of consumer protection and as an indirect means of standard terms regulation. (4) Outside of child pornography laws, there is little in the way of digital content regulation due to the US Constitutions' freedom of speech rights; however, federal law does impose some responsibilities on Internet Service Providers, along with a broad exemption from liability for digital content.[1] (5) US common law has yet to effectively deal with the problems related to network contracting. The rules of privity of contract should be reviewed just, as they were for products liability in the early part of the twentieth century, to allow downstream purchasers or users to pursue claims against upstream suppliers and providers. (6) The 'product' of extended warranties is a multi-billion-dollar industry that is unregulated in the US and has been subject to abuse.[2]

---

1 See, e.g., Digital Millennium Copyright Act (DMCA), 112 Stat. 2860, Public No. 105–304 (1998).
2 See, Better Business Bureau, *Vehicle Service Contract Industry: How Consumers Lost Millions of Dollars*, http://stlouis.bbb.org/storage/142/documents/vehicleservicecontractstudy2011.pdf; Money Crashers, "Six Reasons Why You Should Never Purchase an Extended Warranty", *U.S. News & World Report* (24 April 2012) (warranties are not cost-effective; necessity of repairs is

This review will focus on consumer contracts in the area of sales of goods or B2C; however, the distinction between the sale and supply of digital content has become increasingly blurred due to the commodification of information. Over the last few decades, there has been an acceleration of the commodification of information most noticeably the sale of consumer sourced personal information. Thus, the value and transferability of databases have increased many folds over the years. In addition, the distinction between sale and licence continues to be debated in relationship to software, shareware and other such 'goods'. More recently, the expanded scope and sophistication of internet marketing and platforms have created a virtual marketplace that targets consumer tastes and preferences in a way that traditional sale of goods and advertising are unable to do. The explosion of internet platforms for the direct sale of goods, services and digital content poses many new issues for consumer contract law and consumer protection. The arrival of platforms as 'intermediaries' has blurred the lines between sellers-providers and consumers-users.

I. The US consumer market

In 2012, the US consumer goods market was the largest in the world, with more than 3.6 million retail establishments' total sales reaching $2.5 trillion.[3] The Federal Trade Commission (FTC) conducts an annual survey, through its Bureau of Consumer Protection (BCP), of consumer complaints relating to the sale of goods and services. The FTC BCP's stated purpose is to stop unfair, deceptive and fraudulent business practices by: (1) collecting complaints and conducting investigations; (2) suing companies and people that break the law; (3) developing rules to maintain a fair marketplace and (4) educating consumers and businesses about their rights and responsibilities. The collection of consumer complaints is used to bring enforcement actions and is shared with law enforcement agencies worldwide to assist them in the enforcement of law.[4]

A list of the most frequent consumer complaints gives a quick sense of the BCP's priorities in recent times. In 2009, the top nine categories of consumer complaints are listed in Table 9.1.[5]

The survey shows identity theft as by far the largest area of complaints, making up 21% of all consumer complaints. An aggregation of internet-related categories – internet services and internet auctions – total 10% of all complaints. However, the category of 'Computer Equipment and Software' registered only

---

rare), http://money.usnews.com/money/blogs/my-money/2012/04/24/6-reasons-why-you-should-never-purchase-an-extended-warranty.
3 See Select USA, *US Department of Commerce*, http://selectusa.commerce.gov/industry-snapshots/consumer-goods-industry-united-states.html.
4 See FTC, *About the Consumer Protection Bureau*, www.ftc.gov/about-ftc/bureaus-offices/bureau-consumer-protection/about-bureau-consumer-protection.
5 A complete list of complaints can be found at: www.ftc.gov/sentinel/reports/sentinel-annual-reports/sentinel-cy2009.pdf.

Table 9.1 Complaint categories[1] 1 January 1–December 31, 2009 Federal Trade Commission (Released February 2010)

Rank	Category	No. of Complaints	Percentages
1	Identity Theft	278,078	21%
2	Debt Collection	119,549	9%
3	Internet Services[2]	83,067	6%
4	Shop-at-Home/Catalog Sales[3]	74,581	6%
5	Foreign Money Offers/Counterfeit Check Scams	61,736	5%
6	Internet Auction[4]	57,821	4%
7	Credit Cards	45,203	3%
8	Prizes/Sweepstakes/Lotteries	41,763	3%
9	Advance-Fee Loans & Credit Protection/Repair	41,448	3%

[1] Federal Trade Commission, *Consumer Sentinel Network, Data Book* (January–December 2015), p. 6, available at www.ftc.gov/reports/consumer-sentinel-network-data-book-january-december-2015.
[2] Internet services includes problems with trial offers from Internet Service Providers (ISPs); difficulty cancelling an ISP account; issues with Internet entertainment services; undisclosed charges; website design and hosting services; spyware, adware and malware issues.
[3] Shop-at-Home and catalog sales includes problems, such as undisclosed costs, failure to deliver on time, non-delivery and refusal to honour a guarantee, with purchases made via the internet (not including auction sales), telephone or mail.
[4] Internet auction includes problems with non-delivery or late delivery of goods; delivery of goods that are less valuable than advertised; failure to disclose all the relevant information about the product or terms of the sale.

22,621 or 2% of all complaints.[6] In the calendar year 2015, the number of complaints in this category fell to 8,119 or less than 1%. The top complaint categories for the calendar year of 2015 are listed below (see Table 9.2) and can be used to spot trends over the last 6 years (2009–2015).

In comparing 2009 with the 2015 list of consumer complaints, a number of surprising and not so surprising outcomes can be seen.[7] The explosion of complaints relating to debt collection rose from 119,549 complaints or 9% of all consumer complaints to 897,655, or 29% of all complaints. This was most likely the product of the 2008 financial crisis that reflected high levels of consumer debt and the inability of many consumers to repay personal debt

6 Computer Equipment and Software: includes problems with computer software, hardware and computer equipment purchases, unwanted or unauthorised software installations, and downloads.
7 The complaints categories on the 2015 list that did not rank highly (less than 2% of all complaints included): (1) Credit Bureaus, Information Furnishers and Report Users (43,939); (2) Credit Cards (37,750); 3) Health Care (34,669); (4) Investment-Related Complaints (26,453); (5) Foreign Money Offers and Counterfeit Check Scams (25,3240; (6) Advance Payments Credit Services (24,433); (7) Travel, Vacations, and Timeshare Plans (24,171); and (8) Business/Job Opportunities (17,314).

Table 9.2 Complaint categories[1] 1 January 1–December 31, 2015 Federal Trade Commission (Released February 2016)

Rank	Category	Complaints	%
1	Debt Collection	897,655	29%
2	Identity Theft	490,220	16%
3	Impostor Scams	353,770	11%
4	Telephone/Mobile Services	275,754	9%
5	Prizes, Sweepstakes & Lotteries	140,136	5%
6	Banks and Lenders	131,875	4%
7	Shop-at-Home/Catalog Sales	96,363	3%
8	Auto-Related Complaints	93,917	3%
9	Television/Electronic Media	47,728	2%

[1] Federal Trade Commission, *Consumer Sentinel Network, Data Book* (January–December 2015), p. 6, available at www.ftc.gov/reports/consumer-sentinel-network-data-book-january-december-2015.

(most noticeably, credit card debts and home loans). Identity theft complaints remained high, but as a percentage decreased from 21% to 16% of all complaints. Most interestingly, a new category of 'imposter scams' made the list as the third largest category, making up 9% of all complaints. Surprisingly, complaints related to Internet services and auctions fell off the list with only 2,430 complaints or far less than 1% of all complaints, although complaints related to telephone and mobile services appear for the first time at number 4, making up 9% of all complaints. This is likely a reflection of the rise in popularity of smartphones as the most favoured type of electronic device. Finally shop-at-home and catalog sales dropped by 50% from 6% to 3% of all complaints, from number 4 to number 7 on the list.

What should not be lost in the comparison is the tremendous increase of total consumer complaints from 1,330,426 in 2009 to 3,083,379 in 2015, or a 232% rise. If we expand the longitudinal comparison to 10 years and then to 15 years, the total numbers of complaints starting at 906,929 in 2006 and 325,519 in 2001. This translates to an increase of 279% over the last 10 years and 947% over the last 15 years. In real numbers, there has been a rapid rise in the number of consumer complaints, but the rate of growth has slowed, using the 15-year comparison, the numbers of complaint increased on an annual basis of 63%, while the rate of growth over the last 10 years has been 27.9%. But, when viewing the rate of growth over the last 5 years (2011–2015), the rate of growth has been accelerating again (210% over 5 years) at the rate of 42% per annum. What are the causes of the rapid rise in consumer complaints and the rising growth rate over the last 5 years? A number of causal connections that seem plausible include heightened enforcement (Obama Administration); economic recovery; new laws and regulations; and greater dissemination of information (internet, websites).

Table 9.3 categorises fraud complaints by method of contact – telephone, e-mail, internet (website) and ordinary mail. Counter-intuitively, over a 3-year

150   *Larry A. DiMatteo*

Table 9.3 Fraud complaints by company's method of contacting consumers[1] (Calendar Years 2013–2015)

Contact Method	2013 Complaints/%	2014 Complaints/%	2015 Complaints/%
Phone	230,462 41%	386,807 54%	485,481 75%
E-Mail	184,469 32%	166,545 23%	54,089 8%
Internet/Website	82,757 15%	79,900 11%	39,728 6%
Mail	29,089 5%	29,113 4%	28,127 4%
Others	41,878 7%	48,143 7%	43,392 7%
Total	568,655	710,508	650,817

[1] Ibid at p. 9.

period (2013–2015), there has been a dramatic rise in fraud complaints in which the contact method was by telephone (41% to 75%), a precipitous drop of complaints related to frauds committed via e-mail (32% to 8%) and through internet websites (15% to 6%). Plausible explanations include the shifting of communication preferences from e-mail to texting via smartphones, as well as heightened awareness and increased filtering against unwanted e-mails or spam and increased security to prevent the infection of computers by viruses transmitted via e-mail.

II. Access to justice for consumers and enforcement of consumer law

American consumers are protected from unsafe products, fraud, deceptive advertising and unfair business practices through mandates given to the Federal Trade Commission (FTC) and Consumer Product Safety Commission (CPSC), as well as a mixture of national, state and local governmental laws and the existence of private rights of action. These public and private rights both protect consumers and, at a formal level, equip them with the knowledge needed to protect their interests. Although US mechanisms for consumer protection often exist separately from each other, what the overall scheme lacks in centralization, it gains in depth and variety of protections. Its strength is the array of governmental actors, formal legal rights, and remedies available to consumers. Its weakness lies in the reality of unequal access to the courts.

Given, the large, dynamic, innovation-driven and diversified nature of the US economy, consumer contract regulation suffers from the duality of the need for simplified legal structures and the complexity of the regulatory environment. The result is a fragmentation of the government among a multitude of regulatory authorities and government agencies (federal-state). The regulatory framework is a mix of freedom of contract norms, government regulation, third-party governance (watchdogs) and self-regulation. I have previously stated that the diversification of the consumer marketplace with the rise of the share or gig economy has shown the strengths and weaknesses of the American regulatory system:

> The sharing economy continues to evolve and present potential legal issues for regulatory and private law. American law on the subject is fragmented between federal and state regulatory authorities, as well as by private law, mainly tort, property, and contract law found in the independent common laws of each state. The types of regulations include government regulation, self-regulation (private), and non-regulation.[8]

The regulation of the share economy, especially electronic platforms, as with other areas of consumer protection, have come at all levels of government – local ordinances, federal and state regulatory agencies, and through the federal and state court systems.

Individual enforcement by consumers

One problem facing consumer rights victims is the relatively small amount of economic damages, they suffer as a result of a company's improper conduct. When a consumer falls victim to fraud by purchasing a product or service that does not measure up to the seller's promises, the consumer may suffer a loss equal to the amount paid, and perhaps some incidental expenses as well. But in all likelihood, the loss to the consumer will represent only a fraction of the amount of money it would take to bring a lawsuit against the seller. Consumers have the option of filing a complaint with federal or state authorities in an attempt to have sanctions brought against a fraudulent company, but this does not allow consumers to recover damages.

A class action lawsuit tips the balance of power in favour of the consumer. Consumers whose rights have been violated can join together with others to merge their claims against the same manufacturer-seller (consumers are able 'opt-out' and pursue their claims individually). Due to the economy of scale that exists with a class action lawsuit, a group of victims can present a serious litigation threat to even the largest corporations. The nature of the claim will determine its likelihood of being certified by the courts. For example, certification of class action lawsuits for common law fraud is difficult because US courts require a high degree of commonality among all the plaintiffs' claims in order for the class lawsuit to proceed.[9]

Some federal and state statutes provide private standing to sue. There is no private right of action under the Federal Trade Act, although there are private

---

8 L. DiMatteo, "Regulation of the Share Economy: A Consistently Changing Environment" in R. Schulze and D. Staudenmayer (eds.), *Digital Revolution: Challenges for Contract Law in Practice* (United Kingdom: Nomos & Hart, 2016), p. 89.
9 Federal Rules of Civil Procedure, Rule 23.

rights under the more specific statutes enforced by the FTC and the Bureau of Consumer Financial Protection. Each state also has consumer protection laws, which are modelled after the Federal Trade Commission Act, prohibiting 'unfair and deceptive' trade practices. These state laws normally allow consumers to sue for damages and injunctive relief.

Public enforcement

The Consumer Product Safety Commission (CPSC) was established by the Consumer Product Safety Act of 1972, which defines CPSC's basic authority and authorises the agency to develop product standards and pursue recalls and bans on defective or unsafe products. CPSC staff promotes safety by monitoring or providing technical support for voluntary standards activities for a wide range of consumer products. Through collaboration with voluntary standard organisations, such as the American National Standards Institute (ANSI) and Underwriters Laboratories (UL), the CPSC develops and advances safety standards for consumer products. In many cases, these standards bring industry groups, government agencies and consumer groups together to agree on best consumer product safety practices. Congress provided the Commission authority to enact regulations in the area of consumer product safety. By law, the Commission must follow a standard process for federal government rulemaking, known as the Administrative Procedure Act (APA). The APA requires the Commission to solicit input from the public on proposed regulations and to respond to public comments in issuing its regulations.

The FTC is the main federal agency charged with policing the consumer marketplace and to prevent fraud and advantage taking. It derives its consumer protection authority primarily from Section 5(a) of the FTC Act,[10] which prohibits 'unfair or deceptive acts or practices in or affecting commerce'. According to the FTC, deception occurs when there is a material representation, omission or practice that is likely to mislead a consumer who is acting reasonably under the circumstances. Unfair practices are those, which cause, or are likely to cause, reasonably unavoidable and substantial injury to consumers without any offsetting countervailing benefits to consumers or market competition. In addition to its authority under Section 5(a), the FTC has enforcement and administrative abilities under 46 other statutes, 37 of which relate to the FTC's consumer protection mission, such as the Consumer Credit Protection Act, Truth in Lending Act, the Fair Debt Collection Practices Act, the Consumer Leasing Act, the Equal Credit Opportunity Act, the Electronic Funds Transfer Act, the Fair Credit Reporting Act and the Children's Online Privacy Protection Act.[11]

---

10 5 U.S.C. § 45(a)(1).
11 S.W. Waller, J. Brady and R.J. Acosta, *Consumer Protection in the US: An Overview*, www.luc.edu/media/lucedu/law/centers/antitrust/pdfs/publications/workingpapers/USConsumerProtectionFormatted.pdf.

The newly created Consumer Financial Protection Bureau (CFPB)[12] has also attempted to buttress informed consumer consent with its enforcement of the Credit Card Act of 2009. The Act provides that credit card holders must at least be given *notice* of substantial changes to their agreements, along with notice of their right to terminate prior to the changes' activation, for those modifications to be valid. The Bureau is charged with

> Conducting financial education programs; collecting, investigating, and responding to consumer complaints; collecting, researching, monitoring, and publishing information relevant to the functioning of markets for consumer financial products and services to identify risks to consumers and the proper functioning of such markets; supervising covered persons for compliance with Federal consumer financial law; and issuing rules, orders, and guidance implementing Federal consumer financial law.[13]

Although the CFPB's main mission is to prevent predatory lending and other consumer abuse relating to finance and lending, the full scope of its regulatory powers is still to be determined.

III. Legal framework for consumer sales

A brief review of the UK Consumer Rights Act of 2015 will provide an avenue to compare American and UK consumer sales laws.[14] In March 2015, the UK Parliament enacted the Consumer Rights Act 2015 (CRA), which is a major consolidation of consumer law. In some areas, the CRA supplants the Sale of Goods Act 1979. For example, quality of goods and related remedies are found in Chapter 2 of Part 1 of the CRA.[15] There is a separate chapter dealing with digital content (Chapter 3) that provides that if goods include digital content and proves to be defective, then the defect in the digital content is to be treated as an issue affecting the goods themselves.[16]

Goods are of satisfactory quality if 'they meet the standard that a reasonable person would consider satisfactory, taking account of (a) any description of the goods, (b) the price or other consideration for the goods (if relevant), and (c) all the other relevant circumstances'.[17] Relevant circumstances include the state and condition of the goods, as well as (a) fitness for all the purposes for which goods of that kind are usually supplied; (b) appearance and finish; (c) freedom from

---

12 Dodd-Frank Wall Street Reform and Consumer Protection Act, H.R. 4173 §1011(a), 111th Cong. (2nd Sess. 2010).
13 §1021(c)(1–5).
14 For a critical review of EU consumer contract law see, Oren Bar-Gill and Omri Ben-Shahar, "Regulatory Techniques in Consumer Protection: A Critique of European Consumer Contract Law" (2013) 50 *Common Market Law Review* 109.
15 S.3(2) CRA.
16 S.16 CRA.
17 S.9(2) CRA.

minor defects; (d) safety; and (e) durability,[18] The relevant circumstances include public statements made by the trader, the producer or their represensentatives, particularly in advertising or labelling.[19] If the consumer makes known to the trader any particular purpose for which the consumer requires the goods, then the goods must be reasonably fit for that purpose, even if this is not a purpose for which the goods are usually supplied.[20]

The US has no such counterpart to the CRA, at least not at the federal level. There are a number of underlying reasons that help explain the current regulatory make-up and lack of consumer rules in certain areas. The shortfall of consumer contract regulation is exemplified by certain themes and myths that underscore the American view of such regulations including, the curse of freedom of contract and American individualism, as well as market-legal illusions. The list of illusions include the myth that all market failures are minimised by sophisticated buyers that force market corrections toward efficiency; illusion of the rational consumer; and illusion of consent in standard form contracting. Nonetheless, many of the protections in the CRA are found in the mix of federal and state-level regulations in the US.

Examples of the fragmentary nature of American consumer protection can be seen in recent examples of intervention in the marketplace, the means of the intervention and the sources of the interventions:

- Federal Trade Commission (FTC) Rule Making: Funeral Rule, which requires funeral directors to disclose price and other information about goods and services; Cooling-Off Rule, which gives consumers three days to cancel sales for $25 or more made away from the seller's place of business; and the Used Car Rule, which requires dealers to post on each used car a 'Buyers Guide' disclosing warranty and other important information.
- Do-Not-Call Implementation Act,[21] which allows individuals to register to block receiving unsolicited phone calls.
- State regulatory authorities, such as in the case of *Berwick v. Uber Technologies*,[22] where the California Labor Commissioner's Office ruled that Uber drivers were employees deserving of workplace protections.[23]
- Local ordinances, such as the new City of Santa Monica law regulating house sharing (renting) made famous by the Airbnb online platform.

---

18 S.9(3) CRA.
19 S.9(5)/(6) CRA. Exclusionary provisions for this are found in s.9(7) CRA.
20 S.10(1)–(3) CRA.
21 See D.C. Nelson, "The Do-Not-Call Implementation Act: Legislating the Sound of Silence" (2003) 16 *Loyola Consumer Law Review* 63.
22 Case No. 11–46739, Labor Commissioner State of California (3 June 2015). See also, *O'Connor v. Uber Technologies, Inc.*, 2015 WL 1069092 (N.D. Cal. Mar. 11, 2015); *Cotter v. Lyft, Inc.*, 2015 WL 1062407 (N.D. Cal. Mar. 11, 2015).
23 See generally, *Restatement (Second) of Agency* § 220(2) (a party's right to or actual control of work activities of another party characterizes the employment relationship).

- Consumer Financial Protection Bureau (CFPB) established in 2012,[24] to regulate consumer-financing contracts.
- State and local consumer protection bureaus and offices.
- The Better Business Bureau (BBB) offers programmes focusing on consumer protection for sales and services sold on the Internet at www.bbbonline.org and Direct Marketing Association at www.the-dma.org/channels/consumers.shtml.
- Using existing legal constructs, such as, contract, privacy, fraud, trespass and property in the pursuit of civil litigation.
- Small claims court is a simplified civil court that exists in almost every state to resolve disputes under a certain dollar amount set by law.

American standard terms regulation

In the US, the idea of a separate consumer contract law has been rejected. However, in the sale of goods, there is what is known as the merchant-consumer distinction found in Article 2 of the Uniform Commercial Code (UCC). Karl Llewellyn the drafter of Article 2 (Sale of Goods) wanted to have separate rules for business transactions and consumer transactions, as well as, having business sales disputes decided by specialised 'merchant courts'. The drafting committee rejected both of those ideas. However, Llewellyn was able to write some sales law rules that reflected the power discrepancies often found in B2C transactions. In some areas, Article 2 provides added protections for consumers, and in other cases, it provides rules that only pertain to merchants. A merchant is defined in Section 2–204(1) as

> a person who deals in goods of the kind or otherwise by his occupation holds himself out as having knowledge or skill peculiar to the practices or goods involved in the transaction or to whom such knowledge or skill may be attributed by his employment of an agent or broker or other intermediary who by his occupation holds himself out as having such knowledge or skill.

Therefore, in some situations a person may be acting as a merchant and in other situations the person would be considered as a consumer.

UCC consumer rules

As noted above, Karl Llewellyn drafted a number of consumer rules into Article 2 of the UCC. In the sale of goods, a common scenario involves an exchange of forms or what is referred to as the battle of the forms. In the B2B situation,

---

24 The CFPB was the centerpiece of the *Dodd – Frank Wall Street Reform and Consumer Protection Act*, P.L. 111–203, 124 Stat. 1955 (21 July 2010).

Section 2–207 holds that despite the existence of conflicting terms between the forms an enforceable contract is formed with the additional terms of the offeree entering the contract unless there is a timely rejection by the offeror. However, in a B2C transaction, Section 2–207 requires that the consumer must expressly agree to any additional or different terms, in an exchange of forms situation. Other explicitly pro-consumer provisions found in Article 2 include:

- Section 2–312 (express warranty): 'In the case of consumer goods sold by a merchant with respect to such goods, the description affirms that the goods are fit for the ordinary purposes for which such goods are used'.
- Section 2–719 (limitation of remedies): 'Limitation of consequential damages for injury to the person in the case of consumer goods is prima facie unconscionable but limitation of damages where the loss is commercial is not'.

However, except for these few exceptions in the law of sale of goods, and specific consumer protection laws, there is no general law of consumer contracts.

Enforceability of standard terms in consumer contracts

Standard terms are considered to be a necessary consequence of a mass-market economy; anything else would create prohibitive transaction costs, especially in the market for fungible goods sold in regional, national, and international markets. However, 'the consensus in American academic thought is that the reasons for enforcing terms in a standard from contract as written must be different from the usual reasons for enforcing contracts as agreed upon'.[25] If some standard terms are unenforceable, the question becomes what is the appropriate regulatory mechanism: statutory law (administrative authorities), courts or the markets.[26] The following list shows that such regulation comes from different authorities.

- An overly one-sided contract clause can be held to be unconscionable under contract law by a federal or state court (UCC and common law).[27]
- The Federal Trade Commission (FTC) voided a so-called gag clause, prohibiting consumers from posting negative reviews and testimonials online relating to a manufacturer or seller's products.
- An arbitration clause in consumer contract that included a class action lawsuit waiver held to be unenforceable.[28]
- Federal Communications Commission (FCC) issued a Citation and Order against Lyft for violating the Telephone Consumer Protection Act (TCPA) and invalidating its contract term that was labelled as an 'unsubscribe clause'.[29]

---

25 William Whitford, "Contract Law and the Control of Standardised Terms in Consumer Contracts: An American Report" (1995) 3 *European Review of Private Law* 193, 193.
26 Ibid., at 194.
27 UCC §2–302; *Restatement (Second) of Contracts* §208 (1981).
28 *Mohamed v. Uber*; *Gillette v. Uber*.
29 Federal Communications Commission DA 15-997, *In the Matter of Lyft, Inc.* (Adopted 11 September 2015).

To receive the service, the consumer-users had to agree to receive marketing materials via e-mail, text message, and telephone calls, if they selected the unsubscribe option their service was terminated.
- The FTC's Bureau of Consumer Protection stops unfair, deceptive and fraudulent business practices by collecting complaints and conducting investigations, suing companies and people that break the law, develop rules to maintain a fair marketplace, and educate consumers and businesses about their rights and responsibilities.

Highly scrutinised consumer contract terms

The 'discovery' of the 1925 Federal Arbitration Act[30] in the 1980s led to the invalidating of state laws voiding arbitration clauses and re-stated that as a matter of US public policy, arbitration is the preferred means of dispute resolution. Nonetheless, arbitration clauses in consumer contracts remain subject to attack. For example, states have different requirements for the enforceability of arbitration clauses – some have no special requirements, while others, like California, require consumers to knowingly waive their right to a jury trial. More recently, the Bureau of Consumer Financial Protection, on May 5, 2016, issued a proposed rule invalidating arbitration clauses in some consumer lending and financial contracts. The underlying rationale for the rule was stated as:

> It would prohibit providers from using a pre-dispute arbitration agreement to block consumer class actions in court and would require providers to insert language into their arbitration agreements reflecting this limitation. This proposal is based on the Bureau's preliminary findings – which are consistent with the study that pre-dispute arbitration agreements are being widely used to prevent consumers from seeking relief from legal violations on a class basis, and that consumers rarely file individual lawsuits or arbitration cases to obtain such relief.[31]

Forum selection clauses are generally enforced,[32] but some courts have invalidated them under the doctrine of unconscionability, using the Supreme Court's utterance that such clauses may be unenforceable when the selection leaves a

---

30 Federal Arbitration Act, 9 U.S.C. §§ 1–16, 43 Stat. 883–86, Pub. L. 114–38, enacted February 12, 1925.
31 Bureau of Consumer Financial Protection, Docket No. CFPB-2016–0020, 12 CFR Part 1040, http://files.consumerfinance.gov/f/documents/CFPB_Arbitration_Agreements_Notice_of_Proposed_Rulemaking.pdf. Unfortunately, the United States Senate repealed the arbitration rule on October 24, 2017 under the Congressional Review Act (to allow the enforcement of arbitration clauses preventing consumers to financial contracts from pursuing class action lawsuits).
32 *Carnival Cruise Lines, Inc. v. Shute*, 499 U.S. 585 (1991) (upheld forum selection clause in a pre-printed cruise contract; unless the selected forum is unreasonably burdensome on the party seeking to bring a claim).

consumer unable to pursue a claim.[33] Choice of law clauses, like forum selection clauses are generally enforced, however, in consumer contracts, state courts have voided such clauses as a matter of policy, when the choice of law deprives consumers of the higher protections of their state's consumer protection laws. This is the same rationale behind the Brussels I Regulation (consumer may bring claim at her place of residence) and the Unfair Terms in Consumer Contract Directive that lists as an unfair term one that 'excludes or hinders the consumer's right to take legal action or exercise any other legal remedy, particularly by requiring the consumer to take disputes exclusively to arbitration not covered by legal provisions'.[34]

IV. Factual scenarios

Scenario 1

It must be noted that defective automobiles in the US are treated differently than many other products due to government regulations and interventions. For example, the federal and state governments are more likely to negotiate a remedy directly with manufacturers, such as in the Volkswagen (VW) case in which the car manufacturer fraudulently tampered with the emissions testing for its diesel-fueled cars. In that case, VW reached a settlement with US regulators to fix or buy back nearly 500,000 diesel cars, at a cost estimated to be above $5 billion. This does not include the settlement of numerous class action lawsuits and substantial penalties to be levied by the US Department of Justice.[35]

The scenario posed in the present case study includes a number of operative facts: (1) An advertising campaign promoting a new automobile under the slogan of 'Top Reliability, Low Fuel Consumption, Best for the Environment', including a television commercial showing a family driving across the United Kingdom; (2) An oral representation that the low fuel consumption would be consistent whether on long or short trips; and (3) After the sale, the automobile underperformed (slowness of braking, transmission noise when using lower gears, larger than expected fuel consumption, failure to meet emission standards). What causes of action or avenues of redress does the consumer have relating to the manufacturer and the automobile dealership? What if the transaction involved a 3-year-old automobile?

(i)(a) Brake and engine noise (new car)

Under CRA 2015, a new car that suffers from slow braking and engine noise would be considered as a breach of the implied warranty of 'satisfactory quality'.

---

33 Ibid.
34 Council Directive 93/13/EEC of 5 April 1993 on unfair terms in consumer contracts, Annex (q).
35 J. Ewing, "Volkswagen Reaches Deal in US Over Emissions Standards", *NY Times*, International Business Section (21 April 2016).

The same would be true under the UCC doctrine of implied warranty of merchantability. However, implied warranties are easily disclaimable under the UCC. The primary rights of the consumer are controlled by the new car warranty provided by the manufacturer. These warranties are likely sufficient due to government regulations, industry standards (state of the art), as well as the regulatory-market forces of consumer reports and rating services.

If the braking and noise problems rise to the level of making the automobile unsafe, then enforcement of existing regulations and intervention by the US National Highway Safety Administration would be likely. But, this would only be the case if the defects related to the model of automobile and not if the defects affect a single or a small number of automobiles.

Unlike the CRA, there is no federal right of rejection in the sale of automobiles. However, most US states have passed what are called 'Lemon Laws'. The typical lemon law statute covers defects or conditions that substantially impair the use, value or safety of a new or demonstrator vehicle ('non-conformities').[36] These defects must be first reported to the manufacturer or its authorised service agent (dealer) during the 'Lemon Law Rights Period' of 24 months after the date of delivery of the motor vehicle to the consumer. If the manufacturer fails to conform the vehicle to the warranty after a reasonable number of attempts at repair, the law requires the manufacturer to buy back the defective vehicle and give the consumer a purchase price refund or a replacement vehicle.

(i)(b) Brake and engine noise (used car)

The 'reasonable person' has lower expectations in the purchase of used cars; therefore, the quality measures for such cars are of a diminished nature. However, sharp practices are common in the used car sales market. Thus, the oral representations of the seller in the used car context are of greater importance then in the new car market, and lay the bases for misrepresentation and fraud claims. Complaints may also be filed at the state level with Consumer Fraud Bureaus.

(ii) Higher-than-expected fuel consumption

The representations made by the manufacturer in its marketing of the automobile are likely to be considered to be seller's puff and not representation of facts. The more vague and abstract the claims (fuel efficient, able to travel across the United Kingdom), the less successful will be a claim of misrepresentation. An actual statement of miles per gallon or litre would be considered a statement of fact. Under US law, in new car sales, this would not be an issue since manufacturers and new car dealers must conspicuously place the fuel mileage ratings on a window of the car. The statements of the sales representatives are generally expunged by the express warranty and the merger clause in the sales contract. However, if the misrepresentation is widespread in the sales force, then a claim of

---

36 See "Motor Vehicle Warranty Enforcement Act," Florida Statutes, Chapter 681.

misrepresentation or breach of the implied warranty for a particular purpose may be possible. But, such claims could be blunted by the reasonable person standard since it is common knowledge that local or city driving ratings are almost always higher than for highway driving.

(iii) Failure to meet emissions standards

The failure of meeting emissions standards would most certainly make the automobile of insufficient quality, likely breaching the implied warranty of merchantability due to the fact that such a misrepresentation would be of a material fact and result in a diminishment in the value of the car. However, as was seen in the VW case, mentioned above, if the fuel emissions tests show that the emissions are higher than advertised then the seller would be liable for breaching an express warranty under the UCC, entitling the purchaser to a repair or replacement (with a car that meets the advertised emissions standards). If there is no such fix or replacement car, then the consumer has a right to a full refund. Further, such a misrepresentation would be a violation of federal law and would result in government intervention on behalf of consumers, as well as prosecutions to obtain civil and criminal penalties.

Scenario 2

The young consumers' mantra of 'access not ownership' is shaping a new relationship with retailers and service providers'.[37] The rise of laptop and tablet computers and, more importantly, smartphones have dramatically changed the consumer marketplace in a number of ways. First, it has lead to a new billion-dollar industry that produces an endless amount of apps to be used on these types of devices. Second, the movement from desktops to laptops, tablets and smartphones created the synergistic outcome of connectivity. Instead of a stand-alone electronic device, the average consumer owns a number of interconnected electronic devices. The power of this interconnectivity has become a common expectation of consumers. The issue becomes what is the responsibility of the sellers of these devices and associated software-apps as to their interconnectivity? What responsibility, if any, does the consumer have in assuring the interconnectivity of electronic devices and the functionality of apps across the different devices?

(i) Failure of the app and failure to patch the problem

The failure of the 'running' or vital signs app is analogous to defective goods. The CRA is a more modern law, compared to those that can be found in the American

---

37 Euromonitor International, available at www.euromonitor.com/consumer-lifestyles-in-the-us/report (report of July 20150.

United States 161

UCC and common law. The failure to adopt the proposed UCC Article 2B, the licensing of goods, prevented American law from moving in the direction of formal regulation of digital content. As a result, there is no counterpart to Chapter 3 of Part 1 of the CRA, which recognises contracts for the supply of digital content ('data which are produced and supplied in digital form'), and its extension of the satisfactory quality standard to digital content and by analogy to the interconnectivity of electronic devices. Under the CRA, the failure of the running app would breach the warranty of satisfactory quality, including the warranty for a particular purpose that the app would have uninterrupted functionality.

(ii) Interference with other apps

The non-conforming running app also affected the functionality of the home monitoring app, including the remote operation of the digital TV recorder and central heating system. An investigation would be needed to determine whether the running app has a virus-like effect on the other apps loaded onto the electronic devices, or whether the home app seller was contributorily negligent in producing an app that was incompatible with other apps. The *ABA Consumer Law Guide* cautions that 'the consumer is responsible with familiarising herself with the technical specifications and performance characteristics of different hardware and software combinations'.[38]

(iii) Damage done to the Wi-Fi connector

An expert found that downloading the 'running' app prevented the 'home' app from working and disengaged the tablet's Wi-Fi connectivity. What recourse does the purchaser have against the manufacturer of the tablet and the supplier of the running app? What are the liabilities of the tablet manufacturer and the app supplier for the failure of the running app; the disabling of the different apps, and the damage to the Wi-Fi connector? Again, as noted above, if the running app was below industry standards of compatibility with electronic devices, then the app seller would be liable for the damages caused to the home app and the Wi-Fi function in the tablet's hard drive. On the other hand, the liability would rest on the seller of the tablet if it were defective in its ability to download apps or inhibit their functionality. Finally, the seller of the home app would be liable if it proved to be incompatible with other apps or easily corrupted based on industry standards. A related question unanswered in American law is whether there should be an implied warranty that software or apps are virus-free? If a seller's software is corrupted by a virus unbeknownst to the seller and not due to seller's negligence (performed all procedures and practices based on industry standards or state of art), can the seller still be liable for the damage caused by the transfer of the virus

---

38 ABA Consumer Law Guide at Chapter 14: "The Computer Superhighway: Consumer Rights in the Computer Age."

to the consumer's electronic devices? Should such liability be transferred to the seller under a strict products liability approach?

V. Specific issues in the US: neglected areas of regulations, issues, and recommendations

There is a growing recognition in the US that consumer contracts should be treated differently than business contracts. Mandatory rules and orders from federal and state agencies continue to play an important role in targeted regulations of abusive terms and practices in consumer contracts. Examples include: (1) FTC Fair Credit Practice Rule that prohibits cross-collateral clauses made famous by the seminal case on unconscionability: *Williams v. Walker-Thomas Furniture*;[39] (2) the Credit Card Accountability, Responsibility, and Disclosure Act of 2009 requires credit card companies to allocate any payments first to the accounts with the highest interest rates. The American Bar Association's *ABA Consumer Law Guide* summarises American consumer sales law as follows:

- Consumers who choose to order merchandise through television shopping channels are usually as well protected as those who buy by mail – often better, since they usually use credit cards. Under American credit card law, consumers' liability on their credit card debt related to fraud or identity theft is capped at 50 dollars.[40]
- The FTC's Mail or Telephone Order Rule covers goods ordered by mail, telephone, internet and fax. Under this Rule, goods that are bought through these means must be shipped within the time the seller has advertised. If no time period is specified, the goods must be shipped within 30 days of placing the order. The seller also has to offer to cancel your order and send you a refund within 1 week if the consumer elects not to wait any longer.[41]
- Consumers who receive unordered merchandise in the mail should consider it a gift, unless the consumer inadvertently joined a 'club' with regular purchasing requirements when participating in a sweepstakes or ordering 'trial' or 'free' merchandise. Furthermore, a company that sends a bill for unordered merchandise may be guilty of fraud, which is a federal crime.[42]

However, despite the litany of federal and state consumer protection laws, the need for additional protections within a general consumer contract law has been recognised by the American Law Institute, which has launched the *Restatement of Consumer Contact Law* Project. The project's premise is that because

---

39 350 F.2d 445 (D.C. Cir. 1965).
40 *ABA Consumer Law Guide*, Chapter 6, www.americanbar.org/groups/public_education/resources/law_issues_for_consumers/books_consumer_home.html.
41 Ibid.
42 Ibid.

ALI's existing *Restatement Second of Contracts* generally takes a one-size-fits-all approach that does not distinguish between commercial and consumer contracts, it is inadequate, and a separate restatement of rules applicable to consumer contracts is needed. The project plans to

- Examine the law on when a consumer is bound to a contract and 'provide a clear conceptual framework that adapts the offer-acceptance model to the passive negotiations environment'.
- Clarify how the 'material breach' doctrine applies to a consumer's right to cancel a contract.
- Formulate 'principles for punitive treatment of some types of willful breaches of consumer contracts'.
- 'Unify the framework' for developing rules mandating pro-consumer terms and banning terms that are deemed to be abusive.
- Clarify the contours of the unconscionability doctrine, including how it applies in the area of arbitration. The outline states that 'one goal will be to translate research on consumer decision-making, and on the limits of consumer understanding, into specific guidelines for the courts'.
- 'Distill the common principles that ought to guide' courts in applying the FTC Act and state laws prohibiting 'unfair or deceptive' acts or practices and the Dodd-Frank prohibition on 'unfair, deceptive or abusive' acts or practices.

The Reporters for the project, Oren Bar-Gill and Omri Ben-Shahar, have prepared a summary of the basic principles that currently or should govern consumer contract law.[43] First, the quality of consent in consumer standard from contracting is illustrated by the following long-debated question: how can the law overcome the fact that consumers fail to understand the terms of their contracts and their obligations under the contracts? One approach would be to mimic the concept of pre-contractual information found in the Draft Common European Sales Law, requiring pre-contractual disclosures as to the meaning of contract terms, penalties for seller's disclosure of false or deceptive information, and the unenforceability of 'invisible' or unknown terms unless the consumer is given the opportunity to access, read and save the terms.

In the area of the regulation of specific contract terms, the Restatement project has focused on modification of contract, termination penalties, forum selection and choice of law clauses. The problems highlighted relating to these clauses include the following: service providers often include a contract term that allows them to change the contract unilaterally; sellers in consumer markets, such as mobile telephones require long-term contracts and assess penalties if the consumer

---

43 Oren Bar-Gill and Omri Ben-Shahar, *Summary of Principles of Consumer Contract Law* (on file with author).

terminates the contract prematurely; and sellers often choose a forum and law that make it difficult for a consumer to pursue a claim. Existing contract law principles that have been used to police these clauses include the doctrine of unconscionability, common law penalty rule, and UCC Section 1–301, which limits the ability of merchants from using of choice of law to avoid mandatory consumer protection laws of the consumer's home state.

In the end, the principles of consent, justice and disclosure of information need to be brought to bear in fashioning a balance between freedom of contract and fairness in the exchange norms. All three of these core principles are interrelated. The greater the disclosure of information to the consumer, the stronger is the case of consumer awareness and of actual consent. The greater the quality of consent the less forceful is the argument of injustice or unfairness (unconscionability). A practical conclusion, considering these principles, would be to require that the seller-provider obtain express consent from the consumer for terms that can be used abusively, such as the case of making unilateral changes to the contract.

An alternative regulatory scheme is to leave it to the courts through contract law to use the tools of contract interpretation to blunt the one-sidedness in consumer contracts, such as the *contra proferentem* rule. However, applications of existing rules and principles need to be modified in the context of consumer contracts. The *parol evidence rule* should be 'softened'[44] to allow the admission of evidence of oral representations made by the seller to the consumer that contradicts the contract, and the *doctrine of good faith*[45] should be used more aggressively to regulate the seller's use of discretion granted under the contract.[46]

---

44 Ibid.
45 See UCC §§ 1–102 (3), 1–201 (19), & 1–203; *Restatement (Second) of Contracts* § 205 (Duty of Good Faith and Fair Dealing).
46 Bar-Gill and Ben-Shahar, *Summary of Principles of Consumer Contract Law* (on file with author).

10 Consumer sales law in Vietnam

Nguyen Van Cuong

I. The Vietnamese consumer market

Before launching the Doi Moi (Renovation) policy in 1986, Vietnam adopted a central planning economy, which did not regard consumer protection as a problem. From 1986, Vietnam gradually transited to a market economy with a rapid growth of private enterprises. State-owned enterprises are also required to engage market transactions on equal footing with private enterprises.[1] Goods and services are basically allocated through market transactions, especially through transactions between traders[2] and consumers. The past 30 years of transition to an open market economy lifted an average Vietnamese consumer's annual income to 2,200USD, that is 10 times compared to the annual income of 1986. From a very poor country, Vietnam is witnessing a social transformation to a consumer society, especially in big cities like Hanoi or Ho Chi Minh city. A national market of more than 92 million consumers in Vietnam is really an attractive place for foreign and domestic investment.

Information and communication technology is also driving up changes in Vietnam. The number of Internet users in Vietnam rose from 1.38% of the population in 2001 to 52% of the population in 2015 (about 47 million Internet users).[3] However, turnover for electronic commerce (i.e. online sale transactions) is only about 4 billion USD in 2016 (accounting for 2.8% of the retail market turnover).[4]

Infringements upon consumer rights are quite pervasive. A survey conducted with 3,000 consumers in 12 cities and provinces in Vietnam by Vietnam Competition Authority in 2016 (the authority in charge of enforcement of the Consumer

---

1 Article 22 of Vietnam's Constitution of 1992 (as amended in 2001) and Article 51(2) of Vietnam's Constitution of 2013.
2 Vietnam has about 570,000 enterprises in operation of which the number of private enterprises accounts for about 99%.
3 Cập nhật ngày, *Năm 2015: Tỷ lệ người dùng Internet tại Việt Nam đạt 52% dân số* (kinh te va du bao, 22 December 2015), http://kinhtevadubao.vn/chi-tiet/174-4869-nam-2015-ty-le-nguoi-dung-internet-tai-viet-nam-dat-52-dan-so-.html, accessed 14 April 2017.
4 Sự kiện NÓNG, *Thương mại điện tử Việt Nam tăng trưởng gấp 2,5 lần Nhật Bản* (Vietnamnet, 17 February, 2017), http://vietnamnet.vn/vn/kinh-doanh/dau-tu/thuong-mai-dien-tu-viet-nam-tang-truong-gap-2-5-lan-nhat-ban-356931.html, accessed 14 April 2017.

Protection Law of 2010) revealed that for the period of 2011–2015, about 56% of these consumers had experienced infringements of their consumer rights.[5]

II. Access to justice for consumers and enforcement of consumer law

1. Individual enforcement by the consumers

Of the 51 articles of the current Consumer Protection Law of 2010 (CPL), there are 17 articles stipulating channels for resolving disputes between consumers and traders. This significant number clearly shows the intention of the authors of the CPL to design a better self-help system for consumers in Vietnam. According to article 30(1) of the adopted CPL, disputes between consumers and traders can be resolved through four channels, namely, negotiation, mediation, arbitration and litigation. Accordingly, consumers can lodge a complaint directly to traders to request them handle consumers' complaint. Consumers can also lodge a complaint to a third party (especially consumer associations or consumer protection agencies) to mediate disputes between consumers and traders. Consumers can also bring their disputes with traders to arbitration centres or courts to settle.

As for negotiation, the consumer is entitled to request the trader to negotiate when he/she/it deems that his/her/its legitimate rights and interests have been infringed. The requested trader shall receive and negotiate with the requesting consumer *within 7 days* from the date of reception of the request.[6] The result of a successful negotiation between the requested trader and the requesting consumer shall be documented, except as otherwise agreed by the parties.

As for mediation, the CPL states that traders and consumers are entitled to submit their disputes to a third party (individual or mediation organisation) to mediate on their behalf.

As for arbitration, article 38 of the CPL acknowledges that disputes between consumers and traders can be resolved through arbitration;[7] however, arbitration clauses in standard contracts are not binding on consumers.[8]

As for litigation, according to the *Code of Civil Procedure* of 2004 (having effect until 1st January 2017), all lawsuits brought by consumers (based on contract rules

---

5 Tuoitre Newspaper, "Hon 56% nguoi tieu dung tung bi xam pham quyen loi" ("More Than 56% of Consumers Experienced With Infringements Upon Their Rights") (Tuoitre Newspaper, 9 September 2016), http://tuoitre.vn/tin/can-biet/20160909/hon-56-nguoi-tieu-dung-tung-bi-xam-pham-quyen-loi/1168602.html, accessed 14 April 2017.
6 Article 31 of the CPL.
7 It is worth noting that arbitration is currently governed by the *Law on Commercial Arbitration* of 2010 (which replaced the *Ordinance on Commercial Arbitration* of 2003). Articles 24 and 25 of this law state that arbitration centres have to get the permission from the Minister of Justice in advance for establishment and they can start to operate only upon registration with provincial Departments of Justice.
8 Article 38 of the CPL. A similar provision can also be found in article 17 of the *Law on Commercial Arbitration* of 2010.

or tort rules) against traders due to violations of consumer laws should follow the normal civil procedure.[9] According to the normal civil procedure rules, consumers may have to wait 4 to 6 months for a trial date.[10] Given the excessive caseload of the current court system, consumers may thus have to wait for years to get their final judgements executed. Consumers had to deposit their court fees in advance. Consumers also assume the burden of proof. This regime of civil procedure was widely seen as unfriendly to consumers, especially individual consumers in cases of low value.[11] In other words, there were no summary or fast-track procedures for consumer claims under this code or under other legal normative documents.[12]

The CPL of 2010 provides for two major new provisions which are seen as being favourable to consumers.[13] The first is the provision on 'simplified civil procedure' applicable to a number of simple lawsuits brought by individual consumers. The second is the provision on the right of consumer protection organisations (or social organisations participating in consumer protection activities) to bring legal actions against offending traders without express written authorization from consumers. The introduction of 'simplified civil procedure' applicable to a number of lawsuits brought by individual consumers is seen as an effort to remove unreasonable legal barriers and enhance consumers' access to justice. Article 41(2) of the adopted CPL stipulates that simplified civil procedure will be applied to lawsuits brought by consumers when these lawsuits meet the following conditions:

(1) the plaintiff is an individual consumer and the defendant is a trader directly supplying goods and/or services to the plaintiff;
(2) the lawsuits are simple, with clear evidence; and
(3) the value of the transaction is equal to or less than 100 million VND [i.e. equal to $ 5,000 USD].[14]

---

9 Article 33 of the *Code of Civil Procedure* of 2004.
10 Article 179 of the *Code of Civil Procedure* of 2004.
11 Tuong Duy Luong, "Role of Courts in Consumer Protection" ("Mot so van de ve vai tro cua Toa an trong viec bao ve quyen loi nguoi tieu dung") in Tuong Duy Luong (eds.), *Civil Law and Practice of Implementation* (*Phap luat dan su va thuc tien xet xu*) (Hanoi: National Political Press, 2009), pp. 306–326. Luong is currently the Vice-Chief Justice of the Supreme People's Court of Vietnam.
12 However, as stipulated in article 19 of Decree 55 (2008), consumers can lodge their complaints with a provincial Department of Industry and Trade or with Vietnam Competition Authority for mediation services. According to article 13(1)(a) of Decree 55 (2008), and consumers can also lodge their complaints with Vinastas or its provincial consumer protection associations for mediation services.
13 Other important provisions include the provision to exempt plaintiffs in lawsuits brought by consumers from the obligation to advance court fees, and the provision to shift the burden of proof from plaintiffs (consumers or consumer protection organisations) to defendants (accused offending traders). Specifically, article 43(2) of the CPL states that 'consumers bringing lawsuits to protect their rights and legitimate interests are exempted from advancing the court fees'. In addition, article 42(2) of the CPL states that 'traders shall prove to be faultless in causing damage to consumers'.
14 See article 41(2) of the CPL.

Given the above-mentioned provision, the CPL does not create a new specialised court in the current court system. Instead, the current court system still assumes the task of resolving disputes between consumers and traders. However, in certain lawsuits (meeting the said three conditions), a simplified rather than normal civil procedure will be applied, with the hope that this simplified procedure will help resolve lawsuits more swiftly. Unfortunately, simplified civil procedure is not found in the current *Code of Civil Procedure of 2004 (as amended in 2011)*. As a result, the provision on simplified civil procedure in Article 41(2) of the CPL was not put into operation until 1st January 2017 (i.e. the time the Code of Civil Procedure of 2004 was replaced by the new Code of Civil Procedure of 2015).

The new Code of Civil Procedure of 2015 (taking effect since 1st January 2017) offers a fast-track procedure (i.e. summary procedure) for handling 'simple civil disputes'. Accordingly, the summary court consists of only one judge rather than one judge and two legal assessors as previously stipulated by the Code of Civil Procedure of 2004. For cases in which summary procedure is applied, the judge has only 1 month to consider the facts of the case before officially opening the trial as compared with 4 months applied in normal procedure. However, whether the concept of simple civil disputes as stated in Article 317 of the Code of Civil Procedure of 2015 include disputes between traders and consumers stated in Article 41 of the CPL or not remains a question. Therefore, fast-track procedure applied to disputes between traders and consumers still faces many obstacles to be put into operation.

The legislative wisdom of drafting provisions in the CPL promoting use of the court system by consumers and consumer protection organisations to assert their rights against offending businesses is a matter of debate. As many previous studies show, litigation is generally not a preferred method of dispute resolution in Vietnam.[15] Lodging complaints to authorities to ask traders to respect consumer rights is also not a very popular way of addressing consumer problems in Vietnam. As previously mentioned, a survey conducted with 3,000 consumers in 12 cities and provinces in Vietnam conducted by Vietnam Competition Authority in 2016 (the authority in charge of enforcement of the Consumer Protection Law of 2010) revealed that for the period of 2011–2015, about 56% of these consumers experienced with infringements upon consumer rights.[16] However, the number of consumer complaints in Vietnam is astonishingly low. In 2016, Vietnam Competition Authority received only 1,567 consumer complaints of which 1,193 complaints were received through a hotline (18006838). Most of these complaints come from consumers in the two biggest cities in Vietnam (i.e. Hanoi and Ho Chi Minh city, accounting for 31.09% and 37.32%, respectively). Types of goods and services most relevant to complaints include banking and

---

15 See Penelope (Pip) Nicholson, *Borrowing Court Systems: The Experience of Socialist Vietnam* (Leiden: Martinus Nijhoff, 2007), pp. 269–272.
16 Tuoitre Newspaper, "Hon 56% nguoi tieu dung tung bi xam pham quyen loi" ("More Than 56% of Consumers Experienced With Infringements Upon Their Rights") (9 September 2016), http://tuoitre.vn/tin/can-biet/20160909/hon-56-nguoi-tieu-dung-tung-bi-xam-pham-quyen-loi/1168602.html.

insurance services, mobile phone services, home electronic appliances and internet services.[17] The above-mentioned survey revealed that about half of these consumers decided to tolerate the situation by being silent and ignoring their bad experience. This result is quite similar to the result of a smaller social survey conducted in early 2010 by Phan The Cong, a lecturer at the Hanoi University of Commerce, involving 583 randomly selected consumers in urban Hanoi. This survey found that 75% of consumers stated that, if their consumer rights were infringed upon, they would simply ignore the infringement and would not lodge complaints or file lawsuits against the perpetrators. The interviewees explained that they did not opt for filing lawsuits because they even did not know where to submit their petitions (37.24% of the interviewees) or they thought they were unlikely to get fair compensation (46.68% of the interviewees). Most of them felt helpless in initiating lawsuits against offending traders.[18]

In addition, as the current court system has many problems in terms of both its caseload and its competence, whether establishing a fast-track litigation actually benefits consumers is doubtful. It is not surprising that at present, almost no disputes between consumers and traders were reported to be settled before the courts. Consumer associations have not initiated any legal suits to challenge offending traders.

2. Public enforcement of consumer law

Public enforcement of consumer protection laws is mainly borne on the shoulders of a number of ministries (especially Ministry of Industry and Trade) and provincial People's Committees. Ministry of Industry and Trade's Market Surveillance Agency and its affiliated local organisations (at the provincial and district levels) possess powerful tools in being able to directly attack specific violations of consumer rights. This Agency and its affiliated local organisations (with about 6,000 staff) is entrusted to investigate many kinds of specific violations against consumer rights, such as improper labelling, selling expired products, and producing or selling counterfeited goods. Specifically, from 2003 to 2007, this force dealt with 48,732 cases in which traders sold shoddy products or counterfeited goods. The number of cases increased year by year. For example, the number of cases dealt with by the market surveillance force in 2003 was 5,808; and this number in 2004, 2005, 2006 and 2007 was 5,977, 8,739, 12,885 and 15,323, respectively. Violators were given administrative sanctions such as fines, withdrawal of business licences and destruction of counterfeited or shoddy products. From 2003

---

17 Vietnam Competition Authority, "Cong tac tu van, ho tro giai quyet yeu cau, khieu nai cua nguoi tieu dung trong nam 2016 cua Cuc quan ly canh tranh" ("Vietnam Competition Authority's Assistance to Handle Consumer Complaints in 2016"), www.vca.gov.vn/chitietbvntd.aspx?ID=3534&Cate_ID=436, accessed 15 April 2017.
18 Cuong Nguyen, *The Drafting of Vietnam's Consumer Protection Law: An Analysis From Legal Transplantation Theories* (PhD Dissertation, University of Victoria, 2011), 138, https://dspace.library.uvic.ca/bitstream/handle/1828/3404/Nguyen_Cuong_PhD_2011.pdf?sequence=1&isAllowed=y, accessed 14 April 2017.

to 2007, this market surveillance force also discovered and dealt with 57,939 other violations of consumer rights such as improper labelling, and employment of wrong weights or measures.[19] A more recent statistics shows that of the past 10 months of the year 2016, the market surveillance force throughout the nation discovered and handled 88,000 violations of consumer rights.[20]

In addition, the provision of Article 19 (1) and (2) of the CPL on control of standard consumer contracts paves the way for the Vietnam Competition Authority and Provincial Department of Industry and Trade (i.e. administrative organs) to directly intervene into the standard consumer contracts currently being used by sellers or providers of certain important goods and services. Provisions on settlement of violations of the CPL based on administrative sanctions have been fully set forth. Concretely, regarding settlement of violations of the CPL, the CPL contains one article[21] 'dealing with violations against rights and interests of consumers' as follows:

(1) Individuals violating laws on protection of consumers' rights and interests, depending on the extent and seriousness of the offence, shall be subject to administrative sanctions or criminal prosecution, and shall provide compensation if causing damage, as stipulated by law.
(2) organisations violating laws on protection of consumers' rights and interests, depending on the extent and seriousness of the offence, shall be subject to administrative sanctions, and shall provide compensation if causing damage, as stipulated by law.

The Law on Dealing with Administrative Violations of 2012 and Decree 185/2013/ND-CP dated 15 November 2013 (hereinafter named as Decree 185) set forth many provisions on dealing with violations of the CPL. Accordingly, no criminal liability is applied against offending corporate entities, as the law in Vietnam states that only an individual (natural person) can be held criminally liable.[22] Decree 185 (2013) indicates more than 60 types of specific behaviours of traders (even contractual behaviours) considered as violations of the CPL which are imposed administrative penalties. For example, Article 65 of Decree 185 states that a fine of between VND 10,000,000 and 20,000,000 [i.e. between 500 USD to 1,000 USD] shall be imposed on one of the following acts of violation: a) fail to clearly and publicly notify consumers on purposes before conducting activities of collecting, using information of consumers as prescribed; b) use

---

19 Ibid.
20 Ministry of Industry and Trade of Vietnam's Website, *Quan ly thi truong xu ly 88.000 vu vi pham (Market Surveillance Force Handles 88,000 Cases of Violations)*, www.moit.gov.vn/vn/tin-tuc/8369/quan-ly-thi-truong-xu-ly-88-000-vu-vi-pham.aspx, accessed 16 April 2017.
21 Article 11 of the CPL.
22 This can be changed soon if the new Criminal Code of 2015 takes effect in which corporate liability is set forth.

information of consumers inconsistently with the purpose informed consumers without consents of consumers as prescribed; c) fail to ensure safety, accuracy and sufficiency of the consumers' information when collecting, using and transferring as prescribed; d) fail to self-adjust or apply measures for consumers to update or to adjust the information when detecting that information is incorrect as prescribed; e) transfer information of consumers to third parties without consent of consumers as prescribed, unless otherwise provided by law.

III. The legal framework for consumer sales in Vietnam

1. Overview

The main current law to regulate interactions between consumers and traders in Vietnam is the Consumer Protection Law, a statute adopted by the National Assembly in 2010. It took effect since July 1st, 2011. The adoption of this Law marked a big shift in approaches to consumer problems in Vietnam. Therefore, evolution of consumer protection laws in Vietnam can be divided into two periods: the period before the adoption of the Consumer Protection Law of 2010 and the period after that.

The emergence of consumer protection provisions was mainly associated with the marketization process; when Vietnam shifted from a centrally planned economy to a market economy beginning in 1986, consumers were gradually liberalised to become more autonomous players in the new game of market interactions. Actually, until 1992, few provisions on consumer protection existed in the legal system. Legal provisions on consumer protection in this period were mainly of a criminal or administrative nature.[23] Such employment of criminal laws for the purpose of consumer protection again seems to repeat the inertia of the traditional view of the state as the benevolent protector of the general public. In 1992 (i.e. 6 years after the legalisation of the private sector and the market economy following the creation of the Doi Moi Policy in 1986), the constitution first made a declaration that consumer protection policy was to be formulated by the state.[24] Until the first Consumer Protection Law (CPL) was adopted in November 2010, legal rules relevant to consumer protection evolved substantially thanks to law reform initiatives following the adoption of the new *Constitution* of 1992. These legal rules were stipulated in many codes, laws and ordinances and their accompanying guiding legal normative documents (LNDs) such as the *Civil Code* of 1995 (amended and replaced

---

23 For example, article 5 of the *Ordinance on Sanctioning Crimes of Speculation, Smuggling, Dealing in Fake Goods, and Illegal Business* of 1982 and Article 167 of the *Criminal Code* of 1985.
24 Specifically, article 28 of the *Constitution* of 1992 contains a commitment from the state that 'The state shall maintain a policy of protection of interests and rights of producers and consumers'.

in 2005 and 2015),[25] the *Commercial Law* of 1997 (amended in 2005),[26] the *Criminal Code* of 1999,[27] the *Ordinance on Quality of Goods* of 1999 (amended and incorporated into the *Law on Quality of Products and Goods* of 2007), the *Ordinance on Advertisement* of 2001 (later replaced by the Law on Advertisement of 2012), the *Ordinance on Price* of 2002 (later replaced by the Law on Price of 2012), the *Ordinance on Dealing with Administrative Offences* of 2002 (later replaced by the Law on Dealing with Administrative Offences of 2012), the *Ordinance on Food Safety* of 2003 (amended and incorporated into the *Law on Food Safety* of 2010) and the *Competition Law* of 2004.

Among these laws, provisions about the obligation of traders and businesses to respect the commercial interests of consumers are found in numerous important laws.[28] Violations of consumers' interests are subject to administrative sanc-

---

25 This code was drafted by MoJ. This code is said to be visibly modelled after the *Civil Code* of Japan (1896), with certain references to the *Civil Code* of Germany (2002), the *Civil Code* of France (1804), the *Civil Code* of Soviet Russia (1922) and the Chinese *Civil Law* (1987). See Nguyen Quoc Vinh, *Freedom of Contract: A Leading Principle in Contract Law of Economically Developed Countries and Its Absence in Contract Law of Vietnam* (PhD Dissertation, Meiji Gakuin University, Tokyo, Japan, 2006) at 171–172 [unpublished]; see also John Stanley Gillespie, *Transplanting Commercial Law Reform: Developing a "Rule of Law" in Vietnam* (Farnham, UK: Ashgate, 2006), 161–162.

26 This law was drafted by the Ministry of Trade (now MoIT) with extensive technical assistance from multilateral and bilateral donors such as the World Bank, the Asian Development Bank, United Nations development programmes, France and Japan. See William A.W. Neilson, "Competition Laws for Asian Transitional Economies: Adaptation to Local Legal Cultures in Vietnam and Indonesia" in Tim Lindsey (ed.), *Law Reform in Developing and Transitional States* (New York: Routledge, 2006), 291 at 308; see also John Gillespie, "Developing a Decentred Analysis of Legal Transfers" in Penelope (Pip) Nicholson and Sarah Biddulph (eds.), *Examining Practice, Interrogating Theory: Comparative Legal Studies in Asia* (Leiden: Martinus Nijhoff, 2008), 25 at 46 [Gillespie, "Decentered Analysis"]. The Ministry of Trade was regarded as the agency in charge of enforcing this law (or conducting state management of commercial activities as stipulated in this law) (article 246 of the *Commercial Law* of 1997 and article 8 of the *Commercial Law* of 2005).

27 This code was drafted by MoJ in a close consultation with the Ministry of Public Security, the Supreme People's Procuracy and the Supreme People's Court. This code is said to be significantly modelled after the *Criminal Code* of the former Soviet Russia (1960) and the current *Criminal Code* of Russia (1997). See Nguyen Thi Anh Van, "Skills of Using Comparative Law to Draft Legal Normative Documents" ("Ky nang su dung Luat hoc so sanh trong cong tac soan thao van ban quy pham phap luat") in Nguyen Dinh Loc et al. (eds.), *Manual for Enhancing the Skills of Drafting Legal Normative Documents (Tai lieu boi duong nghiep vu xay dung van ban quy pham phap luat)* (Hanoi: Judicial Press, 2008), 68 at 92.

28 See article 632 of the *Civil Code* of 1995, which states that 'individuals, legal persons and other subjects producing and/or trading in goods which fail to meet standards of food, pharmacy or other goods, causing damage to consumers, shall be liable to pay compensation'; article 9(1–3) of the *Commercial Law* of 1997, which was later replaced by article 14 of the *Commercial Law* of 2005, stipulates that traders conducting commercial activities are obliged to provide consumers with sufficient and truthful information on the goods and/or services they trade in or provide and take responsibility for the accuracy of such information.

Vietnam   173

tions and criminal penalties according to the nature, extent and consequences of the violations. Traders causing harm to other people are responsible to pay compensation.[29]

Prior to the adoption of the CPL, the highest LND specifically dealing with consumer protection was the *Ordinance on Protection of Consumers' Rights and Interests* (the CPO). This ordinance was adopted by the National Assembly's Standing Committee on 27 April 1999 and took effect on 1 October 1999.[30] This Ordinance is quite short with only 30 articles.[31] The CPO does not have any provisions governing specific transactions between consumers and businesses, nor does it have any specific remedies to deal with offences against consumers. The self-help system for consumers is also poorly designed. Provisions on consumer rights in this ordinance are simply declaratory, without concrete effective and enforceable mechanisms. Within this format, the CPO was expected to have a number of subordinate guiding LNDs to concretize its construction.[32]

In 2006, Vietnam Competition Authority (under the Ministry of Trade) was assigned the task to be in charge of both Competition Law of 2004 and CPO.[33]

Traders conducting commercial activities must be responsible for the quality and lawfulness of the goods and/or services they trade in or provide.

29   See article 321 of the *Commercial Law* of 2005. Actually, the Government has issues many guiding legal normative documents (LNDs) regarding administrative sanctions for violations of commercial law. For example, one of the very first decrees dealing with administrative offences in the area of commercial activities was *Decree No. 01/CP dated 3 January 1996 on dealing with administrative offences in the area of commercial activities* (as amended by *Decree No. 01/2202/ND-CP dated 3 January 2002*). This decree was replaced by *Decree No. 175/2004/ND-CP dated 10 October 2004 on dealing with administrative offences in the area of commercial activities*. *Decree No. 175/2004/ND-CP* was then replaced by *Decree No. 06/2008/ND-CP dated 16 January 2008 on dealing with administrative offences in commercial activities*. *Decree No. 06/2008/ND-CP* was further detailed by MoIT's *Circular No. 15/2008/TT-BCT dated 2 December 2008*. *Decree No. 06/2008/ND-CP* was recently amended by *Decree No. 112/2010/ND-CP dated 1 December 2010*.

30   Actually, this ordinance was initially scheduled to be adopted in 1994 according to the NA's *Resolution dated 23 June 1994 on law-making activities for the second half of 1994*.

31   For example, the *Ordinance on Quality of Goods* of 1999 and the *Ordinance on Measurement* of 1999 had only 38 and 41 articles, respectively.

32   That is why this ordinance was later specified by Decree 69 (2001) and then by Decree 55 (2008).

33   The *Competition Law* of 2004 has been specified by a number of important decrees and guiding LNDs such as *Decree No. 116/2005/ND-CP dated 15 September 2005 providing for details of implementation of the Competition Law*; *Decree No. 120/2005/ND-CP dated 30 September 2005 on dealing with legal violations in the area of competition*; *Decree No. 110/2005/ND-CP dated 24 August 2005 on [state]management of multi-level sales*; *Decree No. 05/2006/ND-CP dated 9 January 2006 on establishing and stipulating the function, tasks, and organisational structure of the Competition Council*; *Decree No. 06/2006/ND-CP dated 9 January 2006 on the function, tasks and organisational structure of the Vietnam Competition Authority*; the Ministry of Trade's *Circular No. 19/2005/TT-BTM dated 8 November 2005 providing guidelines on a number of contents in Decree No. 110/2005/ND-CP*; the Ministry of Finance's *Decision No. 92/2005/QD-BTC dated 9 December 2005 on stipulating*

However, in early days of this Agency, Vietnam Competition Authority did not have sufficient power to fight against violations of consumer law (such as conducting independent investigations concerning violations of consumer law, imposing any kind of administrative sanctions upon traders violating consumer laws).[34] The key mandate assumed by Vietnam Competition Authority was to provide mediation between consumers and traders at the request of consumers and to provide consumer education services.

Actually, before the adoption of the CPL, the existing legal system of Vietnam had certain provisions regulating what are known in developed countries as 'unfair commercial practices' or 'unfair trade practices'. For example, *Decree No. 194/CP dated 31 December 1994* prohibited enterprises and advertisers from providing inaccurate information about goods, services and traders.[35] According to articles 12 and 14 of Decree 54 (2009),[36] producers that fail to produce their products in compliance with their announced standards could be fined to 5 million VND (equal to $250 USD). As for producing or trading in fake goods, Article 156 of the current *Criminal Code* of 1999 (as amended in 2009) states that individuals participating in manufacturing and/or trading in fake goods can be subject to a maximum penalty of 15 years of imprisonment. In reality, quite a few violations regarding counterfeited goods have been prosecuted through criminal proceedings. The statistics from the People's Supreme Court show that in the period 2000–2006, 426 criminal charges of such kinds (including 167 cases relating to counterfeited foodstuffs and 33 cases relating to counterfeited animal feed) were brought before the courts.

Regarding consumer contracts, unlike the situation in developed countries, until the adoption of the CPL of 2010, the concept of 'consumer contract' was unknown in the current Vietnamese legal system. Instead, the concept of 'civil

---

   the level of fees for granting registration certificates for multi-level sales activities; the Ministry of Trade's *Decision No. 20/2006/QD-BTM dated 17 May 2006 issuing forms of decisions on dealing with competition cases*.
34 Except for the power to investigate and impose fines upon deceptive advertisers as stipulated in article 42 of *Decree No. 120/2005/ND-CP*. According to this article, the Director of Vietnam Competition Authority can give warnings to violators, impose fines upon violators, confiscate instruments employed by violators, and force violators to publish correct advertisements.
35 For example, article 5 of the *Ordinance on Advertisement* of 2001 prohibits the following conduct: making false advertisements; advertising products and/or goods which are not yet permitted for circulation and/or services which are not yet permitted for provision by the time of advertisement; and advertising goods and/or services, which are banned by law from business or from advertisement. Article 45(3) of the *Competition Law* of 2004 prohibits enterprises from 'issuing false or misleading information to customers about the following: (a) Prices, quantities, quality, utilities, designs, categories, packages, date of manufacture, use duration, goods origin, manufacturers, places of manufacture, processors, places of processing; (b) Usage, mode of servicing, warranty duration; (c) Other false or misleading information'.
36 *Decree No. 54/2009/ND-CP dated 5 June 2009 on sanctioning administrative offences in the fields of standards, measurement, and quality of products and goods*.

contract' in the *Civil Code* of 2005 was considered a concept broadly defined to cover all types of contractual relationships in society.[37] The *Commercial Law* of 2005 is expressly considered a special law of the *Civil Code*.[38] The *Commercial Law* is expressly designed to regulate relationships among traders. This law will take priority over the *Civil Code* when there are differences between them regarding a particular matter. As for contracts between traders and consumers, they are, in principle, governed by contract rules in the *Civil Code* of 2005.[39] However, consumers can elect to apply the *Commercial Law* if they prefer.[40] Disputes arising from a contract are to be submitted to and resolved through the people's district courts and senior civil courts in accordance with the ordinary civil procedure stipulated in the *Code of Civil Procedure* of 2004.

2. Non-conformity

The *Civil Code* of 2015 (previously the *Civil Code* of 2005) requires that the property in a transaction must satisfy such requirements as (1) matching the description or the sample; (2) being reasonably fit for the purpose for which they were sold; (3) being of merchantable quality and durability. More concretely, article 445 (2) of the *Civil Code* of 2015[41] expressly states that 'the seller must secure that the object for sale conforms to the descriptions on its package, trademark or to the sample that has been selected by the purchaser'. Articles 437 and 438 of this code allow buyers to refuse to accept the delivery of goods which do not conform with the description in the contract. In addition, article 445 (1) of the *Civil Code* of 2015 states that

> the seller must secure the use value or properties of an object for purchase and sale; if after the purchase, the purchaser discovers a defect that devaluates or reduces the use value of the object already purchased, he/she/it must promptly notify the seller of the defect upon the detection thereof and is entitled to request the seller to repair or change the defective or devalued object and compensate for damages, unless otherwise agreed upon.

However, the seller will not be liable for defects in the following cases: (1) the purchaser knew or must have known about the defect when purchasing the object;

---

37 Article 1 of the *Civil Code* of 2005. The *Civil Code* of 2005 was replace by the *Civil Code* of 2015 since 1st January 2017.
38 Article 4(3) of the *Commercial Law* of 2005.
39 Nguyen Van Thanh, "Necessary Contents in the CPL" ("Cac noi dung can co trong Luat bao ve quyen loi nguoi tieu dung") (Paper presented at the workshop "Consumer Protection Law in Vietnam – Reality and Orientation for Improvement" ("Phap luat bao ve nguoi tieu dung o Vietnam – thuc trang va huong hoan thien") Hanoi Law University, Hanoi, 10 September 2010). Nguyen is a legal expert working for Vietnam Competition Authority and one of the drafters of the CPL.
40 Article 1(3) of the *Commercial Law* of 2005.
41 It repeats Article 444(2) of Civil Code of 2005 of Vietnam.

(2) the object was auctioned or sold at a second-hand shop; and (3) the purchaser is at fault in causing the defects of the object. Actually, most of the above provisions in the *Civil Code* of 2015 were already stipulated in the *Civil Code* of 1995[42] and the *Civil Code of 2005*.[43]

3. Consumer contracts

One of the key points worth noting is that the contract rules in the *Civil Code* of 2005 (now the *Civil Code* of 2015) were designed with the key purpose of regulating contracts between private parties of equal footing.[44] The *Civil Code* does not extend any special treatment to consumer contracts corresponding to the fact that these contractual relationships are between two parties of, de facto, unequal footing. The *Civil Code* does not have any special rules exclusively applicable to door-to-door sales, distance sales or sales of used goods. The *Civil Code* of 2005 and the *Civil Code* of 2015 provides for numerous important contract rules relevant to transactions between traders and consumers, especially rules relating to sale of property.[45] Here are some examples:

Standard contract: The *Civil Code* of 2005 and the *Civil Code* of 2015 address the inequality of bargaining power only in the case of standard contracts. A standard contract is defined by the code as a contract which contains provisions prepared by one party and given to the other party for reply within a reasonable period of time; if the offeree gives its reply of acceptance, the offeree shall be considered as having accepted the entire contents of the standard contract offered by the offeror.[46] Article 405(2) and (3) of the *Civil Code* of 2015[47] also stipulates a number of legal constraints to prevent the strong contracting party from exploiting the weaker party.[48] Concretely, article 405(2) states that

> in cases in which a standard contract contains ambiguous provisions, the offeror of the contract shall bear the adverse consequences of the interpretation of such provisions.[49]

---

42 See articles 423 &437 of the *Civil Code* in Baker&McKenzie and Clifford Chance, *Civil Code of the Socialist Republic of Vietnam* (Hong Kong: Asia Information Associated, 1996), 146–150.
43 See articles 436, 437 and 444 of the *Civil Code* of 2005 of Vietnam.
44 Hoang The Lien et al., *Scientific Commentary on the Civil Code of 2005* (*Binh luan khoa hoc Bo luat dan su nam 2005*), vol. 1 (Hanoi: National Political Press, 2008), 18.
45 In accordance with articles 163 and 167 of the *Civil Code* of 2005, goods and chattels, land and houses are all regarded as 'property'.
46 Article 407(1) of the *Civil Code* of 2005 and Article 405(1) of the *Civil Code* of 2015 of Vietnam.
47 Similar provisions were found in Article 407(2) & (3) of the *Civil Code* of 2005 of Vietnam.
48 Similar provisions are widely found in contract law in developed countries. See K. Zweigert and H. Kötz, *An Introduction to Comparative Law*, 3d ed., trans. Tony Weir (Oxford: Clarendon Press, 1998), 338–345.
49 Translated by author. Similar provisions were also contained in the *Civil Code* of 1995 (article 406).

In addition, article 405(3) stipulates that

> in cases in which a standard contract contains provisions exempting the liability of the offeror of the standard contract, while increasing the responsibility or abolishing the legitimate interests of the other party, such provisions shall be void, unless otherwise agreed upon.[50]

However, it is noteworthy that the requirement for clarity of language and terms used in contracts between traders and consumers was not clearly stated in the *Civil Code* of 2005 or in other laws prior to the adoption of the CPL of 2010. In addition, the requirement that detailed information about key terms be contained in a contract between a trader and a consumer was also absent. No special contract rules relating to consumer transactions such as door-to-door sales, distance sales and sales of used goods exist.

One of the key aspects of the CPL of 2010 is its inclusion of various consumer contract rules. These provisions seem to indicate that approach to consumer protection problems in Vietnam is shifted to a contract-based approach, paving the ways for consumers to raise their problems before the court to be addressed. Here are the overviews on these relevant provisions:

The CPL sets forth several provisions as supplements to what already stipulated in the Civil Code of 2005 (now the Civil Code of 2015). For example:

- **Interpretation of Unclear Contractual Terms:** The technique of interpreting contracts in favour of consumers was also used by the CPL. In fact, a similar technique was already used in the *Civil Code* of 1995 and in the *Civil Code* of 2005; these two codes contain provisions stating that a contract between 2 parties of different bargaining power should be interpreted in favour of the weaker party. However, these two versions of the *Civil Code* did not expressly state that consumers were the weaker parties in contractual relations. The CPL overcomes this shortcoming of the *Civil Code by* states at Article 15 that 'in circumstances in which there are different understandings of the content of a contract, the organisation and/or individual having the mandate to resolve the relevant dispute shall interpret this content in favour of the consumer'.[51]
- **Invalidity of Unfair Contractual Terms:** The CPL (article 16 (1)) explicitly stipulates nine types of contractual terms deemed to be invalid as follows:
  (a) terms that exclude the responsibilities of the trader towards consumers as stipulated by law;
  (b) terms that exclude or limit the right of a consumer to lodge complaints or file lawsuits;

---

50 Translated by author. Compared with the *Civil Code* of 1995, this provision is new.
51 Article 15 of the CPL.

(c) terms that allow the trader to unilaterally modify other terms of the contract already made with the consumer or to unilaterally modify terms and conditions of sale and provision of services that are not concretely stipulated in the contract;
(d) terms that allow the trader to unilaterally determine that the consumer has to perform an obligation;
(e) terms that allow the trader to determine or change the price at the time of delivery of goods or provision of services;
(f) terms that allow the trader to unilaterally interpret the terms of the contract when there are different interpretations of the contract;
(g) terms that exclude the liability of the trader in the event that the trader deals in goods and/or services through a third party;
(h) terms that coerce the consumer to perform his/her obligations even when the trader does not perform his/her obligations; and
(i) terms that allow the trader to transfer his/her rights and obligations to a third party without the consent of the consumer.[52]

- **Control of Standard Consumer Contracts:** Article 17(1) of the CPL states that 'in entering into a standard contract, the trader shall grant the consumer a reasonable period of time to examine the contract'. In addition, according to article 19(1) of the CPL, 'traders supplying goods and/or services categorised as essential goods and/or services designated by the Prime Minister[53] have to register their standard contracts . . . with the competent state management body on protection of consumers' rights and interests'. Article 19(2) of the CPL states that 'the competent State management body on protection of consumers' rights and interests, at its discretion or at the request of consumers, may request traders to repeal or modify standard contracts . . . in cases in which these standard contracts . . . are found to infringe upon consumers' rights and interests'. This provision is interpreted together with article 48(2) of the CPL to mean that Ministry of Industry and Trade (Vietnam Competition Authority) is empowered to police the unfairness of terms and conditions in standard consumer contracts and in general transaction conditions.[54]

---

52 See article 16(1) of the CPL.
53 Prime Minister's Decision No. 02/2012/QD-TTg dated 13/1/2012. This Decision requires nine types of standard contracts to be registered with Vietnam Competition Authority such as (1) Supply of electricity for residential consumption; (2) Supply of clean water for residential consumption; (3) Pay television; (4) Fixed telephone subscription; (5) Postpaid mobile phone subscription; (6) Internet connection; (7) Air transport of passengers; (8) Rail transport of passengers; and (9) Purchase and sale of apartments, daily-life services provided by apartment-managing units. This document was recently amended by Decision 35/2015/QD-TTg dated 20/8/2015 with an addition that standard contracts relating to (1) 'Issue of inland debit cards, open and use payment account service (applicable to individual customers), individual borrow service (for consumption purpose)' and (2) 'Life insurance' shall be also registered.
54 Decree 99/2011/ND-CP states that the Vietnam Competition Authority shall review standard contracts used by enterprises operating in two or more provinces. The Provincial

Vietnam   179

- **Door-to-door Sales and Distance Sales Contracts:** Article 14(4) of the CPL contains a provision that 'the Government issues provisions on specific transactions with consumers'. This provision has been supplemented by Decree 99 (2011) with provisions on door-to-door sales contracts and distance sales contracts.[55] However, contracts of sale of used goods (such as motors, cars, etc.) are still not specifically regulated except for general rules in the *Civil Code* regarding sale contracts.

It is quite interesting that the current consumer sales laws in Vietnam even consider certain contractual behaviours of traders in interaction with consumers as administrative offences. For example:

- Articles 67 and 68 of Decree 185 state that 'a fine of between VND 5,000,000 and 10,000,000 [i.e. 250 USD and 500 USD] shall be imposed on one of the following acts of violation: a) Sign contracts with the consumers in the forms or contractual languages which are improper with regulations; b) Fail to let consumers to consider the entire contract before concluding in case of signing contracts by electronic means as prescribed'. A fine of between VND 20,000,000 [equal to 1,000USD] and 30,000,000 [equal to 1,500 USD] shall be imposed on acts of failing to comply with the requests of competent state agencies on cancellation or modification of contents of standard contracts which violate law on protection of consumer rights or contrary to general principles on concluding into contracts. A fine of between VND 30,000,000 [equal to 1,500 USD] and 50,000,000 [equal to 2,500 USD] shall be imposed on one of the following acts of violation: a) Fail to register or re-register standard contracts with the competent state management agency to protect the rights of consumers under regulations; b) Fail to notify consumers about changing standard contracts as prescribed.
- Article 69 of Decree 185 states that a fine of between VND 5,000,000 [equal to 250 USD] and 10,000,000 [equal to 500 USD] shall be imposed on acts of using standard contracts, general transaction conditions in dealing with customers which have one of following violations: a) There is a font size smaller than as specified; b) Contract language is not Vietnamese, unless otherwise agreed by the parties or other legal provisions; c) Paper background and ink colour reflecting the content of standard contract or general transaction conditions do not contrast each other.
- Article 71 of Decree 185 states that a fine of between VND 10,000,000 [equal to 500 USD] and 20,000,000 [equal to 1,000USD] for traders of goods and services who enter into contracts with consumers in which have invalid terms as prescribed. In case of standard contracts, traders may be

---

Department of Industry and Trade shall review standard contracts used by enterprises operating within that province.

55   Decree 99/2011/ND-CP dated 27 October 2011.

fined from VND 20,000,000 [equal to 1,000 USD] to VND 30,000,000 [equal to 1,500 USD].

- Articles 72 and 74 of Decree 185 state that a fine of between VND 10,000,000 [equal to 500 USD] and 20,000,000 [equal to 1,000USD] shall be imposed on acts of signing distance contracts with consumers for one of the following cases: a) Fail to provide full and clear information as prescribed; b) Fail to refund money within 30 days since the consumer declares unilateral termination of the concluded contract or fail to pay interests on the amounts delayed in payment to the consumer as prescribed. A fine of between VND 10,000,000 [equal to 500 USD] and 20,000,000 [equal to 1,000USD] shall be imposed on traders who provide door-to-door sale of goods and commit one of following acts of violations: a) Door-to-door sellers do not introduce names of traders, telephone numbers, addresses, head offices or addresses of entities that are responsible for proposals of signing contracts; b) Door-to-door sellers deliberately get in touch with consumers to propose signing contracts in case the consumer has refused; c) Refuse consumers from withdrawing their agreements in case the consumers send written notice on the withdrawal of their agreements within 3 working days from the date of signing of the contract; d) Force consumers to pay or to perform other obligations under the contract before the expiry of 3 working days from the date of signing of the contract, unless otherwise provided by law; e) Disclaimer for sales activities of the door-to-door sellers in case such sellers cause damages to the consumers.

IV. Factual scenarios

Scenario 1

In this scenario, the contract of sale is between Billy (the trader) and Alison (the consumer). This contract is regarded as a consumer contract regulated both by the *Civil Code* of 2015 and the Law on Consumer Protection of 2010

(i) Brake and engine noise

The new car Alison bought is not of the satisfactory quality as she expected due to defective brakes and unusual engine noise. Based on the provisions of Article 445(1) of the Civil Code of 2015, Alison is entitled to (1) get the car *repaired or (2) change the defective car to get a new one or (3) ask for a price reduction and get compensation for damages*. In accordance with the *Civil Code* of 2015, Alison is not entitled to reject the defective car; however, Article 21 of the Law on Consumer Protection of 2010 allows Alison to reject the defective car and get money back if the manufacturer can not repair the defects during warranty period (if any).

The story will be very much different if the sold car is a second-hand one. Article 445(1) of the Civil Code of 2015 is not applicable to sale of a second-hand car. In other words, if Alison buys a second-hand car, she is not entitled to get the car repaired or change the car to get another or ask for a price reduction.[56]

(ii) The higher-than-expected fuel consumption

If Alison's new car consumes more fuel than she expects, which is not consistent with what she was assured by the seller at the time of sale, she can also refer to Article 445(1) of the Civil Code to ask the seller for a price reduction. In this case, the manufacturer is not held liable.

(iii) Failure to meet emission standards

Article 432 of the *Civil Code* of 2015 states that 'the quality of an object for sale shall be as agreed by the parties'. However,

> where the quality of an object has been proclaimed or is provided by a competent authority, the quality of the object agreed by the parties shall not be lower than the quality proclaimed standard or the stipulations of the competent authority.

If there is no quality standard, regulations of a competent authority and industry standard in terms of an object for sale, its quality shall be determined according to *normal standards* or separate standards in conformity with the purposes of entering into contract and as prescribed in the Law on Consumer Protection.

Emission standards are regarded as an element of the quality of the car for sale. These standards are stipulated in Decision No. 49/2011/QD-TTg dated September 1st, 2011. All car manufacturers have to comply with these standards. Therefore, if the car Alison bought failed to meet emission standards, this car can be also considered as failing to meet the satisfactory quality. In accordance with Article 423 of the *Civil Code*, this breach of contract can be considered as a fundamental breach of the contract, and the buyer can terminate the contract, send the car back to the seller and get the price refunded.[57]

Scenario 2

Vietnam currently does not have any specific laws directly regulating contracts providing digital content similar to Consumer Rights Act 2015 in the United

---

56 Article 445(2) of the *Civil Code* of 2015.
57 Article 423 of the *Civil Code* of 2015 states that 'a party has the right to cancel a contract and shall not be liable to compensate for damage in any of the following cases: . . . b) The other party fundamentally breaches the obligations in the contract'. This Article also explains that 'fundamental breach of contract means the failure to fulfill obligations properly by a party leading the failure to achieve the purposes of entering into contract by the other party'.

Kingdom. However, in accordance with Article 115 of the *Civil Code* of 2015 of Vietnam, a software can also be considered as a kind of property. Provisions on sale contract in the *Civil Code* of 2015 can be also applicable to David's contract of buying a new sports application.

(i) Failure of the app and failure to patch the problem

In this case, Article 432 and Article 445 of the *Civil Code* of 2015 shall be applicable. This Article requires that object for sale must at least meet the 'normal standards . . . in conformity with the purposes of entering into contract'. Therefore, if the failure of the app and failure to patch the problem occurs, the app shall be regarded as not meeting the satisfactory quality. Article 445 of the *Civil Code* allows David to ask for a repair of the app or ask for a price reduction.

(ii) Interference with other apps and damage done to the Wi-Fi connector

It seems that Vietnamese legal system does not have specific solutions to the problems raised in the scenario. No courts in Vietnam have so far faced similar disputes relating to contract of supplying digital contents.

V. Specific issues in Vietnam

The adoption of the Consumer Protection Law of 2010 in Vietnam marks a new development in the evolution of consumer law in this country. This Law paves the ways for provisions on consumer contracts that are inserted into the Vietnamese legal system. This Law and its following guiding documents continue the inertia of using administrative instruments to detect and handle violations of consumer rights. In addition, this Law also paves the ways for administrative authority to exercise the functions that could be better assumed by the judiciary when it requires certain standard contracts to be registered with administrative authorities before being used.[58] It seems that, with a traditionally strong administrative state, a mixed model of contract-based approach with state sanction-based approach seems to be the preferred choice made by Vietnamese policymakers in this field.

---

58 From 2012 to the present, more than 200 companies have registered with Vietnam Competition Authority their standard models.

Index

Note: Page numbers in italic indicate a figure and page numbers in bold indicate a table on the corresponding page.

ABA Consumer Law Guide 161
acceptable quality test 5–6
Adäquanztheorie 68
ADICs 83–84
ADR, development 3
Alternative Resolution of Consumer Disputes, Directive 2013/11/EU 49
American Law Institute, *Restatement of Consumer Contact Law* 162–163
American National Standards Institute (ANSI) 152
Äquivalenztheorie 68
arbitration clause, invalidation 157
Australia: Australian Competition and Consumer Commission (ACCC) 17, 21; Australian Consumer Law (ACL) 19; Australian Consumer Law (ACL), consumer guarantees 27; Australian Consumer Law (ACL), contravention 24; Australian Design Rules, emissions governance 24; *Competition and Consumer Act 2010* (CCA) 19; Consumer Affairs Victoria 17; consumer law, enforcement 17–18; consumer market 15–16; consumer sales law 15; consumer sales, legal framework 19–22; consumers, justice (access) 17–18; External Dispute Resolution (EDR) 17, 18; factual scenarios 22–30; gross domestic product (GDP), retail market percentage 15; issues 30; *Motor Vehicle Standards Act 1989* 24; New South Wales (NSW) Civil and Administrative Tribunal (NCAT) 18, 23; New South Wales (NSW) Fair Trading 17; responsive regulation, impact 17; retail, multi-channel industry 15–16; Trade Practices Act 1974, reenactment 19
Australia, car scenario: advertisement, assertions 25; brake/engine noise 23; emissions standards, meeting (failure) 24; fuel consumption, expectations 24; remedies 25–26; scenario 22–26
Australia, tablet computer scenario: apps, interference 29–30; patch/app failure 27–29; scenario 26–30; Wi-Fi connector, damage 30
Autoriteit Consument en Markt (Dutch Competition and Consumer Authority) 119

Berwick v. Uber Technologies 154
Billy, recourse 61
breaching, consequence 78
Broadcasting Ordinance (Cap. 562) 73
Brussels I Regulation 158
Bürgerliches Gesetzbuch (BGB) 50–51
Business Criterion for Second-Hand Vehicle (BCSV) 89–90

capital requirements directive (CRD) 45–47
cars: consumer sales, scenario 8–9; emission standards, meeting failure (scenario) 10–11; fuel consumption, scenario 10
China *see* People's Republic of China: China Food and Drug Administration (CFDA) 84
CISG *see* United Nations Convention on the International Sale of Goods 1980
civil liability, impact 4

Index

collective redress (EU) 35
Common European Sales Law, development 1
comparative consumer sales law 1
compensatory damages (People's Republic of China) 87
Competition and Consumer Act 2010 (CCA) 19
Cong, Phan 169
consumentenbond (Dutch consumer association) 117, 119
Consumer Council (Hong Kong) 70–74; Code of Practice, launch 72
Consumer Council Legal Action Fund (Hong Kong) 71
Consumer Guarantees Act 1993 (CGA 1993) 5
consumer markets 2–3
Consumer Protection (Fair Trading) Act (CPFTA) 5
Consumer Protection Law of 2010 (CPL) 166–168, 170
consumer sales: factual scenarios 7–13; law (Germany) 48; legal framework (EU) 36–39; legal rules 4–7; parties, liability 7; quality standards 5–6; remedies 6
consumers, justice (access) 3–4
Consumption, increase 2–3
contra proferentem rule 164
Control of Exemption Clauses Ordinance (CECO) 74–76
Cox & Coxton Ltd v Leipst 105
criminal liability, civil liability (impact) 4

dealing as consumer, defining 74
defeat devices, usage (prohibition) 44
digital content: damage, CRA provision 143–144; sale rules, absence 58; specificities 12; supply contracts 45
doctrine of implied warranty of merchantability (UCC) 159
doctrine of unconscionability 157–158
Dodd-Frank law 163
Durovic, Mateja 31

Einführungsgesetz zum Bürgerlichen Gesetzbuch 49–50
English Law remoteness test, steps 68
equivalence, principle 34
European Consumer Organisation (BEUC) 33
European Union (EU): ADR procedures 130; capital requirements directive (CRD) 45–47; *Car labelling Directive* 43; collective redress 35; conformity, absence 38, 40; Consumer Awareness Campaign 31–32; Consumer Conditions Scoreboard, publication 31–32; Consumer Law and Policy, focus 32; consumer market 31–32; Consumer Markets Scoreboard, publication 31–32; Consumer Sales Directive 5, 8; Consumer Sales Directive (1999/44/EC) 4; consumer sales law 31; consumer sales, legal framework 36–39; Consumer Scorecards, publication 31–32; consumers, justice (access) 32–35; defeat devices, usage (prohibition) 44; defective goods, repair/replacement 38–39; Directive 93/13/EEC 36; Directive 1999/44/EC 36, 51; Directive 1999/94/EC 43; Directive 2005/29/EC (UCPD)_ 37; Directive 2009/22/EC 35; Directive 2011/83/EU 36, 45; Directive 2013/11/EU, adoption 34; equivalence, principle 34; *ex officio* application 36; *ex officio* doctrine, development 34; *ex officio* grant 41; factual scenarios 39–47; gross domestic product (GDP), consumer spending percentage 31; human rights, justice (consumer access) 32–33; individual redress 33–35; issues 47; Member States, contracting parties 33; Online Dispute Resolution (ODR) 130; Proposal for a Directive, publication 32; Regulation 524/2013 35; repair/replacement, efficiency 41; top reliability statement 40; Unfair Commercial Practices Act (UCPD) 37, 39, 43; Unfair Terms in Consumer Contracts Regulation (UTCCR) 120–121
European Union (EU), car scenario 39–44; app/patch failure 45–46; apps, interference 47; brake/engine noise (new car) 40–42; brake/engine noise (second-hand car) 42; emissions standards, failure 43–44; fuel consumption, expectation 42–43; Wi-Fi connector damage 47
ex officio doctrine/application 34, 36
External Dispute Resolution (EDR) *see* Australia

Index 185

factual scenarios 7–13
Federal Trade Commission (FTC) 150, 156; Mail or Telephone Order Rule 162; Rule Making 154

gag clause, voiding 156
Germany: *Adäquanztheorie* 68; Alternative Resolution of Consumer Disputes, Directive 2013/11/EU 49; *Amtsgerichte* 49; app/patch failure 67; apps, interference 68; *Äquivalenztheorie* 68; *Bürgerliches Gesetzbuch* (BGB) 50–51; Civil Code, rules 4; Civil Code, Section 478 59; Civil Code, Section 823 60; Civil Procedure Act 49–50; consumer law, collective enforcement 50; consumer law, enforcement 49–50; consumer market 48; Consumer Sales Directive 52; Consumer Sales Law 51; consumers, justice (access) 49–50; contract breach 67; contract conclusion period 67; Contract Law 58; damage, inflicting (liability) 60; digital contents, sale rules (absence) 58; Directive 1999/44/EC 51; *Einführungsgesetz zum Bürgerlichen Gesetzbuch* 49–50; *große Lösung* (big solution) 51; *Gütestelle* 49–50; individual enforcement, consumers (impact) 49–50; issues 68; *Landgerichte* 49; *Minderung* 54; *Nachbessrung* 54; *Nachfrist* 54–56; *Nachlieferung* 54; Oberlandesgericht Hamm decision 66; *objektive Zurechnung* 68; Online Resolution of Consumer Disputes, Regulation 524/2013 49; producer statements, repetition 64; Product Liability Act, Section 1 60; *Produkthaftungsgesetz* (Product Liability Act) 59–60; quality, expectation 61, 64; *Rechtskauf* (Civil Code, section 453) 51; remoteness test, steps 68; *Rücktritt* 54; Sales Law, remedies 56–57; *Schadensersatz neben der Leistung* 56; *Schadensersatz statt der Leistung* 56, 67; *Schuldrechtsreform* (Reform of the Law of Obligations) 50–51, 56; Small Claim Procedure, Regulation 861/2007 50; *Stückschuld* 63; *subjektiv-objektiv Sachmangelbegriff* 52; supplier application, problem 68; *Unterlassungsklagengesetz* (Injunctions Act) 50; *Verbraucherstreitbeilegungsgesetz* 49; *Werklieferungsvertrag* (Civil Code, section 651) 51; Wi-Fi connector, damage 68
Germany, car scenario: brake/engine noise (new car) 61–62; brake/engine noise (second-hand car) 63; complications 65; emissions standards, failure 66; fuel consumption, expectation 63–65
Germany, consumer sales: buyer rights, limitation period 53–56; contracts, particularities 57–58; digital content 58; law 48; legal framework 50–58; non-conformity 52–53
Germany, factual scenarios 59–68; Billy, recourse 61–66; Reliable, recourse 59–60
goods, definition (extension) 12
große Lösung (big solution) 51
gross domestic product (GDP), consumer spending percentage 2

Han, Shiyuan 82
Hong Kong: breaching, consequence 78; Broadcasting Ordinance (Cap. 562) 73; Census and Statistics Department (C&SD) survey 69; Chief Justice's Working Party on Civil Justice Reform (Final Report 2004) 71; complaint statistics 69–70; complaint venues 70–74; Consumer Council 70–74; Consumer Council, Code of Practice (launch) 72; Consumer Council, Complaints Statistics 69–70; Consumer Council Legal Action Fund 71; Consumer Council Ordinance (Cap. 216) 70–71; consumer law, enforcement 70–74; consumer market 69–70; consumer safety 77; consumers, justice (access) 70–74; Control of Exemption Clauses Ordinance (CECO) 74–76; Customs and Excise Department, role 72–73; dealing as consumer, defining 74; Estate Agents Ordinance (Cap. 511) 77; factual scenarios 77–81; fitness centre chain malpractices 81; implied condition, breach 75; industry self-regulation bodies 72; Insurance Claims

186   Index

Complaints Bureau, setup 72; issues 81; Laundry Association 72; Law Reform Commission 71; malpractices, deployment 81; merchantable criteria 78; Misrepresentation Ordinance (MO) 80; Money Changers Ordinance (Cap. 34) 77; Personal Data (Privacy) Ordinance (Cap. 486) 77; public enforcement 72–74; reasonable time, direction 78–79; Refund Protection Scheme (Registered Shops) for Inbound Tour Group Shoppers 72; Rules of the High Court, Order 15 Rule 12 71; Sales of Goods Ordinance (SOGO) 74–81; service contracts 75; Small Claims Tribunal 71; Small Claims Tribunal Ordinance (Cap. 338) 71; Supply of Services Ordinance (SSO) 74–76; Telecommunications Ordinance (Cap. 106) 73; Trade Description Ordinance (TDO), description (falsehood) 80; Trade Descriptions (Unfair Trade Practices) (Amendment) Bill 2012 81; Trade Descriptions Ordinance (TDO) (Cap. 362) 72–73; Trade Descriptions Ordinance (TDO), violation 70; trademark infringement 73–74; trade practices 77; Travel Agents Ordinance (Cap. 218) 77; Travel Industry Council (TIC) 72; Unconscionable Contracts Ordinance (UCO) 74–76; Weights and Measures Ordinance (Cap. 68) 77
Hong Kong, car scenario: brake/engine noise (new car) 77–79; brake/engine noise (second-hand car) 79; emissions standards, failure 80; fuel consumption, expectation 79
Hong Kong, consumer contracts 74–77; implied condition 75; implied terms (SOGO) 74–75; implied warranty 75
Hong Kong, consumer sales: law 69; legal framework 74–75
Howells, Geraint 1, 69

implied condition, breach 75
implied warranty 75; misrepresentation/breach 160
individual redress (EU) 33–35
International Consumer Protection and Enforcement Network 18
internet of things phenomenon 7
Internet Service Providers, responsibilities 146

Koh Wee Meng v Trans Eurokars Pte Ltd 123

legal normative documents (LNDs) 171, 173
Lehman Brothers 117
Lei, Chen 69
Lemon Law Rights Period 159
Llewellyn, Karl 155
Low, Gary 113
Lyft, FCC Citation and Order 156–157

material breach doctrine, application (clarification) 163
Minderung 54
Misrepresentation Ordinance (MO) 80
Motor Vehicle Standards Act 1989 24

Nachbesserung 54
Nachfrist 54–56
Nachlieferung 54
NCAT *see* Australia
New South Wales (NSW) *see* Australia
New Zealand (NZ): Advertising Standards Authority, codes 101–102; app/patch failure 109; apps, interference 109–110; assertions of fitness, supplier input 103; Commerce Commission, calls/emails 99; complaints 96–97; consumer contract term, unfairness 111; consumer, definition 102–103; Consumer Guarantees Act 1993 (CGA 1993) 5, 95, 98, 105, 109; Consumer Guarantees Act 1993 (CGA 1993), rights/remedies 100; consumer law, enforcement 97–99; consumer market 95–97; consumer sales law 95; consumer sales, legal framework 100–105; consumers, justice (access) 97–99; Contract and Commercial Law Act 2017 100; Contractual Remedies Act 1979 (CRA) 98; *Cox & Coxton Ltd v Leipst* 105; Disputes Tribunals Act (1988) 97–98; factual scenarios 105–110; failure 104; goods, guarantee compliance 103–104; goods, services (contrast) 96–97; hidden defects 104; individual enforcement, consumers (impact) 97–99; issues 110–112; loss of a bargain 109–110; Motor Vehicle Disputes Tribunal 98; online, offline (contrast) 97; post-contract law 102–105; pre-contract law 100–102;

public enforcement 99; quality, guarantee (breach) 109; Sale and Supply of Alcohol Act 2012 102; Sale of Goods Act 1908 (SOGA) 100, 102, 109, 122–123; Smoke-Free Environments Act 1990 102; third-party app (TPA), connection (absence) 108; trade, meaning 103; transparent, definition 111; unfair contracts law 110–111; Wi-Fi connector, damage 110

New Zealand, car scenario: brake/engine noise (new car) 105–106; brake/engine noise (second-hand car) 106–107; emissions standards, failure 108; fuel consumption, expectation 107–108

New Zealand (NZ), Fair Trading Act 1986 (FTA) 95, 96, 98; amendments 107; product recall 108; prohibitions 101; transparent, definition 111; unfair contract terms law 102

Nicoll, Chris 95

non-conformity: Germany 52–53; remedies (People's Republic of China) 86

non-conformity (United Kingdom), rights/remedies **135**

non-conformity Vietnam 175–176

non-major failure defect, remedy (supplier failure) 22

Obama Administration, enforcement (increase) 149

Oberlandesgericht Hamm decision 66

objektive Zurechnung 68

Online Resolution of Consumer Disputes, Regulation 524/2013 49

parol evidence rule 164

Pearson, Gail 15

People's Republic of China (PRC): ADICs 83–84; app/patch failure 91–92; *Business Criterion for Second-Hand Vehicle* (BCSV) 89–90; China Consumer Association, complaints (increase) 2–3; China Consumer Association, consumer complaints report 82; China Consumer's Association lawsuits 85; Chinese Law on the Protection of Consumer Rights and Interests (LPCRI) 5, 87, 91, 94; compensatory damages 87; consumer law 86; consumer law, enforcement 83–86; consumer market 82; consumer organisations 85–86; consumer protection policy 83; consumer sales law 82; consumer sales, legal framework 86–87; consumers, justice (access) 83–86; contract law 86; Contract Law (1999) 89; *Contract Law* (1999, CCL) 86; Contract Law (CCL) 91–92; factual scenarios 87–94; fake, purchase 94; General Administration of Quality Supervision, Inspection and Quarantine of the PR China (AQSIQ) 84; individual enforcement, consumers (impact) 83; issues 94; *Law of the PRC on the Protection of Consumer Rights and Interests* 86; National Bureau of Statistics (NBS) data 82; National Health and Family Planning Commission report 84; non-conformity, remedies 86; Product Quality Law of the People's Republic of China (PQL) 93; *Provisions on the Liability for the Repair, Replacement and Return of Household Automotive Products* (3R Provisions) 88; public enforcement 83–86; public state organs 83–85; punitive damages 87; *Sale, Spare Part, Service and Survey* (4 S) 88; *San-bao* 86; Sanlu milk powder case 84–85; statutory obligations 92; Supreme People's Court (SPC), law source 86; *Tang Hong-bo v Zhuzhou City Yida Auto Co. Ltd and Dandong Huanghai Auto Co. Ltd* 90–91; 3R Provisions 9; Tort Law 2009 (CTL) 93; Wi-Fi connector (interference), apps damage (impact) 92–94

People's Republic of China, car scenario: brake/engine noise (new car) 88–89; brake/engine noise (second-hand car) 89–90; emissions standards, failure 91; fuel consumption, expectation 90–91

post-contract law (New Zealand) 102–105

pre-contract law (New Zealand) 100–102

Produkthaftungsgesetz (Product Liability Act) 59–60

Provisions on the Liability for the Repair, Replacement and Return of Household Automotive Products (3R Provisions) 88

public enforcement 3

punitive damages (People's Republic of China) 87

punitive treatment, principles (formulation) 163

Rechtskauf (Civil Code, section 453) 51
Refund Protection Scheme (Registered Shops) for Inbound Tour Group Shoppers 72
Reliable, recourse 59–60
remoteness test, steps 68
responsive regulation, impact 17
Restatement of Consumer Contact Law (ALI) 162–163
Rücktritt 54

Sales of Goods Ordinance (SOGO) 74–81; court allowance 79
Sale, Spare Part, Service and Survey (4 S) 88
samenwerkingsprotocol (legally binding memorandum of cooperation) 119
San-bao 86
Sanlu milk powder case 84–85
Schadensersatz neben der Leistung 56
Schadensersatz statt der Leistung 56, 67
Schuldrechtsreform (Reform of the Law of Obligations) 50–51, 56
shopping patterns, change 2
Singapore: app/patch failure 126; apps, interference 126–127; *Autoriteit Consument en Markt* (Dutch Competition and Consumer Authority) 119; claim, prosecution 125; *consumentenbond* (Dutch consumer association) 117, 119; consumer law 113; consumer market 113–115; Consumer Protection (Fair Trading) Act (CPFTA) 5, 115, 120–126; Consumer Protection (Fair Trading) Act (CPFTA), enforcement 117–118; Consumer Protection (Trade Descriptions and Safety Requirements) Act of 1975 120; consumer redress 115–116; consumer rights, private enforcement 117; consumer sales, legal framework 119–122; Consumers Association of Singapore (CASE) 114, 117; enforcement issues 115–119; factual scenarios 122–127; Financial Industries Dispute Resolution Centre (FIDReC) 116–117; Free Trade Agreement, signing 120; gross domestic product 113; household interest penetration rate, growth 113; Injunctions Proposals Review Panel approval 117–118; issues 127; justice, access 115–119; *Koh Wee Meng v Trans Eurokars Pte Ltd* 123; latent defects, complaints 115; market regulation 120–121; Ministry for Trade and Industry (MTI) 117–118, 120; Ministry for Trade and Industry (MTI), remit 121; Product Standards and Testing subcommittee, impact 118–119; retailtainment strategy 114; root-and-branch overview, commencement 120; Sale of Goods Act (Cap 393) 119–120; *samenwerkingsprotocol* (legally binding memorandum of cooperation) 119; Singapore Tourism Board (STB) 117; Small Claims Tribunal (SCT) 115–116; Small Claims Tribunal (SCT) decisions, enforceability 116; *Speedo Motoring v Ong Gek Seng* 124; SPRING Singapore 118; Unfair Contract Terms Act (Cap 396) 119–120; Voluntary Compliance Agreement (VCA) 117–118; Wi-Fi connector, damage 126–127
Singapore, car scenario: brake/engine noise (new car) 122–123; brake/engine noise (second-hand car) 124–125; emissions standards, failure 125–126; fuel consumption, expectation 123–124
Small Claim Procedure, Regulation 861/2007 50
Small Claims Tribunal (Hong Kong) 71
Speedo Motoring v Ong Gek Seng 124
Stückschuld 63
subjektiv-objektiv Sachmangelbegriff 52
Supply of Services Ordinance (SSO) 74–76

tablet computer: consumer sales, scenario 11–12; problem, patch/app failure (scenario) 12; sports application, interference 12–13; Wi-Fi connector, app damage 13
Tang Hong-bo v Zhuzhou City Yida Auto Co. Ltd and Dandong Huanghai Auto Co. Ltd 90–91
Telecommunications Ordinance (Cap. 106) 73
Telephone Consumer Protection Act (TCPA), Citation and Order 156–157
third-party app (TPA), connection (absence) 108
3R Provisions *see* People's Republic of China

Index 189

top reliability statement 40
Trade Descriptions Ordinance (TDO) 70, 72–73, 77
Trade Descriptions Ordinance, violation 70
trademark infringement 73–74
Travel Industry Council (TIC) 72
Twigg-Flesner, Christian 1, 128

Unconscionable Contracts Ordinance (UCO) 74–76
Underwriters Laboratories (UL) 152
Unfair Commercial Practices Act (UCPD) 37, 39, 43
Unfair Terms in Consumer Contract Directive 158
Uniform Commercial Code (UCC) 5, 146, 159; Article 2B, adoption failure 161; consumer rules 155–157; doctrine of implied warranty of merchantability 159; Section 1-301 164
United Kingdom (UK): app/patch failure 142–143; apps, interference 143–144; Citizens Advice Bueraux (CAB) research findings 129–131; Competition and Markets Authority 131–132; Consumer Contracts (Information, Cancellation and Additional Charges) Regulations 2013 134; Consumer Credit Act 127; consumer law, enforcement 129–132; consumer market 128–129; Consumer Rights Act 2015 (CRA 2015) 4–6, 12, 92, 139–140, 153, 158; Consumer Rights Act 2015 (CRA 2015), enactment (impact) 132; Consumer Rights Act 2015 (CRA 2015), quality/fitness provisions 142; Consumer Rights Act 2015 (CRA 2015), s.46 13; consumer sales law 128; consumer sales, legal framework 132–136; Consumers' Association 131; consumers, justice (access) 129–132; Department for Business, Innovation and Skills (BIS) 48; Department for Business, Innovation and Skills (BIS) survey 128; digital content damage, CRA provision 143–144; enforcement order 132; goods, services (contrast) 129; individual enforcement, consumers (impact) 130–131; issues 145; non-conformity, rights/remedies **135**; Ombudsman Services 129; online, offline (contrast) 129; Oxford Economics report 129; price reduction, meaning 136; public enforcement 131–132; remedies, range 141; repair, request 138–139; replacement, remedy 140; Sale of Goods Act 1979 119–120; Supply of Goods (Implied Terms) Act 1973 132; Supply of Goods Act 1979 132; Supply of Goods and Services Act 1982 132; Trading Standards Departments 132; Unfair Contract Terms Act 1977 119–120; UTCCR 76; waiting period, initiation 135; Wi-Fi connector, damage 144
United Kingdom (UK), car scenario: brake/engine noise (new car) 137–139; brake/engine noise (second-hand car) 139–140; emissions standards, failure 141–142; fuel consumption, expectation 140–141
United Nations Convention on the International Sale of Goods 1980 (CISG) 5, 52
United States (US), car scenario: brake/engine noise (new car) 158–159; brake/engine noise (used car) 159; emissions standards, expectations 160; fuel consumption, expectations 159–160
Unterlassungsklagengesetz (Injunctions Act) 50

Van Cuong, Nguyen 165
Verbraucherstreitbeilegungsgesetz 49
Vietnam, car scenario: brake/engine noise 180–181; emission standards, failure 181

Werklieferungsvertrag (Civil Code, section 651) 51
Williams v. Walker-Thomas Furniture 162